LAND WITH
NO SUN

The Stackpole Military History Series

THE AMERICAN CIVIL WAR

Cavalry Raids of the Civil War
Ghost, Thunderbolt, and Wizard
Pickett's Charge
Witness to Gettysburg

WORLD WAR II

Armor Battles of the Waffen-SS, 1943–45
Army of the West
Australian Commandos
The B-24 in China
Backwater War
The Battle of Sicily
Beyond the Beachhead
The Brandenburger Commandos
The Brigade
Bringing the Thunder
Coast Watching in World War II
Colossal Cracks
D-Day to Berlin
Dive Bomber!
Eagles of the Third Reich
Exit Rommel
Fist from the Sky
*Flying American Combat Aircraft of
    World War II*
Forging the Thunderbolt
Fortress France
The German Defeat in the East, 1944–45
German Order of Battle, Vol. 1
German Order of Battle, Vol. 2
German Order of Battle, Vol. 3
Germany's Panzer Arm in World War II
GI Ingenuity
Grenadiers
Infantry Aces
Iron Arm
Iron Knights
*Kampfgruppe Peiper at the Battle
    of the Bulge*
Luftwaffe Aces
Massacre at Tobruk
Messerschmitts over Sicily

Michael Wittmann, Vol. 1
Michael Wittmann, Vol. 2
Mountain Warriors
The Nazi Rocketeers
On the Canal
Packs On!
Panzer Aces
Panzer Aces II
The Panzer Legions
Panzers in Winter
The Path to Blitzkrieg
Retreat to the Reich
Rommel's Desert War
The Savage Sky
A Soldier in the Cockpit
Soviet Blitzkrieg
Stalin's Keys to Victory
Surviving Bataan and Beyond
T-34 in Action
Tigers in the Mud
The 12th SS, Vol. 1
The 12th SS, Vol. 2
The War against Rommel's Supply Lines

THE COLD WAR / VIETNAM

*Flying American Combat Aircraft:
    The Cold War*
Here There Are Tigers
Land with No Sun
Street without Joy

WARS OF THE MIDDLE EAST

Never-Ending Conflict

GENERAL MILITARY HISTORY

Carriers in Combat
Desert Battles

LAND WITH NO SUN

A Year in Vietnam
with the 173rd Airborne

Command Sergeant Major Ted G. Arthurs

STACKPOLE
BOOKS

Published in 2006 by
STACKPOLE BOOKS
5067 Ritter Road
Mechanicsburg, PA 17055
www.stackpolebooks.com

Printed in the United States of America

10 9 8 7 6 5 4 3 2

FIRST EDITION

Library of Congress Cataloging-in-Publication Data

Arthurs, Ted.
    Land with no sun : a year in Vietnam with the 173rd Airborne / Ted
Arthurs.— 1st ed.
        p. cm. — (Stackpole Military history series)
    Includes index.
    ISBN-13: 978-0-8117-3290-1
    ISBN-10: 0-8117-3290-8
    1. Vietnamese Conflict, 1961–1975—Personal narratives, American. 2.
Arthurs, Ted. 3. Vietnamese Conflict, 1961–1975—Regimental histories—
United States. 4. United States. Army. Airborne Brigade, 173rd—History.
I. Title. II. Series.

    DS559.5.A78 2006
    959.704'342092—dc22
    2006005152

In memory of Dennis Richard Cooney

and

James Robert Lester	*Robert Eric Lochridge*
Daniel Walter Jordan	*Norbert L. Froelich*
John C. Borowski	*John Michael Olszewski*
Arthur Albert Erwin	*Michael Ferguson*
Roger William Clark	*Sylvester Wright*
Jesus M. Torres	*Steven M. Haniotes*
Harry Diwain Spier	*Edward Oran Claeys*
Larry Allen Doring	*David Lee Fennessey*
Michael S. Mitchell	*Walter Douglas Williams*
Ronald Russell Jones	*Myron Stanley Beach, Jr.*
Lindsay David Baldoni	*Franklin S. Shepherd*
Robert Lee Fleck	*Walter A. Samans, Jr.*
Robert H. Darling	*William A. Scott*
Clarence A. Miller, Jr.	*Jimmy Earl Darby*
Linwood C. Corbett	*Malton Gene Shores*
Willie Alfred Wright	*Siegfried Koffler*
James Dudley Shafer	*Kenneth Lloyd Brown*
Richard Arlan Stone	*Bobby Horace Sorrells*
William A. Collins	*John Robert Bamvakais*
Harry Conrad Wilson II	*Rodney Barrette Cline*
Arthur Turner, Jr.	*Joaquin Palacios Cabrera*
Louis George Arnold	*Rufus John Dowdy*
David Ricahrd Reynolds	*David Frank Burney*
Robert W. Lindgren	*Sherman Lawrence Jones*
James Worrell	*Richard Francis Laird*
Raymond W. Michalopoulos	*Edrick Kenneth Stevens*
Gerald Klossek	*Richard Dale McGhee*
William Lloyd Cates	*Charles H. Robinson*
Richard Floyd Mason	*Roy Ronald Lee*
Billy Ray Cubit	*Roland Will Manuel*
Lawrence D. Greene	*Leonard J. Richards*
James Calvin Bodison	*Roger Dale Mabe*
Robert Charles Peters	*Angel R. Flores-Jiminez*
John Henry Tigner	*Earl Kennon Webb*

John Lewis Ponting
Robert Edward Paciorek
John William Smith
John Henry Curtin
Miloslav J. Martinovski
Alvin John Wesolowski
Edward Eddy Cervantez
Brad John Szutz
Jack Roger McKee
Peter Wellesley Foote
Gary Lee Jatich
Richard James Grooms
Lawrence E. Philyaw
Winfred Alderman
Gerald Chales Hague
Joel Michael Sabel
William Joseph Deuerling
Oris Lamar Poole
David Harold Johnson
David Paul Crozier
Frazier Daniel Huggins
James Fabrizio
Arthur C. Retzlaff
Gerald Edward Davis
Edward Barden
Daniel Ralph Meador
Charles G. Bowersmith
Louis Charles Miller
Robert John Bickel

James Lee Ellis, Jr.
Dewain V. Dubb
Emery Lee Jorgensen
Michael A. Crabtree
Douglas G. Magruder
Thomas Curtis Mays
Jesse E. Smith
Michael J. Gladden
Thomas Joe Wade
Kenneth Grant Owens
Thomas Louis Corbett
Merrel P. Whittington
Tracy Henry Murrey
Charles E. Willbanks
Le Roy Edward Fladry
Larry Edwin Hill
Arthur Floyd Elliott
Thomas Henry Swinnea
James M. Larouche
David Wayne De Priest
Jimmie Paul Wall
William Thomas Jarvis
John Davis Willingham
James Richard Biernacki
John Clair Bonney
William Coy Turner
David Joseph Johnson
Gene Autry Ross

And all the other heroes on The Wall.

Table of Contents

Preface: Red and the Other Heroes

As stated, this book was written in memory of Dennis Richard Cooney and 125 specific troopers killed in my battalion during my year with the Fourth Bat, as well as all the other heroes on The Wall.

Why pick out a special low-ranking rifleman like "Red" Cooney? We had over seven-hundred fine riflemen, so what sets him apart from all his comrades? Red was not only one of our best riflemen in that jungle, but he was so dependable that they kept on trying to make a leader out of him, but he turned all those promotions down. He didn't want the responsibility for maybe causing injury or death to any of his comrades, though he willingly volunteered for dangerous ambush patrols and other missions.

Red reminded me of the World War II hero Roger Young, who was losing his hearing and afraid for his men, so he turned in his stripes and died saving others from a machine-gun nest as a private rifleman.

Now don't get me wrong. Red was a hero, first class. On the July 10, 1967, on Hill 830 at Dakto, Red was badly wounded in combat while saving some of his buddies.

Many of our men died that day, or were wounded like Red. During a lengthy hospitalization in Walter Reed, he was decorated there with the Nation's third highest award for valor and gallantry in action, the Silver Star.

Now think about this: While many others of that era dodged the draft, went to Canada, or performed other subterfuge in order to avoid combat, Red volunteered for the Airborne Infantry.

At the time of his hospitalization, no one in the world realized that the blood supply had become tainted with the horrible hepatitis "C" virus which lies dormant for many years and may then crop up as liver cancer.

Red and I kept in touch over the years. I watched with great satisfaction as his fortunes increased through hard work and skillful investments until in his mid-fifties this fine hero had become a wealthy man in more ways than one. He had more friends than the average man, and not only because he helped anyone in financial need.

At the apex of his life, this brave warrior found that he had to battle liver cancer, induced by all those transfusions in the hospital.

The nearest thing to a panacea to all this is twofold:

First, anyone, particularly wounded veterans, who received blood transfusions during that era should be tested for the virus periodically, so that early action may be taken against existing cancer.

And second, the average citizen can become a life-saving hero like Red through participation in the organ donation program. A timely transplant from such a program would undoubtedly have saved Red's life, but sadly, after a valiant struggle, he passed away.

All his friends and loved ones, and I, miss him terribly.

In respectful memory of Dennis Richard Cooney
January 16, 1944—April 4, 2002

And to all the others who died like him.

Acknowledgments

My lovely wife, Marlene, who promised the padre in '51 to be there through thick and thin and always has been.

Three great kids—Christine, Barbara, and Patrick—who attended schools on different continents, emerging well.

My folks, Hugh Theodore and Clarice Estelle Arthurs, who taught me that one can be poor and remain honest.

Great captains like Harold L. Barber, Robert A. "Tex" Turner, and William Brown, who taught me leadership by example.

All my terribly wounded friends and comrades, such as Dennis Richard Cooney, Earl Joseph Soucie, and Wayne Lee Hughes, maimed in body but not spirit, who loved their country beyond comprehension and gave their all to her.

Gary Linderer, unsung Vietnam hero, and Ed Murphy, whose generous, experienced guidance has helped me and many other neophyte soldier-authors.

Rick Redfern, whose encouragement and graphic expertise has helped me immensely over the years.

Another friend of fifty years, Jim Mendell, for having convinced me to exclude any bitter memories.

The brave little lioness, my hopelessly crippled sister, Millie Jo, who taught me to never, ever give up.

And finally, all my gung ho friends from the Marine Corps and Paratroops, who taught me how to live and, sometimes, how to die.

Thank you all.

Introduction

Almost twenty-five centuries ago, Simonides wrote the epitaph for the brave Spartan troops slain in 480 B.C. during their famous heroic stand against the numerically superior force of Persians during the battle of Thermopylae:

> *Go tell the Spartans, thou who passeth by,*
> *that here, obedient to their laws—we lie.*

Although they were overwhelmed in the end, the outnumbered Spartans fought to the last man.

Not much has changed in the past two thousand years: think of what has happened since. At this writing, my son is joining all our other brave warriors in quelling the despotism of Sadaam Hussein in Iraq.

And there will be more to come.

In my dedication, I have attempted to honor those brave men who died in my battalion between May 1967 and May 1968. I was the proud sergeant major of the 4th Rifle Battalion, 503rd Airborne Infantry, of the 173rd Airborne Brigade. During normal periods, we averaged a bit more than 700 riflemen—divided among four rifle companies—in the jungle each day.

At full strength, such a rifle company was composed of three forty-eight-man rifle platoons, a smaller weapons platoon, and a headquarters section consisting of the captain, who commanded the company, and his six-striper first sergeant, plus communications personnel.

Each rifle platoon was led by a lieutenant and a five-striper platoon sergeant and had three twelve-man rifle squads and a smaller weapons squad armed with two M-60 light machine guns. Each squad leader was a four-striper.

The weapons platoon was also led by a lieutenant and platoon sergeant. Its mission was to carry the heavy 81mm mortars and as many of the thirteen-pound high-explosive mortar rounds as was humanly possible in order to provide immediate and accurate fire support for the entire company during battle.

We were a rucksack outfit. Each trooper's load-bearing harness and rucksack contained everything he needed to survive in the jungle for five days and nights. On the fifth night, a Huey "firefly" resupply chopper would rendezvous with each company at a predetermined jungle clearing, replenishing "C" rations, ammo, and other supplies, as well as water during the dry season. At this time, replacements were also delivered, and men going home were extracted.

Most outfits in Vietnam went to the jungle for a few weeks and then returned for a "stand-down" period of rest and training, but sadly, from the standpoint of my men, we did not operate like that. A new man could look forward to staying in the jungle, being resupplied every fifth night, for his entire year, except for a week of R&R, when the first thing he did was to take a shower.

Every five days, the cooks in the rear filled the insulated marmite cans with hot meals and loaded them onto the fireflies as a treat for the poor rucksack soldiers who had no socks or underwear, only the jungle fatigues he wore. Once, because of one thing or another, we went more than forty days wearing the same set of fatigues.

Several of our more severe battles were fought in the Dakto region of the Central Highlands, near the confluence of the three borders of South Vietnam, Laos, and Cambodia. The North Vietnamese Army (NVA) would send a fresh regiment or two across the border to lock horns with the troopers of the 173rd and those of the 4th Infantry Division, to which we were attached for operational control. At one time, we faced several of these infiltrated regiments.

This situation and our status as full-time jungle residents combined to cause the 173rd to have the highest per capita casualty rate of any unit in Vietnam. For example, during my year, I tabulated our casualties in a green book that I kept wrapped in plastic in my rucksack. We lost 125 killed in action and well over 500 wounded. Our policy was to move a thrice-wounded rifleman to the rear. The law of averages was catching up to him, and humping a rucksack weighing more than eighty pounds required a great deal of exertion. A small guy carried exactly the same load as a former linebacker! Nothing's fair in love or war.

When people ask me about Vietnam, I am reminded of the clever story of the three blindfolded people being asked to feel an elephant and then render a physical description. The one who felt its side described a wall, the one who felt its trunk came up with a different description, and so forth. This aptly describes Vietnam's countryside. Any of the hundreds of thousands who served in the Delta region or the coastline areas would be hard-pressed to understand why my men referred to the Central Highlands as the "Land with No Sun." Most of them were almost constantly exposed to bright, sometimes harsh sunlight—except during the country's lengthy monsoons. But in the thick, dark, triple-canopied jungle of the mountainous Central Highlands, it was a different story.

The Chaine Annamitique Mountains extend for hundreds of miles from China down to the Pleiku area of Vietnam. They have never been truly conquered by the hordes of invaders who have tried over the centuries. Invaders encountered problems trying to understand the dialects of the several dozen principal Montagnard tribes that dwell there. If you can't understand 'em, you can't govern 'em.

In dealing with the Central Highlands, just about any problem comes right back to the impossibly thick triple-canopied jungle that covers all those mountains and peaks. At one time or another, most everyone has walked in the woods. This is comparable to a single-canopied jungle, where you could easily read a newspaper and where the sun shines down in spots all over. This was true in much of Vietnam, where trees stood sixty or eighty feet, but in the Central Highlands, as the elevation increased, so did the height of the trees, which, at heights of more than 100 feet, spread thick vines to form a double canopy. Once trees reach 200 feet, they form yet another canopy that interweaves with lower canopies. The result is one huge canopy—almost like a spiderweb of vines, leaves, boughs, and branches—that covers the jungle floor in darkness. In such an environment, which was dark as well as damp, troopers would acquire a jailhouse pallor, sometimes with the horrible ulcers of jungle rot.

This was all in addition to the mortal dangers of combat. It took a while before it dawned on a "newbie"—or "FNG"—that he had almost a 100 percent chance of becoming a casualty. Troopers who had served the longest there knew the score and held out hope for a "stateside wound" in lieu of a body bag. A rucksack soldier under such conditions didn't have much to look forward to during the summer and fall of 1967.

The Fourth Battalion actually made two trips to Dakto during a six-month period. The first time, the brigade had been operating west of Pleiku in the vicinity of the Plei My Special Forces camp when Gen. William Westmoreland ordered it north to Dakto in the Kontum Province, at the confluence of the borders of Laos, Cambodia, and South Vietnam, where masses of NVA troops had been pouring into the Dakto area.

Accordingly, the Fourth Bat found itself operating in thick jungle by the last week in June. On July 10, it fought its first big battle with the NVA in the vicinity of Hill 830. Soon after this battle, it became apparent that the bulk of the NVA had departed the area, re-crossing the border in order to regain its strength for another try at Dakto. Meanwhile, in September and October, the Fourth Bat was moved to Tuy Hoa in order to protect that province's rice harvest from the NVA.

On November 1, when the NVA returned to the Dakto area in force, the Fourth Bat was loaded into Air Force C-130 transport aircraft at Tuy Hoa and airlifted back to Kontum, below

Dakto. The troops were then swiftly transported back to Dakto on trucks, and by November 2, 1967, the battalion was moving in the deep jungle west of Dakto in order to meet the enemy threat there.

By the afternoon of November 6, Dog and Alpha Company found themselves deep in battle with a superior force of NVA in the vicinity of a hill mass known as Ngok Kom Leat, while Bravo Company fought an identical action on Hill 823. Following this action, the men of the Fourth Bat referred to that entire battle as Hill 823. During this battle, Charlie Company's fight on nearby "Dog Hill" involved less NVA, but Chargin' Charlie was to get its turn five days later when it saw some fierce action as it went to the aid of Charlie Company of the First Bat, which was in dire danger of being overrun.

No one could know that less than two weeks later, the Fourth Bat would be tasked to assault the slopes of Hill 875, up through the remnants of our sister Second Bat, which had not only been chewed up by superior NVA forces, but had suffered the tragedy of being on the receiving end of two 500 pound bombs from a mis-directed friendly airstrike.

Hill 875 came to be known as one of the fiercest battles of the Vietnam War, with both battalions having suffered severe casualties while taking on the superior numbered NVA forces.

In mid-December, the Fourth Bat was once again returned to Tuy Hoa in Phu Yen Province, in order to aid the Third Bat in "Operation Bolling."

In late January, with the advent of the "Tet Truce," suspicious leaders, experienced at past chicanery by enemy forces during such "truces," designated the Commanding Officer of the Fourth Bat to provide an ever-ready reaction force which could become immediately moved to the city of Tuy Hoa in the event of an enemy double-cross.

This became the background for the Tet Offensive's Battle for Cemetery Hill in the vicinity of the city of Tuy Hoa. Dog Company, having been designated as the above-mentioned reaction force, ended up becoming nearly decimated during the two day battle commencing during the early morning of 30

January, 1968. By the time the battle ended, most of the battalion was involved in the almost complete destruction of the NVA's Fifth Battalion of the Ninety-Fifth Infantry Regiment.

As previously mentioned, the entire 173rd Airborne Brigade had been awarded the coveted "Presidential Unit Citation" for covering itself in glory during the Dakto Campaign.

Almost thirty-five years later, our Fourth Bat was awarded a separate "valorous unit citation" for their superb performance during the Battle for Cemetery Hill.

Ironically, that battle had started at about four o'clock in the morning, and our magnificent Lt. Col. James H. Johnson, whom we nicknamed Colonel Johnnie, was due to be replaced by a new commander around five hours later, but it was not to be. The way things turned out, he personally led the assault upon Cemetery Hill, earning himself the coveted Distinguished Service Cross and almost getting me killed in the bargain! He's a retired two star in South Carolina now, and we are still the best of friends.

I have taken the liberty of sprinkling some other stories in here too, which had a distinct bearing upon my overall career of thirty years with infantry fighting soldiers.

The purpose of this book is to salute those brave heroes, wherever they may be.

"I asked for all things, that I might enjoy life,
and was granted life, that I might enjoy all things."
—Anonymous Civil War Soldier

CHAPTER 1

The Coward

Arney was a coward. Cowardice was definitely an exception to the rule in my battalion of 750 brave paratroopers who were fighting like tigers against a numerically superior enemy in the rugged mountains of Vietnam's Central Highlands in the summer and fall of 1967.

At the time, I was sergeant major of the 4th Rifle Battalion of the 173rd Airborne Brigade. The brigade was a direct descendant from the famous 11th Airborne Division's 503rd Parachute Infantry Regiment. In February 1945, the 503rd covered itself in glory by wresting the island fortress of Corregidor from the Japanese Infantry after a lightning parachute assault upon its craggy cliffs. During a week of fierce fighting, the 503rd captured Corregidor, killing 4,500 Japanese with the loss of 450 of its own brave troopers.

The 173rd was deployed to Vietnam from its home station of Okinawa during May 1965, its two infantry battalions (the 1st and 2nd) augmented by the arrival of my 4th Airborne Rifle Battalion from Fort Campbell, Kentucky, a year later. Oddly enough, it would be another year before the 3rd Battalion reached the Central Highlands in October 1967.

It was during the aftermath of one of the 4th's battles at Dakto that Arney's cowardice was discovered. My investigation immediately brought some ominous facts to light. Arney was a coward—a live coward. His men were all dead or badly wounded except for two—and they were live heroes.

I interviewed these two, who were the sole surviving members of Arney's squad. All the others had been lost during our recent terrible battle with the North Vietnamese Army at Dakto, which is located in the steep, verdant, mountainous jungles near the confluence of the three borders of Vietnam, Laos, and Cambodia.

Arney had been squad leader for these two riflemen during the battle. Bravo Company had been the hardest hit of our four rifle companies, and the few soldiers who still survived were very proud warriors. They knew that they were very lucky to have made it through the battle, and they were extremely proud of their buddies who had not. Both of the lads I was talking with ranked private first class. Collins, the black one, was more aggressive and did most of the talking; his buddy, Smitty, simply nodded grimly or interjected a "right" or "hell yes" as the story unfolded. Both looked dead tired.

"Sergeant Major Arthurs," Collins said, "what we have to tell you makes us both very ashamed—doesn't it, Smitty?"

Smitty grunted, nodding his head.

"Our squad leader's a coward—a dirty, stinkin' *coward*—and I'm gonna kill 'im, first chance I git," Collins continued.

I had heard this kind of talk before and knew better than to condone or encourage it, but I didn't want to interrupt immediately and risk turning them off completely. I looked at each of them closely. They were as sincere as could be, and my long years of troop experience urged me to hear them through.

"Go on," I said softly.

"When he comes back to the jungle from that hospital, he's a dead man. If somethin' happens to me first, Smitty's gonna kill him—ain'cha, Smitty?"

The lanky Smitty shifted the cud of chewing tobacco that he was thoughtfully working on, eyed Collins a bit and then nodded.

"Damn right, Collie."

"They won't be no proof neither," continued Collins emphatically, "'cause we'll git him first time the slugs start flyin'," he nodded.

Looking at their serious faces, neither impressed me as an idle braggart; rather, they were stating simple, honest facts of life as they saw them. The two young men came across to me as country boys who were seeking their own brand of justice. It was a bad situation. The rain had ceased for the time being, but the monsoon still raged relentlessly in the Dakto region.

"Well, let's sit down here right now," I suggested, "and you guys can give me the story from scratch."

We turned our steel helmets upside down and sat on them. Collins had the reputation for being a very brave soldier, as did his friend.

"Yes, sir," he licked his lips earnestly. "Well, Smitty an' me an' the other squad members always thought that Arney was an all right guy. Outside o' him bein' a big city slicker, he seemed like a good leader who knew his job. He went out of his way lots of times to take care of us better than some other squad leaders we knew."

"He," Smitty spit a stream onto the muddy ground, "sure had *us* fooled, way it turned *out*!"

"Like how, Smitty?" I asked.

"Well," he wiped his mouth on his jungle fatigue shirt's sleeve, "like when the balloon went up an' we got hit so bad. He bugged *out* on us an' left us holdin' the *bag*! Way we figure it *now*, the minute the column got hit up ahead, an' we all took cover in the very deep an' heavy jungle, when the word come to move out, he must've stayed *hid*—an' that's the only way it could've happened!"

The tall, slim, sad-eyed Smitty was chewing faster, and I could see in his eyes that he was reliving those awful moments as Collins continued the story.

"Before it was through," said Collins, "just about the whole platoon bit the dust one way or the other. They killed the lieutenant and the platoon sergeant almost immediately. Our squad got hit the hardest. If our Dog Company hadn't come in from our flank and rousted 'em, they'd 'a killed Smitty an' me *too*! They really saved our bacon."

I asked, "Who could witness that Arney hid and didn't join in the fight?"

"Nobody," replied Collins."How do ya think I feel on this deal? Me an' Arney is both soul brothers. Two of the soul brothers who died in our squad were the best friends I ever had—along with Smitty, here—an' now they're gone. Not to mention the others, who me an' Smitty also thought the world of."

"We started with a twelve-man squad," said Smitty, "an' now we're down to me an' Collie . . . an' that coward in the hospital!"

"If," Collins continued, "Arney had been doin' his job an' organizin' the rest of us, we could've got through with only losin' *half* as many as we did. I know we could've!"

Smitty spit and closed his eyes. "Amen," he breathed, fingering his M-16 menacingly, as though he was thinking what Arney was going to get for his cowardice.

I had to proceed cautiously and attempt to convince them that there was a better way to punish Arney.

They knew that there was no way for a court martial to prove that Arney had bugged out with no witnesses, so they were determined to take the law into their own hands.

"Talk to Earl, the medic, Top," suggested Smitty.

I took pens and writing pads from my rucksack and had them write statements. I promised them that I would talk to the medic, and that Colonel Johnnie would bust Arney and ship him to another rifle company in our battalion. I convinced them that I would personally see to it that he went to a military prison if he continued his cowardly acts. I didn't want these two fine riflemen to endanger their own freedom to get revenge.

Then I went and interviewed Earl, the platoon medic. He was a fine black trooper and one helluva medic. He would be killed a few weeks later. Turned out that Earl had seen Arney limping around the loading zone after the battle, and it had been quite obvious that Arney had shot himself between two of his toes. Earl told me that Arney had thrown his boot away to conceal telltale powder burns but that he had given Arney a tetanus shot because of the powder burns. He specified, however, that he did *not* tag Arney for evacuation.

"He acted like a whipped dog, sergeant major," said Earl, "a cowardly soul brother. What a disgrace. I can't get over it." He shook his head in disgust. "He couldn't look me in the eye when I accused him of being guilty of a self-inflicted wound, but he denied doin' it."

Earl told me that there was absolutely no doubt that Arney's suspicious wound was self-inflicted. He said that he had told Arney that he was okay for full duty and would not be evacuated with scorched toes.

"Minute my back was turned," snorted Earl, "he snuck onto the next outgoin' chopper. On the chopper's return trip, the one door gunner told me. He had gotten off at the hospital."

I got a written statement from Earl and gave all three of them to Colonel Johnnie and told him the whole story.

When we flew to the 91st Evacuation Hospital to visit our wounded, we talked to the angry doctor, who willingly gave us a statement against Arney and discharged him to our custody.

We brought Arney back with us on our chopper and within fifteen minutes of our arrival back in the jungle, Colonel Johnnie had busted him for AWOL. The colonel had some choice words of wisdom for Arney, who could not bear the AWOL charge. Of course, Arney denied any wrongdoing, but the colonel busted him anyway and turned him over to me. I took him off to where no one could hear what I had to say to him.

"How long have you been in the Army, Arney?

"About nine years."

"Nine long years. Ever been in combat before?"

"No, sir."

"Okay. Now that it's all over with, what did you do it for, Arney?" I stared at him.

He decided to continue his bluff and told me that he was a victim of circumstances—and some liars to boot.

"Why didn't you demand a General Court Martial for cowardice in the face of the enemy, Arney. Your own troops won't shoot you unless they know that you are guilty, and that's definitely what is going to happen to you if you ever get around Bravo Company again. They have people standing in line for the privilege of gunning you down, Arney—and I can't say that I blame them after the way you conducted yourself."

He hung his head.

"By the time your own troops got through testifying against you, they'd probably have put you so far into the stockade that they'd have to pump sunlight into you. Dead soldiers and badly wounded ones—all because you didn't do the job you have been trained to do for years. All those poor kids died because of you."

He couldn't meet my eyes.

"The colonel knows what I know, Arney. There is no such thing as a dyed-in-the-wool coward. There are only soldiers like *you*, who didn't have their mind made up in advance that they'd do their duty—no matter—and who took the easy way out."

He looked uncomfortable and shuffled his feet.

"Everyone's going to think that you got off easy, Arney, but I know better." I looked at him sternly. "What would you give to be able to turn back the clock and get another chance to lead that fine squad of honest privates, who thought the world of you? Wouldn't you willingly die rather than to be branded a coward and to live the torment you do now?"

Tears rolled down his cheeks. "Yes, sir," he whispered, "I would."

I told him that his wife and three kids would never know of his cowardice—if he now did his duty. I told him that if he did not do it, he would be court-martialed and would go to prison, and that I would personally go and see his family and tell them the truth.

"Those were my troops that you betrayed, Arney. You owe them. You think about that. I am putting you in Charlie Company"—which I did that very afternoon.

The word got around, and the troops shunned Arney. From time to time I got progress reports from his new first sergeant that Arney was going great guns and going out of his way to attempt to redeem himself but the rest of the troopers still shunned him.

I took turns visiting my rifle companies for a week at a time, and several weeks later, I was with Charlie Company when they were ambushed by a superior North Vietnamese Army force.

We were hit hard, with heavy initial casualties, and the company's leaders tried very hard to form a perimeter of defense quickly, but there were ragged areas, and some of the wounded still lay outside the perimeter, helpless and pinned down, because the enemy was still bellied up there in force.

In most situations like this, the enemy used our wounded as bait to try to get their comrades to come save them and then gunned them down. It is difficult to listen to wounded comrades screaming in pain and fright, and three of our men had already been wounded—one seriously—trying to reach their buddies. One seriously wounded soldier wasn't too far from our perimeter.

Arney, who had been wounded in the neck and face by grenade fragments, was now safely within the perimeter. He was a sure thing to get evacuated—legitimately, this time—once a dustoff chopper could safely land. Calling to his other squad members to cover him, Arney sprinted to where his fellow rifleman lay, catching the enemy unawares and meeting only sporadic fire on the way out.

Arney made it back inside the perimeter with his wounded comrade, but both had been hit several times by the enemy, despite the heavy covering fire the squad laid down. As the guys dragged them in, they discovered that the man Arney rescued had been shot through the head and killed. Arney himself had been struck six or seven times, including in both lungs and once in the armpit, which is critical because of its proximity to the aorta. The great aorta, in a grown man's body, is almost as large as the inside of a garden hose. If someone's aorta is severed in the parking lot of a large, modern hospital, he might have a good chance to survive. Out here, Arney needed a miracle.

Jungle miracles are few and far between. I was lying beside Arney, trying to help "Greek," the platoon's medic, who was futilely trying to keep him from bleeding to death. The sun had set, and the light in the jungle—like the light in Arney's eyes—was rapidly fading. He might have been trying to shout, but it came out as a bubbly, garbled whisper.

"Sergeant major . . . sergeant major . . ." he gasped. The medic tried to quiet him, and the burbling gasps from his two chest wounds were hard to listen to. I dropped what I was bandaging and sat up to cradle him in my arms. It sounded as though he had only a few seconds to live. Incoming rifle fire cut down the bamboo around us, so I hustled to get flat again and placed my ear against his lips.

"Is the kid livin'," he gasped, "that I brought in?"

"Sure he is, isn't he, Greek?" I lied.

"Sure, Arney," the medic joined me in the lie.

Arney convulsed and wheezed.

"Ughhhhh . . . the kids . . . their pa . . . ughhhh . . . good soldier?"

I don't know if he heard me tell him that his kids would know that their father was a hero, because Greek suddenly shook his head "no" and crawled toward the next wounded soldier within the jungle's gloom. I looked into Arney's eyes and saw that he was dead.

Arney had earned a posthumous restoration to the rank of sergeant. He had partially redeemed himself. The Silver Star Medal, which his wife and kids would receive on his behalf, read in part, "Through his gallant acts, above and beyond the call of duty, he laid down his life for a comrade."

Arney was a hero. For him and his squad, the battles for Dakto had ended.

There were more to come.

Earl the Medic

Earl had three strikes against him from the start, three important reasons why he should never survive the Battle of Hill 875 at Dakto. First, he was a medic. Second, he was a medic in a rifle platoon. Third, he was a medic in a rifle platoon in combat. I knew, from bitter past experience in Korea and Vietnam, that this is the very deadliest combination of factors to have working against you.

There's a reason why so many medics get killed under fire. Troopers are severely wounded in the initial burst of fire, and things are quite disorganized for a time. Usually, the wounded soldiers are isolated from the rest, and if there is a large number of enemy in the area, one can count on being pinned down while the lead is really flying. But for the medic, it goes downhill from there. While everyone else is hugging the ground, the medic has to leave a safe spot and move to aid the wounded, or else someone bleeds to death or dies of shock. His creed calls for him to aid the wounded—no matter where, no matter when. Pound for pound, more medics get blown away under fire than any other soldier. When he gets to the wounded, he is at the center of the action, and the enemy knows that if he takes out your medic, you are in even worse shape.

Earl had been in the outfit for a long time, and so had I; he was scheduled to rotate to the states a couple of weeks before I was. He was a little older than our average trooper. Earl was a super-intelligent guy who had always been interested in medicine. He told me that his goal was to attend medical school after he left the military, taking advantage of the G.I. Bill. After basic and jump schools, he had attended the Medical Aidman's Course at the Fort Sam Houston, Texas, Medical Center. He was an expert in his field, and everyone admired him for it.

Immediately upon graduation, he had received orders for the 173rd Airborne Brigade. The 173rd had four rifle battalions, and we were lucky to get him in my battalion, the 4th. Over the months, he and I had become great friends. We kidded each other about being black and white buddies. Earl told me that he felt that a black medic had to soldier twice as hard as a white one, just to show that he could do it. Earl was a fine fellow and a good family man. His lieutenant, Carl Noyes, thought the world of Earl, who had already earned several decorations, and quickly nominated him for an expeditious promotion to sergeant.

Being a medic, Earl was armed with a .45 pistol. According to the rules of the Geneva Convention, no one shoots a medic. Therefore, medics carry pistols explicitly to protect the wounded, and wear the red cross armband so that the enemy won't shoot them.

Evidently our enemy in Vietnam wasn't too worried about little things like the Geneva Convention. Early on, our medics learned that the enemy used that red cross armband for target practice.

"Top," said Earl, "Earl is carryin' that pistol to protect *Earl* with!"

None of my medics would even think about wearing an armband. Earl said that all an armband brings you is free advertisement for a coffin.

Earl didn't have day-to-day experience in handling a rifle like the rest of us.

During this time, we had a new HQ Company Commander who was kind of strict. I thought he was out to make a name for himself. The only problem was that he didn't have much combat experience and sometimes he wasn't being entirely fair with the men—and they knew it. He stayed back in the rear all the time and as such, he didn't get to know the combat troops like Earl, and share their dangers and hardships on a daily basis like the rest of us.

He was nominally in charge of the medics, as they were all assigned on his morning report. As such, he had a lot to say about who went on R&R and so forth, but outside of that he did not have any control over a medic who was assigned to one of our rifle companies in the jungle, like Earl was.

A rifle company, performing "search and destroy" jungle missions, had to be supported by artillery to keep large numbers of enemy from overrunning it. The artillery pieces were slung beneath helicopters and flown into a jungle clearing already secured by our infantrymen.

We would keep one of our rifle companies dug in around the artillery to provide them around the clock protection, while our other three rifle companies fanned out and hunted the enemy down.

The colonel and his staff remained within this perimeter along with our 4.2 inch heavy mortars. In this fashion, the commander could control all our firepower.

After a couple of weeks, the whole process would be repeated with the fire support base being moved into a new location in another part of the jungle in our area of operations.

As an aftermath to the ferocious battle where Arney had been killed, choppers brought into the fire support base all the weapons and equipment and rucksacks belonging to all the troopers who had been evacuated as dead or wounded.

The monsoon still raged, and all that gear was in a big pile, just wallowing in the mud. You have to see a mess like that to really comprehend what it looks like.

The correct procedure at a time like this would be for the unit's S-4—the supply staff section—to clean up the gear for reissue to incoming replacements.

Earl was assigned to Bravo Company and this rifle company was performing the perimeter guard for the fire support base.

The new HQ Company Captain overstepped his bounds of authority by pulling Earl off Bravo Company's perimeter and ordering him to clean rifles from the pile of gear.

The captain should have stayed out of the act, because it caused a big, unnecessary fiasco. Some people call this "stepping on it while wearing golf shoes."

This young captain had Earl and two other medics cleaning and oiling the weapons while squatting beneath their ponchos, next to the big, muddy pile. It was a stupid deal from the start. The captain should have simply let the supply folks pick up the gear and clean it back in the rear area. We were about fifteen miles out in the jungle in our artillery fire support base, and it was raining to beat hell.

Anyway, it all came out in the wash when a shot rang out. I was talking to the colonel when—BLAM—the shot filled the air and everyone ducked because there's no way of knowing initially who is on the business end of a rifle being fired in a combat area. You must assume it's a catastrophe until proven otherwise.

After all the excitement was over we found that one of the rifles lying in the pile of gear had still contained a round in its chamber. While Earl had been cleaning it, lying beneath his poncho to keep out the downpour of rain, he had pointed it up in the air and snapped the trigger. The round had whizzed off harmlessly through the trees. No harm done.

About five minutes later the HQ Company Captain brought Earl to the colonel and demanded that he bust him down two stripes to private, and to fine him under Article Fifteen punishment for having accidentally discharged the weapon. There's a very good basis for being strict on accidental discharges, for many a good soldier has lost life or limb by accident due to this very thing.

I thought, however, that there were quite a few extenuating circumstances to consider, and as sergeant major, it was my duty to participate in any action of this nature.

It was still raining heavily, so, the colonel and I and the captain and Earl were gathered in the colonel's little six foot by eight foot tent which was kept in the fire support base for him.

The colonel was doing most of the listening, along with poor Earl and me, as the captain ranted on and on. It was obvious to me that he was trying to impress the colonel, but I could see that he wasn't.

Colonel Johnnie had served in many rifle units in all kinds of leadership positions during his infantry career and the colonel knew what I knew: that in the final analysis, Earl had taken the precaution of pointing the weapon skyward while he snapped the trigger, which is standard procedure.

"Sir, it's within your authority to reduce this man from Specialist Fourth Class to Private and that's what I want you to do. I think it's a disgrace that a man with his rank could pull such a dangerous, ignorant stunt, and I want his stripes and that's all there is to it!"

Colonel Johnnie stared at the captain. Then he looked at Earl. "What have you got to say about all this?"

Earl looked the colonel right in the eye. "Nothing, sir—except that I'm sorry that it happened. I guess he's right because he's the captain. I am guilty, sir. I pointed the muzzle skyward and snapped the trigger, thinking it unloaded—because it was dark beneath that doggone poncho, sir!"

Colonel Johnnie was no fool. By this time, he had surmised just about the same things that I had about the matter. He was impressed that Earl was truthful and not trying to muddy the water with a bunch of excuses to try and worm out of it. The colonel looked at me.

"Sir," I said, "Earl's our best medic. He's number one on the list for promotion to sergeant. He has been awarded the Silver Star for gallantry in action, plus two Bronze Star Medals for valor. He's been wounded three times and shouldn't even be here."

The colonel nodded. He was well aware of the regulation which required that after three wounds, we transfer a trooper to a safe job in the rear.

"He has voluntarily stayed with the 4th Rifle Battalion for the sake of our troops because we are short of medics. He was cleaning someone else's weapon and a rifle is not his basic firearm—"

"Sir," interrupted the young captain, "the sergeant major's siding in with a man who endangered my life and yours and I want—"

Colonel Johnnie stuck up his hand. "Now, we'll get back to your turn to speak in just a minute, captain. Continue, sergeant major."

"Yes, sir. Well, it was an idiot deal from the git-go. Who in hell ever heard of putting three medics to cleaning forty rifles in a dad-blamed tropical downpour—under ponchos? It's dark as hell under a poncho in the rain and before we go any further, I think that we should find out right here and now, who ordered such a half-witted stunt, sir."

"Now," the colonel's eyes twinkling, he said, "it's your turn, captain."

"Well, um, sir," the captain stammered, "I saw the stuff all piled up there and I thought I'd take action to, um, get the job done, um as soon as possible, sir!"

"In a pouring rainstorm? Did you tell these men to clean those rifles beneath their ponchos?"

"Um, yes, sir, I did."

Colonel Johnnie scratched his face with his left hand, like he did when he was perplexed. "Fine. Fine. Well, I feel Earl has been punished enough for scaring the wits out of everyone. Sergeant Major Arthurs, you and Specialist Earl are dismissed. Captain, I have a few points for you to ponder, if you will kindly remain here."

Earl and I saluted and departed.

The word got around. Earl had deserved the good break and all the combat troopers were reassured that they were in a good outfit where they weren't going to be punished unless someone took a good hard look at all the circumstances.

That's what makes the difference between a good outfit and a poor one. Under Colonel Johnnie, we had the finest battalion in Vietnam.

Earl was an outstanding human being, medic and soldier. He vastly respected his mother and sent her money and wrote to her at least as often as he did to his girl friend back home. He would make an outstanding doctor in civilian life, as he had already made his mark with us.

Then came the battle for Hill 875. Our sister battalion, the Second, had been hard hit partway up the hill and was out of action. They had so many wounded that their units had to form perimeters in place, keeping their wounded in the center while they defended their stand against a vastly numerically superior enemy.

Their Chaplain, Father Watters, had been in my company in the states. I was his first sergeant and got him into shape to attend jump school and become a paratrooper. He was the

Chaplain for the Second Battalion when he was killed on Hill 875 and was subsequently awarded the Medal Of Honor posthumously.

It was no accident that the Second Bat had suffered so many casualties. The NVA had fortified the "military crest" of the tall, steep hill, with bunkers and tunnels. When the Second Bat brought in air or artillery strikes, the enemy soldiers simply ducked into the tunnels to escape and then bobbed out unscathed to once again man their fighting positions, mowing down the Sky Soldiers as they assaulted up the rugged hill.

On top of everything else, the Second Bat was accidentally bombed by one of our own jets, killing several dozen and wounding most of the rest.

This was the situation when our Fourth Bat was ordered to assault through the area occupied by the Second Bat and to take the hill after evacuating what was left of the Second Bat.

A few able members of the Second Bat attached themselves to the Fourth Bat.

It was during one of these assaults upon the hill that Earl was killed. The law of averages had caught up with him while he was up front tending to a seriously wounded trooper.

Several weeks later, we were in another area and I received a surprisingly fresh and well-packed cake and a letter from Earl's mother. It, and all my possessions later became lost, so all I have is my memory of the letter's contents.

She thanked me for having been Earl's friend and for being someone that he had looked up to. She stated that the cake was for his friends. When I removed the waxed paper, I saw that on the white icing, words had been laboriously printed in infantry-blue wording: HAPPY BIRTHDAY, EARL, WHEREVER YOU ARE

The medics and I and some others who remembered Earl well ate the cake. I had a lump in my throat the size of a golfball, but I ate my share.

Earl was some soldier and one helluva medic. I think of him often and of what might have been for him and all the others.

For Earl, the Battle for Hill 875 had ended.
For the rest of us, there were more to come.

In memory of Earl Kennon Webb

CHAPTER 2

Killer's Tunnel

Killer didn't look like John Q. Public's concept of what a hero looks like. When you come right down to it, what does a hero look like? Killer was a slim teenager with brown hair. I had spent three years in the U.S. Marine Corps, and two dozen years in the airborne infantry—the Paratroops—and had met my share of heroes. They were just ordinary looking people. In fact, some of those considered to be most likely to become heroes, never did, and some of the very least likely came through with flying colors when the chips were down.

Killer originally picked up his nickname from his own squad leader, due to his eagerness to volunteer to walk point when it was his squad's turn, or to go on nightly ambush patrols. In civilian life, Killer's hobby had been weapons and he knew a lot about them. He was a crack shot with a rifle and pistol, and it wasn't very long before the first sergeant of Dog Company convinced the captain that they should leave Killer on the point all the time, with one other expert rifleman as backup for this position.

With only one hundred men, our Dog Company was our smallest rifle company and in many instances acted as our battalion's recon element.

Killer soon acquired the vast knowhow and expertise to become a legend in Dog Company. He instinctively steered them out of ambush situations with a uncanny sixth sense concerning the whereabouts of the well-concealed enemy.

Up until that day late in November, when Dog Company encountered the tunnel complex, Killer had never been wounded—not a scratch.

Killer had been in Dog Company for several months when the action occurred in the fall of 1966. The 173rd had been in Vietnam a little more than a year at that time. Reactivated on Okinawa in May 1963, it had been the first U.S. Army unit into Vietnam in May 1965.

This particular operation was being conducted in War Zone D, just north of Saigon. Local V.C. units had been located here for years and had dug a tunnel complex which was magnificent.

The entrances to these tunnels were so cleverly camouflaged that you could be standing right beside one and never see it.

When the fight started, Killer saw this enemy soldier shoot and kill his old squad leader with a rifle and then duck down into a tunnel. Quick as a flash, while Killer was getting out of his rucksack to go into action, two more enemy soldiers appeared seemingly from nowhere and ducked down into that same hole.

That didn't slow down Killer one bit. Although he knew that there were three armed enemy in that tunnel, he grabbed his .357 Magnum Python which he had brought from the states and carried as a sidearm, and scurried down that hole before anyone knew what was happening. The tunnel ran back beneath the paratroopers' feet who were still up on top of the ground.

There was the sound of scuffling, thumping, and shouting and howling—and then quiet. Then, farther into the tunnel, it happened again and then quit. Everyone up top side did some fast mathematics and figured that the second enemy soldier must have done Killer in. If not, why hadn't they heard him gunning the third soldier in the tunnel?

Nobody knew quite what to do at this point. They started calling into the hole for Killer. No dice. They called the Vietnamese words for "surrender"—*Chieu Hoi*—which every GI knew. Still no answer.

About this time they heard this grunting and dragging sounds and gasping going on inside that tunnel and everyone jumped back. Out popped Killer, bleeding like a stuck hog, from an open, sucking chest wound. He hauled a dead Clyde out of the hole by the neck and threw him down at the feet of his platoon leader.

"Lieutenant," he gasped triumphantly, "there's the rotten son of a bitch who killed my old squad leader—signed, sealed, and delivered!" Then he fell over on the ground and the medic began working on him.

Everyone looked at each other. They couldn't figure it out, because the dead body didn't have a mark on it. Not so much as a scratch. Killer had that bad sucking chest wound, and they were trying to hold him down long enough for the medic to bind this serious wound and then lay him on the wounded side like the book says to do, to keep him from drowning in his own blood.

Killer howled with glee. "He shot me as I crawled to him, but then his rifle jammed! That'll teach that dumb-assed Clyde to clean his friggin' weapon," he chided!

"He had me dead to rights," he continued, "'cause I was re-loadin' my Magnum after killin' the last two who went into that hole, an' when he shot me in the dark, I heard him—not two foot away—fiddlin' with his jammed rifle, an' I just up an' grabbed him an' choked his ass to death."

At that point, everyone could see the marks on the body's neck. As an afterthought, Killer addressed the lieutenant.

"Sir, please do me a favor an' have someone crawl into that tunnel an' bring me my .357 Magnum. It's about ten feet past the second body an' down a little sharp left turn, like!"

Killer was just as calm as if he was giving directions to the school house.

That was Killer's number-one feet-first go-round in South Vietnam. He was awarded the Silver Star, the Vietnamese Cross of Gallantry with Gold Star, and the Purple Heart for this episode. Most of the troops thought that wasn't nearly enough, but Killer couldn't see what all the fuss was about.

He was evacuated and in the process, some rear echelon type stole his expensive pistol from off his litter while he was unconscious!

One could see why Killer kept a very special place in his heart for rear echelon soldiers . . .

For Killer, the battle for War Zone D had ended.

There were more to come.

The Chinook

Killer was evacuated from the jungle about five or six months before I arrived in the Fourth Bat. When I went out on an operation with Dog Company, I heard many stories about his prowess as pointman. Eyewitnesses told me about his bravery during the tunnel incident.

I was pleasantly surprised, therefore, when he approached me at An Khe, where I was attending a Sergeant Majors' meeting.

"These REMFs won't listen to me, sergeant major," he began, "and send me back to the Fourth Bat. They're cuttin' orders on me, sendin' me to the Second Bat. Will you help me?"

Of course I did. While at An Khe, I talked an Ordnance Sergeant out of a beautiful M-14 rifle with a powerful scope already mounted on it, and I presented this to Killer when I assigned him back to his beloved Dog Company. It became his proudest possession.

Our mission placed us in open country for a few weeks in coastal rice paddies and during that time, he killed more enemy soldiers with that rifle, than any single squad in my battalion.

Then we went into Dakto, located in Kontum Province, right near the confluence of the Laotian and Cambodian borders. It was like being a nut in a nutcracker: because of the political ramifications involved, we fought the North Vietnamese Army with one hand tied behind our backs.

We couldn't cross either border in pursuit of them, so they would just sit across the border, build up their forces, and when they were at their strongest posture, they'd cross the border and attack in force, gobbling up American units which were only a fraction of their size.

As soon as our airstrikes and other firepower would start to overwhelm them, the NVA would swiftly retreat over a border and repeat the process.

Meanwhile, the American battalion which had been chewed to pieces would receive two or three hundred brand new replacements and be sent right back into that jungle for the next round with the NVA.

This happened to my battalion of about seven hundred riflemen on three separate occasions. During my year, this battalion of fine paratroopers suffered 125 killed in action and 503 wounded—some, two or three times.

An infantryman going into the Dakto area had a one hundred percent chance of being killed or wounded—but not captured. The enemy headshot every wounded soldier in every case that I ever knew about where they trapped wounded.

They would play cat and mouse games with them in order to entice their comrades into coming to rescue them, and then they would add those scalps to their belt, too. They were a cruel, unfeeling, ruthless foe and it sickens me when our high-ranking officers return to Vietnam and hug their counterparts of former battles as though they were respected comrades-in-arms.

My bitter memory is longer than that.

My troops called the deep, dark jungle the "Land with No Sun." The triple-canopied mountainous jungle was so thick that you had to squint to see your watch clearly in broad daylight. Many of those trees are over two hundred feet tall and six feet thick at the base. The next interlacing canopy of trees might be one hundred and fifty feet tall, with its myriad vines running to the taller trees and down to the single-canopied forest of one hundred footers. It was like standing beneath three separate circus tents consisting of very thickly interlaced vines and normal foilage. Not a very pleasant way to spend a year—seldom seeing the sun while humping an eighty pound rucksack half the day, everyday.

Our rifle companies were conducting search and destroy missions—three out in the jungle and one dug in around the artillery fire support base. They took turns a week at a time guarding the FSB, which was a good deal for a lot of reasons, not the least of which was the fresh cooked food from the mess tent as opposed to the jungle "C" rations.

While in the jungle, the rifle troops ate canned "C" rations, five days straight. On the fifth night, the "firefly" resupply chopper would bring in "C"s for the next five days. The poor, tired and wet troops looked forward to this because at the same time, they were fed a meal of "A" rations—freshly cooked food—from the FSB. This food was transported in insulated "marmite" five gallon containers similar to the current picnic cooler.

The monsoon was in full force, and the troops had been soaked, week after week. It gets cold at night in the mountains of the Central Highlands. People give me a very curious look when I tell them that I had several of my troops med-evaced from the jungle with pneumonia, but it's the truth.

Dog Company had "laagered" for the night on the side of a steep ridge which had been partially leveled by an "arc light," or B-52 strike. The term "laager" evolved from an Afrikaan term describing a defensive encampment encircled by wagons.

Humping an eighty pound rucksack could be likened to carrying your living room TV set on your back. After eight or ten hours of this, the troops had to dig foxholes in the extremely hard mountain laterite soil. After this, right before dusk, some would then go on an all night ambush patrol to cover avenues of likely enemy approach.

It was about this time that Dog's firefly had deposited two cooks, along with the coveted food for the hungry troopers, and Killer got himself into some very serious trouble. It took all the pull that I had and all that the colonel had to keep him from being court martialled.

The incident involved the pilot of a CH-47 "Chinook" double-rotored helicopter. This is a huge ship, capable of carrying over thirty fully equipped troopers and is most often used as a heavy cargo ship for delivering supplies or sling-loaded artillery pieces to jungle positions.

The hitch is that the ship is so powerful—it must be, to do the things for which it has been designed—that its twin rotors blast away Hell and half of Georgia with the turbulence it causes on landing or taking off.

Now, flying a chopper in combat in the jungle is a tough racket, but so is being a grunt. A grunt, or rifle soldier, leads an extremely cruel life in the jungle. After all that humping and digging, he can only sleep about fifty percent of the night for he must be awake half the time on an ambush patrol, or taking his turn on perimeter watch during the night. There's not one ounce of fat on a grunt, for obvious reasons.

The grunt knows that for every guy like him in actual combat, there are several rear echelon personnel with normal jobs, who have it made compared to him. He thinks that no one cares about his plight outside of his immediate outfit and this is magnified when a chopper pilot pulls a stupid stunt like this Chinook Pilot did on Killer and his friends.

Those who have stood anywhere in the vicinity of a landing Chinook know all about the terrible things which usually happen to a bunch of grunts huddling beneath their poncho shelters, trying their best to keep the rain out—their clothing already soaking wet—and no way to ever get dry. Fires were forbidden.

One could almost write a book about the experiences of troops who were exposed to such blasts. At any rate, a chopper pilot must take a bunch of things into consideration when taking off or landing; wind direction, trees and other natural obstacles and myriad other things. The troops understand this.

All things considered equal though, an astute, considerate pilot will consider any troops he sees on the ground and avoid landing near them and tearing up their gear—where possible. There are many astute ones. There are some inconsiderate ones also. It was Killer's misfortune to run into one of the latter jerks at the wrong time.

The Verdict

Dog Company had hardly settled for the night and it was still drizzling rain. The troops had gone through some serious fighting in recent days and they were exhausted both physically and mentally. They had eaten "C" rations until they were coming out their ears. Everyone was looking forward to some freshly cooked hot chow.

The two cooks had the chow line set up and they were just getting ready to feed the first hungry squad when in comes this Chinook with its rotors blasting the whole world away. Instead of the pilot approaching the landing zone from an intelligent angle, which he could have done as the wind and everything else was right, he came in quite low over the chowline.

The horrible blast upset all the chow from the marmite containers onto the ground and blew all the pans and lids off into the jungle. Paper plates were used in the jungle to prevent dysentery. Paper plates flew for miles.

Dog company's beef stew, green beans, vegetable soup and the jello and cake were strewn for thirty or forty yards along the jungle floor. Two thousand slices of fresh bread went into orbit like huge snowflakes in reverse.

As the mystified Colonel Johnnie and I watched this fiasco, I thought of the Biblical manna from Heaven. The mess tent ballooned into a huge ball, divested itself of its tent stakes and, flapping like some gigantic monster manta ray, took off from the jungle clearing, out over the thickly matted jungle rooftop to its final unknown destination—probably in some two-hundred-foot treetop.

There was no joy in Mudville; the Chinook pilot had definitely struck out. There would be no fresh chow for Dog's combat troops.

There wasn't a smile in our entire outfit as the hungry, battle-hardened paratroopers craned their necks to prevent being brained by flying pots, lids and everything else you could think of. No one could believe that it was happening. Then, to top it all off, the pilot overshot his landing spot, made the full run of the edge of the jungle clearing, gaining altitude for another try, but in the process, he ruined every poncho shelter in Killer's platoon. Most of those troopers, discerning what was about to happen, had deserted the chowline, grabbing their precious, fragile shelters and hung onto them for dear life.

Those who weren't near enough to grab their own, watched helplessly as their rainproof ponchos, which they had rigged as tents, and their camouflaged nylon poncho liners, used like comforters in the cold mountains, wafted up and out high over the jungle canopy never to be seen again.

This sort of thing is equivalent to losing one's entire life's savings in one fifteen second span of unearthly catastrophes. In addition to possible pneumonia, they suspected that they had just been sentenced to go completely without warmth or shelter for a week or two until the supply system could once again provide them with these bare necessities of life.

In one grand, ear-shattering sweep, the Chinook had wiped us out. Some troops were more bankrupt than others, however. It was just too much for Killer. The injustice of this, on top of everything else which had happened, must have caused him to blow his stack temporarily. As the Chinook wheeled back around to make its next pass, Killer jacked a round into his weapon and blasted the full magazine—tracers and all—in the vicinity of the airship's rotors.

He never intended to do any damage to the chopper—and he didn't—but he got that pilot's attention. As the troops all cheered, the flustered pilot had to make still a third pass before he succeeded in making a shaky landing. He came stomping off that huge ship and came up the hill looking for our commander. We found out later that he hadn't been in country very long, and was green as a gourd.

At the same time, Killer could have remained in the obscurity of the rest of the troops on the ground and no one would ever have told on him for simply scaring that stupid Chinook pilot to death. In their mind, he should have gone all the way and shot him. As it was, the only damage had been to the pilot's nerves, and that must have been considerable.

Killer arrived at where the colonel and I stood, just about the same time that the irate pilot got there. He showed the colonel and me his frayed pup-tent rope and confessed to being the shooter, right in front of the ashen-faced pilot.

"Sir," said Killer, "my buddies an' me lost our hootches, ponchos an' shelters an' all. All I got left is this cruddy tent rope because one end was tied to a tree an' the other end was tied to my poncho hootch which is now somewhere on the other side o' the horizon—"

"Listen, you—" sneered the pilot.

"You be at ease," Colonel Johnnie said, holding his hand up, "and listen to this trooper. You might just learn something."

Killer looked from one to the other of us and continued in his soft voice.

"Sir, the only reason I'm bringin' this here pup-tent rope to the sergeant major for safe keepin' is because some of the troops who ain't got no chow nor no hootch, was eyein' my rope, an' mutterin' 'bout hangin' this "shit-hook" pilot here with it from one of his own rotors."

I had to bite my tongue.

"Vacate," Lieutenant Colonel Johnnie told the pilot. "You vacate." He jerked his head toward the Chinook. "Get it unloaded and get out," he said, "and I'm not even going to mention to you how carefully you had better fly it on your way out, either, captain. Are there any questions?"

"Yessir," the young pilot saluted. "What are you going to do to this guy for cutting down on us with that rifle?"

Colonel Johnnie looked at him for a couple of seconds. "I can guarantee you, captain, it's going to cost him. Now, git!"

He got. The colonel turned to Killer. "From now on, you let *me* take care of Chinook pilots. If you ever pull a dumb stunt like that again, I'll put you in jail—and that's a promise. As it is, taking into consideration your fine record as pointman for Dog Company, I'm fining you five cents."

Killer looked sheepish. He looked from the colonel to me and back again. He looked so forlorn, standing there with that silly pup-tent rope dangling from his hand.

"Thank you, sir," he said sadly, "but I ain't even got a nickel. My pay was fouled up when some dumb REMF lost my pay record. I ain't drew a nickel in two months—not that I need money here in the jungle."

"Sentence suspended," the colonel nodded. "You tell your buddies we'll have some ponchos and liners out here one helluva lot quicker than they've been used to getting them. Translated, that means tomorrow morning you'll have them—and that's a promise."

The colonel dismissed him and Killer trudged back across the ruined chowline area with the rope still dangling from his hand.

"What" asked the colonel, "is a REMF?"

"That," I laughed, "stands for 'Rear Echelon Mother Fucker.' The troops don't feel that everyone back there does his utmost, the way all of them have to do just to stay alive."

He laughed good-naturedly.

"By the way, sir," I added, "that was kind of a stiff fine for you to award to a first offender, wasn't it?"

"Yeah," he snorted, and shook his head as we both looked at the backside of the departing Killer.

"Yeah. What in Hell are you going to do to a guy who's just lost his house and home, is going to freeze his ass off in the rain tonight, ain't been paid for months and is very likely to get zapped tomorrow or in the very near future while on point?"

It wasn't long after that when Killer was nominated for the Medal of Honor by the colonel. It was during the Battle for Cemetery Hill.

The AK-47

Two weeks later, the 4th Bat participated in the bloody battle for Hill 875, which I'll describe in detail later. Then, after receiving 335 replacements, we were moved into the coastal plains area of Tuy Hoa—pronounced "Tooy Waw," with the mission of searching the jungle to prevent the NVA from absconding with the area's rich rice harvest.

In most tropical areas, rice is planted twice yearly, in ankle-deep water. It's a backbreaking job, but to the peasants it's a cash crop as well as a guarantee against their own starvation. No simple task, each seedling must be gently planted in the water by peasant farmers wearing the ubiquitous black cotton pajamas.

Even during non-monsoon season, it rains a lot in Vietnam and these simple garments quickly dry while still being worn.

I'd been there about eight months in the jungles and rice paddy warfare was something new to me. We kept one rifle company patrolling the hamlet/village areas where the paddies met the jungle.

A second rifle company guarded our artillery fire support base in the jungle, supporting the other two rifle companies in the jungle and the company in the paddies simultaneously.

During my eight months, this was the first time that our battalion of seven hundred riflemen had been moved out of the jungle and into a rear area, and fate decreed that we'd get only forty-eight hours of such rest before being committed to the jungle once again.

Many other infantry outfits which I had buddies assigned to, operated on a more lenient schedule—staying out in the jungle for a few weeks—then returning to the rear for rest and training of new replacements.

Our 173rd Airborne Brigade, consisting of four infantry battalions, was only about one third the size of a regular infantry division. It could be swiftly moved hither and yon, so it ended up being a "fireball" outfit, moved like a chess pawn— usually from the frying pan into the fire.

My poor raggedy-assed troops looked upon this forty-eight hour rest period as a matriculation into Heaven itself! We coordinated for the nearby air force base to send one of their base exchange vans out to our area, bringing our men the first beer and other goodies we'd seen in over three quarters of a year.

Our outfit allowed absolutely no alcoholic beverages in the jungle. Colonel Johnnie allowed our guys two beers per man the first day, during which time they each laid out their field equipment and weapons for inspection. Our S-4 Supply Section made a valiant attempt at trading unserviceable items for new ones.

I would say that each of our four rifle companies, "A" through "D," had accumulated at least ten percent of extra weapons, acquired as an aftermath of battles. After Lieutenant Colonel Johnnie and I discussed the pros and cons, we let the troops keep them.

"We have a great fighting machine here," said Johnnie, "and if it ain't broke, we ain't fixin' it." He was my kind of guy and richly deserved the two stars which he eventually retired with.

I knew his background. Throughout his military career, when his peers were scrambling for staff jobs or special schools, he opted to command troops. This experience held him in good stead in combat.

"Doc Ed," our battalion surgeon, had his medics handing out suntan lotion to the troops, closely watching for telltale signs of sunburn. "Beats the 'Land with No Sun,' " observed one private whose skin had acquired a jailhouse pallor during his many months of life in the dark, dank and moldy jungles of the Central Highlands.

After our scant hours of paradise, my troopers reluctantly re-packed their rucksacks as the battalion once again made its way into the jungle.

About three weeks had passed, when I saw Killer for the last time in Vietnam. He was lying in his hospital bed in Tuy Hoa. His right thumb had been shot off and he had been shot through the lung again—just like his first "feetfirst exit" from Vietnam fourteen months before.

This seemingly indestructible rifleman was cussing a blue streak about "those thievin' low-life, non-combatant REMFs" who had once again stolen his .357 Magnum Python, only this time they had also stolen the AK-47 that had gotten him nominated for the Medal of Honor.

The group around his bed included the one star general who commanded the 173rd, his sergeant major, "The Pope,"

Colonel Johnnie, and me. Years before, the troops had hung that moniker on "The Pope" because of his stringent religious convictions which prevented him using any stronger profanity than the word, "Cottonpicker," to vent his feelings.

He was one cottonpickin' good soldier, though. One of the best.

"Well, now," beamed the general tolerantly, "ah, Killer, we'll just have to see about getting your weapons BACK for you, won't we, sergeant major?"

"Yes, sir," chorused The Pope and I simultaneously.

Killer squirmed and made a slight maneuver to sit up in his bed, which was countermanded by pain. The nineteen year old hero looked our general right in the eye.

"Well, thank you, sir," he said softly, "but mind ya, though— I'll know if it's the same enemy rifle, so I hope nobody tries to foist off no ringers. If they can't really find the right one, please don't let 'em bring me nothin', sir."

That was typical of our Killer—quiet talking but honest and forward.

Killer was a hero and a half. He had received these terrible wounds during the battle for Cemetery Hill during the January 30-31, 1968, Tet Offensive.

During hand to hand combat, he had killed one enemy soldier with his own rifle after snatching it away from him, and then, badly wounded, he had proceeded to clean out the remaining holes of those still resisting.

No one who made the assault upon Cemetery Hill and survived would ever forget Killer's heroic struggle. We sixty-four who still lived of Dog's original eighty-three in the initial assault force could never forget the nineteen who died on those slopes, either.

CHAPTER 3

The Great Doublecross

Near the end of January, the 4th Bat air-assaulted a prominent terrain feature in the jungle above Tuy Hoa, establishing a fire support base in support of our rifle companies, which were beating the bush in search of the NVA. During this period, Colonel Johnnie was notified that our battalion would provide a reaction force to handle any emergencies that might occur during the forthcoming truce in our area of operations. Dog Company was designated as the reaction force because it was operating in an open area adjacent to rice paddies while two of our other rifle companies were operating in the jungle and the fourth was guarding our FSB.

Both sides had agreed to the truce, ostensibly so that the Vietnamese populace and the enemy soldiers could observe their religious "Tet" holidays. It's a good thing our leaders had anticipated a massive doublecross on the part of the enemy.

As the witching hour approached, the colonel's radio operator and I deepened our foxhole, which turned out to have been a great idea at three o'clock the following morning.

"*In*coming! *In*coming!"

Zzzz Zk—Ka-ROWWWL, Zzzz Zk—Zzzz Zk—Ka-ROWWWL— ROWWWL! The earth around us shook violently as those terrible thirteen-pound 82mm mortar rounds struck in and around the small perimeter. We violently shuddered and vigorously hugged one another, huddling at the edge of the foxhole as the next three rounds walked up to us, their awful explosions promising quick death.

Miraculously bracketing our hole, the waning barrage slowly made its way toward the artillery pieces, mysteriously petering out just short of the nearest gun. Gratefully breathing the acrid cordite fumes permeating the area, the three of us shakily exited our lifesaving foxhole.

"Are your paws," lightly suggested Stanley, the radio operator, "shakin' like *mine* are?"

"Mm-hmm," my shaking voice confirmed.

"Parablast Six, Parablast Six," intoned his radio, summoning Colonel Johnnie, to inform him that the fat was in the fire. The colonel was notified that the enemy was assaulting another artillery FSB that was also supporting us. This base was located beside one of Tuy Hoa North Airbase's landing strips which lay between the sea and the jungle, surrounded by sandy hillocks a few hundred feet in elevation.

Colonel Johnnie immediately notified his staff to coordinate for two Chinook CH-47 helicopters to race to Dog Company's area, while we boarded his "C&C"—that is, his command and control ship, which our pilot, Pete, had expertly flown through the dark night to us. Our outfit did not permit helicopters to remain in jungle fire support bases overnight.

While our friendly forces played by the rules of the truce, fair and square, the enemy—across the country—was already moving large forces in the dark against just about every major city and built-up area in South Vietnam.

As it turned out, it was lucky for the city of Tuy Hoa that our contingency force was ready to react, but it was mighty unlucky for Dog Company. The fortunes of war decreed that before the sun set that night, all but a very few of Dog's eighty-three men would be killed or wounded on Cemetery Hill.

The 5th Battalion of the NVA's 95th Infantry Regiment, about the size of ours, had quietly infiltrated a small village next to the Tuy Hoa North Airstrip on the night of January 29. They had pressed the village's able-bodied civilians into service and forced them to dig fortifications and make other preparations, just in case the NVA became besieged.

A representative of the province chief notified our brigade staff that a grizzled patriarch of the village had somehow escaped and made his way to the South Vietnamese authorities, informing them of the NVA's activities. He couldn't provide a definite figure on the enemy's strength; all he said was that there were "many" of them. We should've listened to him, but our intelligence experts had heard that same story time and again and evidently felt that the enemy had purposely released him in order to embellish their numbers.

Apparently, the commander of the NVA's 5th Battalion of the 95th Infantry Regiment was confident that they could sneak into our area, accomplish their objectives, and then move out again before we could extract our paratroopers from the nearby jungle and fight them. Either that, or he was stark, raving mad. In any event, he ended up killing himself and 188 of his men in order to prove his point. Another thirty of them were wounded and captured before the battle ended.

A couple of hundred yards north of this little village was a huge government prison filled with VC and other prisoners. On the other side of the prison was the large American artillery compound which, according to our radio alert, was being overrun, and it was our intention to move Dog Company to that location in the two Chinooks which were now enroute to Dog's position. The enemy's plan had been to pull a sneak attack on this compound, neutralize the artillery, and take over the prison. They intended to release the prisoners, who would then join forces with the NVA in the effort of taking over the entire city of Tuy Hoa.

If it hadn't been for Dog Company, they might well have accomplished their mission. At about 0300 in the morning, in the pitch blackness, a platoon of these NVA soldiers sneaked down from the village, breaching the wire and taking over several bunkers in the southwestern portion of the artillery compound. They then commenced raising hell with the rest of the compound by sending small groups throughout to shoot it up. The element of surprise was initially on their side. By the time that Colonel Johnnie got the word and alerted Dog Company for extraction, the situation within that compound was terrible.

The thunderous roar of our C&C ship's rotor alerted Captain Jackson and First Sergeant Knight to our impending arrival at Dog's location. I flicked the butterfly on the radio console to Dog's frequency for the colonel.

"Dog Six, this is Parablast Six, over," intoned Colonel Johnnie.

"Dog Six," came the immediate reply.

"Dog Six," answered the colonel, "we are on our way to your location. You have about zero five minutes for your troopers to get packed up and ready to roll. We have a real hot one on the fire. How about giving us a little light down there to guide us in on. Over."

"Dog Six, I roger," came the reply.

I looked down at the black jungle below us and thought grimly to myself, Sure hope that brother Clyde doesn't take this opportunity to go flashing any lights from *his* position.

My fears were allayed moments later as we arrived over Dog's position in the dark elephant grassed area below. Colonel Johnnie advised Dog Six to blink his light one time for each letter of Dog Six's last name, as I smiled to myself over my previous apprehension concerning the light business.

After receiving proper authentication in this manner, the colonel ordered Pete, our pilot, to descend and land within the jungle clearing below. Colonel Johnnie jumped out with me following him and greeted Dog Six Capt. Jimmy Jackson.

"Hi, Jack. Spread your poncho here on the ground and let's crawl under."

Art Knight, Dog's First Sergeant, was busily engaged in getting the troops rolling. I crawled beneath the poncho and held Captain Jack's flashlight while the colonel briefed him with the map on the soon-to-be-launched assault.

"Ummm, looks pretty furry, doesn't it, sir?" Captain Jack observed soberly.

"Yeah," Colonel Johnnie nodded, "and we have to move out *fast*. While we are headed to that compound, I'm having my operations officer back in our FSB arrange for Charlie Company to hump to a jungle clearing as fast as they can for immediate extraction to come and support you at the compound.

The nearest clearing might be three or four hours travel time for them, but I'll make it happen as soon as I can."

"Didn't you say there is only an estimated reinforced platoon in that compound, colonel?"

"Right. But there's a whole battalion known to be in that vicinity. If we run into them you sure could use some assistance from Charlie Company."

"With a mind like that, sir," grinned Captain Jack, "it's a good thing you never turned to crime."

Captain Jack was a good guy, and his troops loved him, just as they did his brave first sergeant, Art. Jack was a black policeman from St. Louis; his ambition was to return to the force there.

"Colonel Johnnie's last day in this battalion is today," I informed Captain Jack. "We are scheduled to attend his doggone changeover ceremony about four hours from now—and he ain't never gonna make it!"

The three of us laughed at the irony of the situation. How could any of us know that fate portended that six hours from then, Colonel Johnnie would lead the initial assault up Cemetery Hill and earn the nation's second highest decoration in the process.

We detected the sound of the Chinooks approaching from somewhere out on the fringe of the horizon as they approached Dog's location. The initial gray fingerlings of light painted the treetops as we shook hands all around.

"We'll be right there with you, Jack," encouraged Colonel Johnnie.

We were shaking hands with First Sergeant Art Knight, one of the finest combat leaders I have known, when Pete jumped from the C&C ship and ran to our group.

"Those hooks will play hell with my rotor if they land on top of us, colonel," he said, so we jumped back aboard and took off while the Chinooks circled, preparing to land.

The colonel would have ordered ten smaller Huey choppers instead of two Chinooks if he'd had a choice. A Chinook is a big target, with lots of eggs in one basket, but no Hueys had been available.

As we circled above, we could see Dog Six's light guiding the two hooks into its clearing. Most of Dog's troopers were quickly loaded, and the rest waited for one more hook to arrive and pick them up. Time was of the essence. The Chinooks took off, and the colonel guided our ship and led the hooks to the vicinity of the compound. When we were still a thousand yards away from our LZ, we could see the bluish-white enemy tracers lacing the compound and the red American tracers zipping about in return.

Reminds me, I thought to myself, of Hollywood's black hat on the bad guys and white hats on the good guys.

Pete made the appropriate approach, and we weren't at all surprised when the enemy tracers stitched the sky around us. I didn't say we weren't scared.

The Compound

Colonel Johnnie led us in from a low angle. We didn't know yet that only about one-tenth of the enemy were in the compound and that the rest of them were lying in wait for us just a few hundred yards away on Cemetery Hill.

Our attempt to evade the enemy's fire proved successful until about the last hundred yards. Up until then, they couldn't see us because of our low altitude. During these last few seconds of the approach, we were perhaps sixty feet in the air when we came into their view and received a hail of tracers among our three-ship formation, bringing down one of the Chinooks just as we had settled to about thirty feet and prepared to land.

Fortunately, the downed chopper didn't blow up. It hit hard and bounced a few feet into the air and bounced again, abruptly coming to a stop, and then canted to one side. The badly shaken troopers and the ship's crew came billowing out the rear like smoke. Colonel Johnnie and Captain Jack had previously decided that the men would leave their rucksacks aboard the hooks.

In the few minutes it had taken us to fly from where we had picked up Dog Company, false light had ended, and we were in that slate-gray predawn period just prior to sunup. None of us knew at that time that we were just practicing in that artillery compound for a horrible assault that would come a few hours later that morning, one which would make our initial one look like a Sunday School picnic.

The troops formed up and entered the compound using fire and maneuver against the part of the perimeter known to contain the bunkers that the NVA occupied. We had no trouble locating them since the spearhead elements of Dog were receiving fire from that direction.

Colonel Johnson immediately located his CP at a huge rockpile that had evidently been formed when engineers had intially graded the ground for the base's location.

As it grew lighter, it became apparent that the compound was composed of large self-propelled 8-inch and 155mm howitzers. These guns were much too heavy to be flown into the jungle by helicopter, unlike our much lighter 105mm artillery pieces. Evidently, the enemy had considered the neutralization of such powerful, far-reaching weapons to have been of primary importance to their overall master plan. Dog Company was the only fly in their ointment, and before the day was over, the enemy commander and his force were to find that Dog Company would also become a terrible thorn in their side.

The 173rd's 3rd Battalion of the 319th Field Artillery Battalion had previously emplaced a radar site within the compound. The 3/319th's commander, Lt. Col. Robert E. Whitbeck, was on his way to the radar site when he was killed by enemy riflemen.

Fortunately, our S-3 had coordinated with the Air Force to place one of their powerful "Spooky" C-47 gunships on station to support Dog's assault, and as Dog's spearhead element began receiving fire from the large rice-paddy area to their front, the colonel notified Spooky to severely hose down the area.

While this was going on, Dog's "spearhead" element of the initial assault group, using fire and maneuver, got into place in order to destroy the first bunker. With Spookey keeping enemy heads down in the rice paddies, Dog's platoon leader gave the signal to attack. One group put down a heavy base of fire while the second group swiftly leap-frogged into position and neutralized their objective using grenades and the powerful Light Anti-Tank Assault Weapon, known as "LAAW."

Several of the artillerymen had been killed during the enemy's initial sojourn through the wire before they could get into foxholes and bunkers. In turn, the Americans had killed several of the enemy as they ran around attempting to shoot up the compound.

The balance of the NVA soldiers were occupying the bunkers in approximately one-third of the perimeter, and as the sun came up, it fell to Dog Company to ferret them out. It hadn't dawned on Colonel Johnson that the nearby government prison was part of the NVA enemy commander's assault plan.

At this point, I would like to mention how cool Colonel Johnnie was under fire. As Dog had been settling into place to assault the bunkers, we had all been vastly surprised by the large, sudden volley of fire being placed upon us by the enemy's hidden support group located in the rice paddies. Everyone took cover except Colonel Johnnie, who led our small group of five in a sprint to an open area between two bunkers which were closest to the paddies. In a very few minutes, he was in radio contact with our supporting Air Force C-47 "Spooky," who, at his direction, began spraying the paddies with its miniguns.

We were lying in the sand near the edge of the partially secured portion of the compound's perimeter when the colonel asked Spooky to bring the fire in a bit closer to the perimeter. I don't know what it looked like to Spooky at their altitude, but from our perspective, it looked like thick raindrops hitting a pond.

What seemed like millions of machine-gun slugs, arriving before their sound, cascaded into the sand around us. Their whirring sounds reminded me of the sound effects of a movie I had once seen where hordes and hordes of locusts were descending.

We five were the closest to the storm of slugs. Some of the slugs splattered the sand between and around us. Miraculously, only one man was wounded in our group.

I thought for sure it was all over for us. Colonel Johnnie was on the radio in a flash, his voice so calm that it belied the shaken feelings he must have been enduring along with the rest of us.

"Spooky," he calmly admonished the pilot of the C-47," you're shootin' us, dammit, please lift your fire and put it a wee bit farther out."

That's all there was to it as far as Colonel Johnnie was concerned, but it was mighty close. He was one cool customer.

Dog's troopers continued the dangerous job of cleaning out the Clydes who still occupied the bunkers. They went about that task, providing covering fire for each other while one force neutralized the bunkers with grenades.

Lieutenant Colonel Johnnie led our CP group back to a big rockpile, the closest point to the government prison, when we got a radio message from the 173rd's one-star commanding general. Up until this time, we had received no fire at all from the vicinity of the government prison, about four hundred yards away. Beyond the prison, Tuy Hoa's tall, sandy dunes stretched into much higher foothills that culminated in a group of what looked to be a mountain range of huge sand dunes covered in vegetation.

Act II began as our general's C&C ship settled amid a storm of sand and dust fifty yards from our rockpile CP as Colonel Johnnie and I ran out to greet it and bring the general and his aide to the scant shelter of our rocks.

At first, because of the noise and turbulence of the chopper, we didn't realize that we were receiving fire from the vicinity of the government prison. At least two snipers were cutting down on our group from one of the prison's watchtowers. Clyde knew that it's usually some high-ranking folks who arrive in such fashion.

As the four of us reached the rock pile and snuggled into its base, I unlimbered my M-79 grenade launcher and opened its 40mm maw, inserting one of the eighteen grenades I carried in my vest. It was obvious that the two snipers were firing from one of the prison's four tall watchtowers, and I decided that the closest one was the culprit.

It took me two rounds to get the sights exactly set, and just as I plopped a round into the tower's parapet, one of Dog's lieutenants expertly hit the tower with a LAAW, and that was all she wrote for the snipers.

My small audience at the rock pile was awed at such accuracy until I explained the simplicity of the M-79. The round that it fires looks for all the world like a huge .22 rifle bullet, firing a highly explosive projectile which is about twice as heavy as a golfball. The weapon is so accurate that three years before, at a demonstration at a range in Baumholder, Germany, I fired a grenade into the opened window of a derelict automobile 350 yards away.

Several hours later, I was to repeat that performance on Cemetery Hill.

By this time, Brig. Gen. Leo H. Schweiter and his aide-de-camp, 1st Lt. Frank H. Akers, had regained their breath after that swift sprint under fire.

Akers had been a platoon leader in our 4th Bat and saw his fair share of action. He had probably heaved a big sigh of relief after having been selected to be our CG's ADC. Most young lieutenants look upon such a plum assignment as the "racket of the century." Following General Schweiter around, however, was no sweet deal, as Frank Akers was soon to find out. He and our S-3 major, Jim Oerding, would both distinguish themselves scant hours later during the battle for Cemetery Hill.

The general was no stranger to enemy fire, having served in World War II and Korea in every leadership position from platoon leader through battalion commander.

Colonel Johnson was on the radio, coordinating with Dog's CO, Captain Jackson, when I presented the general with Colonel Whitbeck's dogtags, wallet, and other personal items, indicating that the poncho-shrouded remains nearby were those of his brave artillery commander.

Sadly, he handed the personal items to his aide for safe-keeping. He placed his hand on my shoulder and told me that it looked like the start of what could be a very bad day for Dog Company. As Colonel Johnson finished his radio conversation, General Schweiter told us that he had just received some bad news from his S-2 intelligence officer. A nearby village was thought to be in the hands of a large NVA force.

The general instructed the officer to immediately get into contact with the Phu Yen Province chief's advisor and to let him know what could be confirmed. I could read between the lines here and soon discerned that if the NVA held hostages, our assault would be costly since there could be no advance "prep" with friendly artillery and air.

"No question of it," agreed the general. "The bad thing is all those hostages. You know what that means."

At this point, Dog Company piled the bodies of eighteen NVA soldiers in front of the compound, and Captain Jack gave them a break to eat a "C" ration breakfast.

The gaunt-looking artillery captain and his first sergeant came to the rock pile to thank us for our help.

I took the artillery first sergeant to one side. "Look," I told him, "you guys are in good shape now, but we have some bad shit facing us. See that hill mass over there?" I told him that I had some very bad feelings about this pending operation and asked him to have his guys scrape up every extra hand grenade they could find, plus ammo. We'd do it all.

Dedicated to the memory of

LTC Robert Earl Whitbeck
1st LT Lawrence D. Greene
S/Sgt Miloslav J. Martinovski
PFC Arthur Floyd Elliott
PFC James Calvin Bodison
PFC Alvin John Wesolowski
PFC Thomas Henry Swinnea
PFC Robert Charles Peters

PFC Gene Autry Ross
PFC Edward Eddy Cervantez
SP4 James M. Larouche
SGT John Henry Tigner
PFC Brad John Szutz
SGT David Wayne DePriest
SGT Robert Eric Lockridge
SGT Jack Roger McKee
PFC Jimmie Paul Wall
PFC Norbert Elliott Froelich
SP4 Peter Wellesley Foote
SP4 William Thomas Jarvis

And to all the others on "The Wall."

Cemetery Hill

The plan called for Dog Company to make an approach march past the prison, neutralize any enemy, then ascend Cemetery Hill from the rear up the lowest hillocks adjacent to the side facing the ocean. Once we reached the assembly area, we were to await gas masks and some new weapons capable of raining "CS"—an irritant similar to tear gas—onto the defenders of our objective.

This was as close to an advantage as we could get although we found out after the battle that most of them had gas masks just like we did. Our only hope was that the enemy force consisted of a rifle company like us, one that had already lost a third of its number to the pile of corpses outside the compound.

It turned out that the enemy had only penetrated the watch towers of the prison before our arrival and were starting to flee as Dog's point element approached. Dog's riflemen cut down four or five.

Another few hundred yards and the unopposed point element began climbing the wild hillocks comprising the gradual inclined surface of the rear slope of Cemetery Hill. So far, so good. At this point, Colonel Johnnie's C&C ship arrived with

Sp-5 Rufus Humphrey, our chemical NCO. Rufe had several duffel bags filled with gas masks and five of the brand new experimental contraptions (known as the E-8).

An E-8 was about the size of a kitchen wastebasket, and contained 64 "roman candle" type cylinders of CS gas with a propellant charge beneath each individual one like a miniature mortar round.

I had never seen one before, and I haven't seen once since. Each had folding legs to be extended as a baseplate, and a device for slanting the business end toward the enemy so that the strike on target could be adjusted.

There was no surprise intended, because the Province Chief, worried about the hostages, asked that we have a "Psy-Warfare" light aircraft fly repeatedly over the village with an interpreter to broadcast that the enemy should surrender and that any noncombatants must be released. We gave them an hour to do so.

Needless to say, it didn't happen. Everyone knew that this maneuver was hopeless and they kept trying to shoot the aircraft out of the sky. When it finally got too hot for them the pilot flew off.

As we couldn't prove if any hostages were held in the village, we had to proceed as though they were. That meant rifle against rifle. Bad odds for the offensive and good for the defensive.

The colonel instructed Rufe to preset the E-8s from fifty yards on up to two hundred. We were ready to roll as soon as the hour went by.

Those who have experienced it know how awful it is, sitting there waiting to attack an objective bristling with armed riflemen. In regular combat, many casualties are victims of shrapnel from mortars, artillery or bombs, but today, Dog's troopers faced bullets and grenades—a deadly proposition.

There were eighty three of us in that initial assault element, sprawled about the ground in a shallow saucer-shaped depression a few feet from the top of the hill, but still out of sight of the enemy below.

Colonel Johnnie, Captain Jack, Art, and I crawled up to the hill and peered over its crest at the objective below. The first thing we could see in front of us was a huge cemetery. From the looks of some of its stones, it must have been there for centuries.

I'd much rather be dug in behind a gravestone than to be the one charging it. Beyond the graveyard existed a very steep slope, bottoming out with some flat, open ground which culminated at the very outskirts of what must be a good-sized village. There wasn't a soul or an animal stirring and it was almost ten thirty in the morning of the January 30, 1968.

Because of superb camouflage, what we could not discern was that on that flat, open ground at the edge of the village, the enemy had prepared three "V" shaped formations of dug-in fighting positions, pointed at us like some great phalanx.

Sprinkled throughout that whole area were numerous equally well-camouflaged "spider-holes." A spider hole is a small foxhole with a cleverly designed cover so that it cannot be detected until you walk by it and the enemy soldier pops up and shoots you in the back. To our practiced eye, this seemingly innocuous scene looked like waiting death.

As it became obvious that there was no turning back, men shook hands with one another and whispered small talk of encouragement. Rufe selected four riflemen, each to jerk the fifteen foot lanyard which was attached to his assigned E-8 device, while he, himself held one.

Colonel Johnnie nodded to Captain Jack and donned his gas mask. Everyone else followed suit. All eyes were upon the colonel and on Rufe's designated operators.

"Fire!" commanded Colonel Johnnie, his voice muffled by the tight rubber gas mask.

Five troopers pulled their lanyards. Nothing happened, absolutely nothing.

We were crushed. This was the only edge that we had on the enemy and now, even this one little ace in the hole was gone.

What none of us realized was that it took a while for the fuses to catch. Suddenly, with no warning, all five devices commenced loudly sputtering at once. Then, the rocket-like containers started taking off skyward like huge Roman candles on the Fourth of July! We watched in fascinated awe as 320 miniature canisters, each streaming propellant and gas, arched high into the air, then plummeted earthward. The enemy saw the origin of the rockets and began placing rifle fire on the crest of the hill, which we had to cross on our way into the cemetery.

I prayed to God that it wouldn't be too hard to die. A searing fire built in my gut and then it felt as though someone were stomping on it with both feet. I vividly recall a mixed feeling of fear and regret that I had been too stupid to retire from the Army instead of volunteering to come here as I watched the enemy slugs splatter the sandy loam around the assembly area.

Just as suddenly, this feeling evaporated and was replaced by a resolute one that not only was I not afraid, I was going to survive this assault, and I was going to tear up some Clydes' asses with that M-79 and AR-15 of mine and make them pay for anything that they did to my troopers.

The colonel extended his hand as we lay side by side, flat on the ground and we shook. It was time! After another second or two, he smacked me hard between the shoulder blades and leaped up.

"GO!" he screamed and ran forward, waving his hand like the "Follow Me" statue of the infantry leader at Fort Benning, Georgia, the home of the infantry. The plaque on the statue contains the inspiring words:

> WHEREVER BRAVE MEN FIGHT AND DIE,
> YOU WILL FIND ME.
> I AM WITH YOU—NOW AND FOREVER—
> I AM THE INFANTRY, QUEEN OF BATTLE!
> FOLLOW ME!

"GO!" he screamed. "GO! GO!'

We charged that graveyard, screaming and firing as we went. Like eighty-three wild, vengeful apparitions, we seemed to float through that graveyard, rifles blazing, and down that

long slope which ended up strewn with Dog's killed and
wounded.

After the battle, we surmised that our initial charge had
carried us through the first phalanx of trenching and into the
second, where we bogged down because we were being shot in
the back from the spider holes which we had inadvertently
bypassed.

Those contesting our conquest of the cemetery during the
first few seconds of our attack never really had much chance as
we completely overran them, killing everyone. The assault continued rolling down that long slope from the cemetery and
almost into the outlying areas of the village itself, but the
enemy riflemen made us pay for every inch of the contested
ground.

We could only partially penetrate the second line; our
losses were too great. By this time, everyone was crawling, using
grenades and rifles at sometimes point blank range on the
holes and bunkers.

We were pinned down, but good, from an element on a
high shoulder of ground to our left. Killer was in the element
in closest proximity to this position when the enemy killed his
lieutenant. This particular lieutenant was a helluva guy and was
well-liked by all the men. Even though his own dad was an
army general, the lieutenant maintained the bearing of a regular guy and really looked after his men.

It was too much for Killer. Just like when he fired up at that
Chinook with his rifle, he had reached his limit.

"Come ON!" he screamed to his other squad members
above the din of the firing. "Let's go git 'em!" No one would
go. They were all hugging the ground and trying to return fire
simultaneously.

"No, Killer!" someone screamed, "There's too many Clydes
over there! Wait!"

A rifle slug took Killer's right thumb off and splintered the
beautiful sniper rifle's scope on the weapon which I had given
to him two months before. That was the last straw. It was all

over for those enemy soldiers on that shoulder, they just didn't know it yet.

Crawling swiftly to his dead lieutenant, the stub of his thumb badly bleeding, Killer grabbed his rifle from beneath his body, inserted a fresh magazine, and set the weapon on semi automatic, to fire single shots only. Those twenty shots were to get him nominated for the Medal Of Honor.

"We come here to kill Clyde!" he screamed, as he charged the enemy foxholes without firing a shot. The rest of the troopers supported him by fire as best they could in an effort to force the enemy riflemen to keep their heads down. Before it was over, enemy slugs had torn through his jungle fatigue jacket and trousers and took the guts out of his wristwatch.

With bullets raising geysers in the sand around him, Killer arrived in the vicinity of the foxholes and began his Clyde-extermination program. After he had cleaned out the third hole full of Clydes and was rushing the fourth, Killer seemed to strike an invisible wall, spinning him around and knocking him down as an NVA in a hole he had yet to see shot him through the chest with a rifle. Killer bounced right up and killed him.

Missing one thumb and with a slug through the lung, this one man army ran out of ammunition. He was in bad shape in the middle of three holes full of Clydes who were very much alive. The only thing that saved him was the heavy fire which his comrades kept pouring into the area around him.

At this point, a confused enemy soldier suddenly thrust the muzzle of his AK-47 from his hole right beside Killer, who jerked the weapon away from the surprised soldier, killing him with his own rifle. Killer now had a loaded weapon and two holes to go to bat a thousand. Killer batted a thousand.

He slumped to the ground. The pressure was finally relieved on our left flank, and we were able to rally our forces.

Killer had saved the day; now we had to save Killer. Other enemy were still in a position to be able to place fire on that position. Using fire to suppress those doing the damage, Killer's squad gained the top of the shoulder and dragged him down to where he wasn't exposed. He had a death grip on that AK-47 and it came down with him.

"Give me another rifle and come with me!" he screamed. "We'll kill every one of these dirty, rotten sons of bitches who killed our lieutenant!"

Killer was a bad man to cross, and a sore loser. He just didn't know the meaning of the word quit.

Colonel Johnnie took stock of the situation and knew our troopers needed a lot of grenades, and we didn't have them. Rolling to me on the sandy ground, he told me to find an able bodied trooper to sprint back up that slope through the cemetery and run to the artillery compound, some seven or eight hundred yards away.

I looked around me at the dead and wounded. I was pushing thirty-nine, didn't smoke, and was in fine shape. I told him that I was going, and he said if I made it to bring back one of the tracked vehicles and park it behind the cemetery so that we could evacuate our seriously wounded with it.

You have to realize that the enemy was in holes, mostly, and we were all lying flat. Anything exposed was fair game. I bounced up and sprinted a few yards in the loose sand and hit the deck and rolled.

Through short relays like that, I made my way quickly to the foot of the long slope leading up through the cemetery. I knew that slogging through that ankle-deep sand up that steep slope was going to slow me down and make me an easier target.

All I had to do was to make it through that cemetery and the contours of the ground would protect me. The following morning, Stanley, the colonel's radio operator, and I measured the long sprint I had made up that slope, and we figured it at sixty-five yards.

"I'm gonna make it," I gasped to myself as I looked up that formidable steep slope. With a quick prayer on my lips, I jumped to my feet and hit that slope, trying my best to bob and weave every few yards.

At least two enemy riflemen took a vast interest in my desperate trip. With slugs kicking up geysers of sand around me, I was almost to the graveyard when one came so close to my ear that it sounded like someone had just missed me with a dump truck.

"Oh, God, oh, God," I gasped, begging for mercy and help as I entered the cemetery. Up until that time, I hadn't been touched until slugs ricocheting off gravestones got to me in the form of a sliver of flying fragment imbedded between my right thumb and wrist. The next day a big bruise appeared on my one thigh where I must have banged into a tombstone in my fright and never realized it at the time.

With one last fearful bound, I was through the graveyard and into our former assembly area on the reverse slope of Cemetery Hill. I had made it. No sooner had I finished congratulating myself than a new thought formed: I have to go back there.

CHAPTER 4

My Journey

My chances seemed better now. I kept going until I reached the smooth asphalt of the airstrip. This was a near-fatal mistake on my part. As I dog-trotted by the government prison, I noted two bodies to my left front which hadn't been there when we had passed through this area on our way to the assembly area for the assault upon the hill.

I was approaching them, perhaps twenty five yards this side of them when I discovered where the bodies had come from. HHOORROPP! The bullet just missed my head and caused me to hit the asphalt and roll. At this time, two more slugs tore fist-sized hunks out of the asphalt around me.

I have heard and read of dog-tired men suddenly finding an extra reserve of energy. I believe it. Terror-stricken, I streaked to my feet and tore for the ditch on the far side of the strip, hurling myself into it and rolling the last few feet from where my adversary had last seen me.

I knew that he was on the slope across that airstrip and that rifle report sounded close.

When I made the cover of the ditch, I wasn't fool enough to try and look for that sniper. He knew exactly where I was, but I intended to change all that. I immediately crab-crawled my way swiftly down the ditch and got the hell out of his private domain. I wasn't looking for revenge.

I believe that fear and panic can make one's body completely unfeeling of pain or weariness. Eventually I found that I had crab-crawled completely past the prison and was right across from the compound. I jumped up and made a run for it back across the asphalt strip. No one shot at me this time.

In very short order, the captain and first sergeant were making things happen. Top motioned for a driver to bring forward one of their tracked vehicles, used to tow the huge 155mm artillery pieces.

"This is our best driver," said the captain, "and he has volunteered to help you. You'll take care of him, won't you?"

"Sure, sir." I looked at the vehicle. Unlike the armored personnel carriers assigned to the infantry, this "prime mover" was open, front and rear, with no armor.

"I got shot at by at least one sniper on this airstrip on the other side of the prison," I leveled with them. "You," I nodded to the driver, "will be exposed, you know."

"So will you, sergeant major," he shrugged. Good kid.

"You guys are catching Hell up there, aren't you?" said the first sergeant sympathetically. "Anything more we can do?"

"No. Thanks. They've got hostages, so we couldn't prep. We've had a dozen killed already, and Pat here is going to be bringing you a bunch of badly wounded on his return trip. Can you folks evacuate them to the Tuy Hoa Airbase Hospital for us?" They assured me that they would send their own medics with our guys, and radio for medevac ships for the more seriously wounded, as dustoff choppers couldn't get anywhere near Cemetery Hill without being blasted out of the air.

They waved farewell to me and Pat Stafiero, probably figuring they'd never see either one of us alive again, as Pat expertly moved us down the strip approaching the prison.

"See those two bodies on the right, Pat? There's an expert sniper on that high bank to the left somewhere, so let's give him a fast moving target!"

Ahead of us lay a lonely, several-hundred-yard trip back to the edge of Cemetery Hill, and I could feel someone's eyes on us like a hawk on a pigeon. I'll never know why that sniper didn't cut down on us again at that point, but he might have moved by then.

I was feeling cocky at this point. I should have known better. A few seconds after Pat had wheeled to the right to start up

Cemetery Hill's reverse slope, I heard the distinct "PHOOON-NFF" of an American M-79 grenade launcher being fired from behind us to the left where Clyde must have infiltrated.

Simultaneously, I heard the "Waaaas—WAAS—WAAAA-SSSSS—SSSHHHH" of the swiftly traveling incoming grenade, followed a second or so later by the terrible sharp "KACHO-WWWOW" explosion of the projectile where it landed several feet away from our carrier. Its shrapnel pinged all over the carrier and sang its song of death.

I knew, because I carried one, that this weapon is so accurate that the next round was very likely to be right in the open rear of the carrier, on top of all those cases of hand grenades and other ammo!

"TURN, DAMNIT, TURN! I screamed to Pat and it seemed to take him forever to skid the vehicle sideways as I heard the inevitable sound of the second round; "PHOOONNFF!"

A second later, its "Waaaas—WAAS—WAAAASSSSSSSS-HHH-KACHOWWOWWW" right on the left side of our carrier. We had turned just in the nick of time. The concussion lifted our eyelids. I urged Pat to turn us completely around so that we could back up the hill, which he expertly did.

From the sound of that M-79, its firer couldn't have been more than 150 yards from us, and at this point, our NVA friend with the captured U.S. weapon was undoubtedly licking his chops at the prospect of such a fat target. He was good, but now he had to make a helluva shot to get us. Maybe he ran out of grenades or he didn't want to waste them, for, to our relief, he quit trying.

We parked the carrier in the original assembly area for the assault, completely concealed from the enemy below as I took Pat forward to point out to him the route we would take in carrying the cases of vital grenades to our troops below.

From our present vantage point above the cemetery, we could see much more of the entire battle area than Colonel Johnnie and Captain Jack could below, due to the contours of the ground around the enemy positions.

"Look at that!" said Pat. I had seen it also. What looked to be two fireteams of enemy riflemen had sprinted across a road and entered a fairly large—by peasant standards—one story building situated where they could better place fire upon our troops.

"Watch this," I said, as I set the sights on my M-79 for one hundred and fifty yards. I still had fifteen projectiles in my vest. Extracting four, I dropped to the ground and took careful aim at one of the two windows facing us. Remembering to slightly compensate for the steep slope, I put two of the grenades in each window. Two of the grenades' victims staggered from the door on the building's right and fell to the ground, flopping around, so I dug a fifth projectile from my vest and put them out of their misery.

Pat whistled in appreciation.

I knew that we had to get down there with those grenades, and looking the ground over from above, I could see a much safer route. Instead of going down through the graveyard, if we went around to our left and then down through a big gully, we would come out right behind the little ridge where Killer had charged on those dugin riflemen.

I furtively looked behind us down the slope where we had been fired upon by the M-79 and calculated our odds. If there were a lot of them over there, they would see us making those trips with the cases of grenades and returning the same way with our more seriously wounded and they could kill us both easily.

On the other hand, those grenades were going to slow us down if we took the more direct route through the cemetery, but I already knew they'd fire us up going that route, because that's the way I had made my sprint.

The medics at the artillery compound had bound up my wrist and thumb, but I still had four good fingers on the wounded hand. A grenade case contains thirty grenades as I recall, and has a rope handle on each end. I figured that Pat and I could handle two cases each because we were going downhill.

I told him the plan, and we each grabbed two of the heavy cases and made our way over the route which I had decided upon. Once we got to the gully, the going was easy, as we simply laid our cases on the ground, grabbed a rope handle in each hand and slid down the slope, finally using the same method to go uphill.

Just as I had figured, we ended up about thirty or forty feet from the nearest troops on that flank, who saved a case and began relaying the other three across the line.

I told Colonel Johnnie that we had NVA behind us.

"Shit," he shook his head cynically. "Just what the hell we need. Our Charlie Company is still at least an hour's walk to the nearest LZ for extraction from the jungle. If anything happens behind us until they get here, we're all dead."

I nodded. I told him about the more protected route up to the carrier, by skipping the cemetery and told him that we had mucho grenades and ammo still in the carrier.

He told Captain Jack to have the four seriously wounded brought to our location with two able-bodied men per wounded and that those eight men would unload the carrier, bringing as much ammo and as many grenades back down as they could, while I accompanied the wounded to the artillery compound. Captain Jack told him that the medics were completely out of plasma and asked if I would try and scrounge some.

Surprisingly, it went off like clockwork and when I got back to the compound, they took care of our wounded and gave me a jeep and driver who knew where some rear echelon unit was in the nearby city of Tuy Hoa which had plasma.

I couldn't believe how cheerful Killer was, lying on that litter, wisecracking about Clyde. The other three wounded were unconscious.

"Thanks, Top," he smiled. "Sorry I lost that great rifle with scope that you gave me, but those Clydes should 'a brought their lunch before they fucked with ole DAWG Company, huh?"

"That's okay, Killer. You did a helluva job on those Clydes with your lieutenant's rifle."

I shook hands with his good hand and bid him farewell. I told Pat to take the carrier back to Cemetery Hill and I jumped into the jeep which the Artillery First Sergeant gave me to go and look for plasma.

Lucky for us, the driver knew right where to go because I had never been near any city in Vietnam and certainly didn't know my way around Tuy Hoa. Fortunately for us, the unit we visited was only about a half mile from the very end of the airstrip.

We picked up the eight or ten units of plasma which they could spare and jumped in the jeep to make the trip back up to where I could climb Cemetery Hill. We were about half way back to the airstrip, and right at the edge of town, when large groups of civilians began running across the road from our left. All of them were screaming and waving both arms at us to go back where we had come from!

"V.C! V.C!" they screamed.

We couldn't proceed because there were hundreds of them crossing the road. We couldn't retreat because we had the precious plasma. We could see a fringe of armed soldiers behind the panic-stricken crowd. We were sitting ducks!

"Go! Go forward," I yelled.

Leaning on the horn, he surged through the milling crowd. I knew we were going to run over some of them, because they feared the V.C. more than they did a moving jeep, but we missed each one of them, and when we broke completely free of the crowd we were home free. At least one of the enemy cut down on us on full automatic, tearing up the air and ground all around us as we tore off amid the fusilade of whizzing rounds.

Many weeks after the action, I learned that the artillery commander had nominated this driver for the Bronze Star for valor and Pat for the Silver Star for their exploits. Good men.

When I got back up on Cemetery Hill, I found that Pat had made another trip with the carrier, bringing more grenades which the artillery first sergeant had scrounged for us at the Tuy Hoa Airbase, and making another trip back with casualties.

Those guys saved our bacon. As the forward element of Dog stretched all the way across the enemy's front line just a few yards apart, those grenades were worth their weight in gold.

A few yards behind that line, the enemy's third—and final—line was providing us with plenty of action, but considering the condition of our troops, there was no way that we could attempt to ferret them out.

A few minutes after my return, the enemy pulled a stupid stunt, tantamount to suicide, as it ended up getting most of them killed. They eliminated their one big ace in the hole.

They began igniting the thickly thatched straw roofs of the dwellings, probably in the hope that they could evacuate that third line of defense through the thick smoke created by such a diversion. The catch to this heartless maneuver was the trapped inhabitants who were being burned to death as a sacrifice to the enemy's escape.

Well, we caught four aces on that deal because our Charlie Company was starting to arrive and set up in a semicircle above and around the cemetery, probably prompting the decision by the enemy commander to burn the dwellings. Charlie Company Capt. Johnny Gilbert, was shot through the abdomen while leading his men into position.

Colonel Johnnie radioed our general that the enemy was murdering the hostages and the general notified the province chief.

Back came the decision; bring in airstrikes. Our general's staff coordinated this intricate procedure and the plan called for us to somehow withdraw back up Cemetery Hill and dig in while Charlie Company provided massive suppressing fire to keep the enemy from shooting us as we climbed the slope. The signal to withdraw would be me blowing my army issue "Whistle, Thunderer" over and over again.

I crawled to Dog's foremost position and asked that squad leader if all his troops were accounted for. We knew that he had several dead strewn to his front and the decision had been rendered that they had to be left down there, rather than for us to lose more killed while trying to retrieve their bodies. I stressed to him the importance that every live trooper would be brought out.

Due to the number of casualties, the withdrawal amounted to the less seriously wounded dragging the more seriously wounded. When Colonel Johnnie gave me the signal to blast that whistle, I almost blew it apart.

Once everyone had been dragged up that hill, we dug in along a sandy ridge and brought in the air strikes. By this time, all the civilians were either burned up, had bugged out and left the village, or would be killed by the bombs. We had no way of knowing.

I can tell you this, though; the screams of burning human beings and animal stock are hard to listen to while you are lying there on the ground among your own wounded and dead.

At the prescribed time, our jets started delivering 500 and 750 pound bombs. The very first bomb killed a soldier in Charlie Company, lifting a big stone about two hundred feet into the air and dropping it right into his foxhole. When a bomb of such strength lands within a hundred yards, the concussion lifts you a foot or two up out of your foxhole and then slams you back to the ground.

Right before the detonation of such a close strike, we would hear a very sharp "VIIT" sound, and you would try and brace for it, but it didn't do you any good. You still got slammed.

Each bomb, no matter where it hit, blew hundreds of stones and other matter into the air, and many times you could see up to three or four torsos swimming around up above, missing an arm here and a leg there. Our troops cheered every time.

The colonel's radio operator, Stanley, hugged my shoulder.

"What's the matter, sergeant major?" he asked. "Why are you crying? We're safe now. Why aren't you cheering?"

"How do you tell theirs from our, Stan?" I sobbed. It was the saddest day of my life, but I knew it would have been worse had we lost more soldiers by trying to recover those bodies.

We avenged our dead. As the enemy attempted to run from the village complex to avoid our bombs, our troopers picked them off. Most were killed, but that was where the balance of the thirty wounded prisoners came from.

The village was completely destroyed. The 5th Battalion of the 95th NVA infantry regiment was decimated with 198 killed.

Dog Company didn't fare much better. Of the eighty-three men who started out that morning, eighteen were killed on Cemetery Hill and most of the others wounded. Colonel Johnnie was awarded a much-deserved Distinguished Service Cross.

Killer was forced out of the infantry by the army because he had no right thumb. They put him into a rear echelon outfit. Killer chose a medical discharge rather than become a REMF. He was definitely one of the finest, bravest soldiers that I ever had the privilege of serving with.

The battle for Cemetery Hill has long been over. It lives on in the memories of those who were there.

Respectfully dedicated to the memory of the late
Sgt. James Eli "Killer" Mahon
Maj. Gen. Leo H. "Hank" Schweiter

and to
Maj. Gen. James H. Johnson (Retired)
Command Sgt. Maj. Vincent D. Roegiers (Retired)
Capt. Jimmy Jackson
Command Sgt. Maj. Artis Knight (Retired)
Col. Johnny Gilbert (Retired)
Sp-4 Pat Stafiero, Battery C, 6th Bn, 32nd Artillery

Our Colors

"SNAP!"

I ducked involuntarily from the bullet from nowhere, my reverie interrupted where I stood in the clearing watching our chaplain and our operations sergeant as they supervised the preparation of the ceremony to commemorate our fallen on Cemetery Hill.

Jarred back to my senses, I looked proudly at our national colors and our 4th Battalion colors as they flapped in the brisk breeze. I had never seen them before.

"Gettin' a little battlerattled, ain'cha, Top," laughed Dick, our operations NCO.

"Yeah," I admitted sheepishly.

I didn't mind at all. Dick had paid his dues on 10 July, 1967, during the battle for Hill 830. With enemy crawling all over the area, our major, call sign "Whisky Six," asked Dick to wait out in the middle of the jungle—in the middle of a big battle, all by his lonesome—with a message for Dog Company's captain, on what to do if, as and when he ever got to Dick's position.

"I hid," Dick told me, "off that trail until I could hear Dog beatin' through that thick jungle, and I sounded off loud and clear, a dozen times. I wasn't about to get shot by their point element." He made it sound easy, but he'd have been skinned alive if the NVA had been the ones to find him.

He received the Silver Star for this and some other feats which he performed that day. Our major, Walter Douglas Williams, and some of his group never made it to sunset. He was one of the very finest, and his story comes later.

Dick made master sergeant and got out. He's an executive in a large company in Charlotte, North Carolina, now.

Dick was a helluva soldier. In the infantry, your best officer and NCO are chosen to run the S-3—the operations and training section of the battalion's staff. In combat, they planned and monitored all operations, and in peacetime, did the same with training.

One of Dick's jobs was to rehearse the ceremony coming up within the hour. He was reading it right out of the book to me and the NCO in charge of the color guard. He placed each of us in our proper positions and we went through our paces. Our communications people had placed a mike at the very front for our colonel to make his farewell speech and for the new one to say a few words, too.

In Vietnam, battalion commanders were rotated every six months and all of us wondered what Colonel Johnnie's replacement would be like. Whoever he was, he had some great jump-boots to fill. We had been lucky so far. Lt. Col. James H. Johnson's predecessor had been a great man, too. Lt. Col. Lawrence W. Jackley had led the Fourth Bat through the first big battle in Dakto, the one where Whisky Six was killed.

Our S-4—supply officer—had provided Dick with twenty sets, consisting of rifles, steel helmets, and pairs of boots, and the chaplain's assistant was busily arraying them in the appropriate symbolic manner. With fixed bayonet, each rifle had been turned upside down and the bayonet shoved into the ground. Atop the butt of every rifle rested a steel helmet and directly in front of each bayonet's blade was a pair of jungle boots. One rifle in front honored the lieutenant who had died leading Killer's platoon, and one single rank of eighteen represented the troopers killed. Off to one side, pointing at an angle to the other nineteen, was emplaced the twentieth, symbolizing all the others who had been killed before. Eighteen had died on the hill, and one more later died of his wounds.

Our chaplain, Father Roy V. Peters, a major, would conduct the religious portion of the ceremony, and after he had led the troops in the Lord's Prayer, it would then fall to me to call the troops to attention, accept the report from our company commanders, render the report to Colonel Johnnie and then participate in passing the battalion's colors for the change of command ceremony.

Chaplain Peters was one of the bravest soldiers I ever met. He was one of the unsung heroes in our brigade, constantly exposing himself to enemy fire in order to care for wounded soldiers. He deserves to be one of the more highly decorated chaplains.

He had finished setting up his portion of the ceremony and joined us for a cup of coffee while we waited.

"Sir," I introduced Dick, "this is 'Dick' Dixon. His real name is 'William R.' and he is one of the best senior NCOs in the airborne infantry."

As the padre shook hands with Dick, I explained to him that this ceremony held particular significance for Dick and me as we had served together in Dog Company for years.

"This Dog Company? Our Dog Company? How could this be?" The major was dumbfounded.

"Yep," observed Dick. "I guess that Ted and I are just about the 'Last of the Mohicans' from old Dog Company when this 4th Bat used to be the 501st at Fort Campbell before it came to Vietnam as our 4th."

Chaplain Peters allowed as how it was certainly a small world. Dick told the padre that I had been his first sergeant of Dog Company for six years and had raised him from a pup.

We regaled him with tales of our fabulous Captain, Harold L. Barber. Harold had fought at Guadalcanal with the First Marine Division at the age of sixteen. The elder marines had referred to him as "Chicken"—a custom among Marine riflemen. Some were making bets that Harold couldn't kill a man. Well, one night the enemy launched a "banzai" suicide charge into Harold's company's perimeter, and the next morning they sent Harold's squad outside the perimeter to eliminate any of the enemy wounded still lurking there.

Wounded Japanese had played possum and killed Marines before, so they all watched with interest as Harold approached a soldier who was sitting up, with the stub of a recently bandaged arm in his lap, holding his good arm behind his back! The older Marines watched warily to see that Harold wasn't ambushed, while Harold decided that to just shoot this guy wouldn't do justice to his goal of the elimination of the hated nickname "Chicken!"

Hearkening back to the many hours of bayonet drill, Harold hauled off and delivered a mighty vertical butt-stroke with the stout nine pound Garand M-1 rifle then in use.

"It would've instantly killed any champion heavyweight boxer," Harold told us, "but instead, the force of the blow also demolished the stock of my weapon, right at the hand-grip." One of the guys shot the Japanese soldier, who had a grenade in his good hand.

With Harold as our C.O., Dog Company became the best one in the entire 101st Airborne Division. Harold had held every rank from private through captain at that time and he taught us everything he knew and made soldiers of us all.

We sure had some great experiences during the years we were together. After his stint commanding Dog, Harold was selected to perform in the operations field, where a smart commander puts his best officers. He and his lovely wife, Mary, are retired near Atlanta and we stay in touch constantly.

When the waiting was over and the troops were in place, I screwed up the detail badly. I was to call the battalion to attention and take the report from each captain. Then, I'd about-face and deliver the report to our colonel. Then I'd face left into the color-bearing detail.

I would grasp the battalion's colors, take them from the bearer, and pass them to the general, who would pass them to Colonel Johnnie, who would pass them to the new colonel.

The new colonel would pass them back to the general, the general to me, and me to the bearer. Then came the speeches from the two colonels and the final one from the general.

Well, we didn't need a microphone, because of my unintentional faux pas. Everything was going smoothly until I got involved. I called the battalion to attention.

"Report!" I commanded.

I was doing all right up there doin' my stuff. As I'd receive each unit's report from its company commander, we'd exchange salutes, and the next commander in line would offer his.

Confidently, I rendered my best parade ground salute and went on to the next, but I met my Waterloo when it came Dog's turn.

You have to remember that during my eight months as the 4th Bat's sergeant major one in four of my men had been killed and nine out of ten had been wounded. Eight weeks before, we had just finished up the horrible Dakto Campaign which had cost us most of those casualties and now, in just a few awful hours, we had all but lost Dog Company.

Companies A, B and C had about 150 men each, standing in ranks. C's captain, Johnny Gilbert, had been shot and evacuated from Cemetery Hill, so a young lieutenant rendered their report.

Finally, it was Dog Company's turn and I guess it was their captain, Jimmy Jackson, who set me off. He and his first sergeant, Artis Knight, and less than a dozen other men were standing in ranks. Tears rolling down his cheeks, Captain Jackson rendered his report.

"D-Dog Company, all p-present and a-accounted for, s-sir!" he sobbed.

That was the end for me. I was rendered completely useless, looking at Dog Company and listening to Captain Jack; peering at one another through the dimness of our tears.

With all the aplomb of a wet noodle, I returned his salute and did an about-face and saw to my consternation that Colonel Johnnie was in worse shape than I was. I rendered the report.

"Fourth Bat, all p-present and ac-ac-accounted for, sir."

It was his turn. He was to command "parade rest," and then give his speech, followed by the other two officers. Taking a death grip on the mike, at least as many tears rolling down his cheeks as I had, he gulped. Then he gulped again. I about-faced.

"Parade REST!" I commanded, and about-faced.

Johnnie stood there, transfixed. I looked at our general and he gave me a kind wink.

I stepped to Johnnie's side, taking his left elbow into my hand.

"Heck with the speeches, sir, let's troop the line."

Together, with me to his left, we marched over to HQ Company, whose commander called his troops to attention and presented arms. We returned his salute as we marched in front of A, B, C, and D Company, repeating the procedure.

Those troops trusted and loved Colonel Johnnie, and there was not one dry eye in that battalion. All those young men were looking at those rifles turned upside down out there and thinking of their own buddies who were going home to their loved ones in a flag-covered casket.

It was one of the most unforgettable spectacles I had ever witnessed in all my years in the infantry.

While serving as our 4th Battalion commander, Lt. Col. James H. Johnson earned the Distinguished Service Cross and Silver Star. After an eventful military career, he retired as a major general in South Carolina. He knows what his troops and I know, that his finest hour was the Dakto Campaign and the Tet Offensive's battle for Cemetery Hill.

His finest award was that his troops respected and trusted him.

One of those troopers, Killer, wasn't ready to hang it up, even after being medically discharged. Killer came and visited me and my family at West Point, New York, in 1969. He told us that he was thinking of going to Israel to see if they could use a "one-thumbed" infantryman.

It was years later, sadly, when our son, Patrick, showed us a magazine article about the ambush of some Israeli settlers in a kibbutz. Killer had been part of the rear guard for a large group of farmers one evening, returning from the fields. Several Arabs had lain in wait on the flat roof of a nearby building, killing him and three others as they passed by, and wounding over a dozen settlers.

In memory of Sergeant James Eli "Killer" Mahon
Killed in action, May 2, 1980

CHAPTER 5

Whisky Six

"Kilo—India—Alpha," spelt the young radio operator phonetically, his voice wavering in terror.

"I say again," he almost whispered, "Whisky Six is Kilo—India—Alpha."

Killed in action. Our battalion operations officer, Maj. Walter D. Williams, had been killed by our enemy.

Lt. Colonel. Larry Jackley attempted contact with the next ranking officer in the ambushed column, now being besieged by a numerically superior enemy, many of whom were efficiently entrenched into the prominent terrain features dominating the approaches to Hill 830, while others tried to flank and surround them with their huge force of riflemen.

"Bravo Six," he called, "this is Parablast Six, over."

The same terrified young voice, trembling with fear and stress, answered again, stating that Capt. Daniel Severson was also dead, as well as our artillery forward observer lieutenant, whose group's task was to call in protective artillery fire.

"Six," in military jargon, denotes the commander.

Temporarily sheltered in the small command post, we were all completely shaken by these tragic events. We knew that unless someone in that ambushed force immediately took command and coordinated artillery fire and airstrikes against that huge force of enemy troops, our paratroopers, now coiled into a hasty defensive perimeter, were in danger of being overrun by the NVA.

"Let's get airborne!" shouted the colonel, exiting the CP and running toward his C&C ship parked nearby. My job was to help run the chopper's big console of radios and our artillery liaison captain would help Colonel Larry bring in artillery fire at the endangered troops' direction. Pete, our pilot, was soon airborne, expertly winging toward the embattled troops below.

This was no quasi-military V.C. force that would hit and run before being retaliated upon. These were NVA Regular Army rifle troops who would fight to the last man! We had already witnessed their merciless tactics which included executing our helpless wounded, and we knew that being overrun meant death for every last one of our men. We took prisoners; the NVA did not.

This fierce ambush, sprung upon two of our rifle companies in column, announced the start of the July 10, 1967, battle for Hill 830, in Vietnam's mountainous Central Highlands in the Dakto vicinity, almost seven months prior to our Battle for Cemetery Hill during the Tet Offensive.

Fortunately, this horrendous beginning was hastily rectified by one of the youngest lieutenants in our battalion. After informing the colonel that his platoon was located nearest to the decimated command group, Lieutenant Peyton Ligon III was placed in command as acting Whisky Six.

In place of the dead artillery lieutenant, whose radio had been shot to pieces, Lieutenant Ligon effectively coordinated all requests for protective fire from our friendly troops. He relayed the requests through our colonel and artillery liaison officer, riding in the chopper with him to the artillery's fire direction center four miles away at the fire support base that we had just taken off from.

This lieutenant's actions saved the day, resulting in the eventual destruction of many enemy troops and the routing of the rest. Of equal importance had been his assistance in adjusting the airstrikes being called in by Colonel Larry.

As I watched these airstrikes, my mind wandered to the day before when Whisky Six and I had flown for several hours together reconning the area in our C&C ship, and last night, I had dreamt about our trip.

Major Williams was a big, cleancut fellow with dark hair and equally dark, inquisitive eyes. He told me that his hobby was riding horses. He really cared for the welfare of our troopers and I knew that they admired and trusted him.

A West Point graduate of some distinction, he possessed a compassionate and pleasing personality, and sincerely cared for our soldiers. The enlisted men who really knew him, respected him because he would never send one of them to fetch his chow for him—he went and got it himself—and he never maintained an aloof attitude toward them as many other officers did.

The day that we had flown together, he had been in very high spirits because he had just received a long newsy letter from his wife.

They had a new baby and he showed me his family pictures. With his tour nearly over, he had conjured in his mind all the usual plans that combat men think about accomplishing upon their return home—the fun the entire family would have, the places they'd go, the things they'd do together.

I remembered that I had listened and looked into his eyes and for some inexplicable reason, I had an eerie feeling that he and I both sensed—deep within our hearts—that none of these plans would be consummated.

I don't know why, but these events must have preyed heavily upon my mind because that night—last night—I had experienced a deep, meaningful dream that bothers me to this very day.

In the dream, we were flying along in the C&C ship, he and I, just as we had done that very day. The Huey was making its usual deafening noise, the WHOP-WHOP-WHOP of its massive rotor forcing us to either yell at one another or else to talk through the ship's intercom system. No one in Vietnam closed the sliding doors, which were wide open as we rode serenely along, searching the thickly jungled mountainsides below for a likely site for us to conduct a heliborne assault within a week or ten days from then.

The dream had been so realistic, I was convinced that it was really happening. We were flying along and suddenly it turned as dark as though there had been a total eclipse of the sun. Simultaneously the deafening rotor noise ceased. Startled,

I looked at the aircraft commander and pilot. Both were obviously dead. I looked at Whisky Six, and he was also dead. Frantically I looked at each door gunner. Dead. Quickly, I looked at myself and I couldn't see a thing. No legs, no arms, nothing! I knew I was there, I could feel myself, but I couldn't see myself.

I looked out the door at the main rotor where it still whirled merrily away in complete silence. The ship was flying itself.

I felt my weight suddenly shift in the nylon seat as the Huey wheeled itself sharply to the right. Everything was turning much darker now. It was the noon hour, yet I could scarcely see into the cockpit up front.

I broke out in a cold, clammy sweat.

"What killed them and not me?" I wondered. "Why was I spared? Where is my body? Where am I?"

It grew even darker outside as the ship slightly canted to one side and then glided silently to earth. The downdraft from the rotor struck the ground and ricocheted back into the ship, striking me with grains of sand. Startled, I jacked a round into the chamber of my rifle, threw off the safety and waited.

I waited, and waited, until some mysterious, irresistible force commanded me to jump from the ship, and in so doing, I barked my shin on a tombstone. As my eyes gradually adjusted to the dark, I saw that we had come to rest in the midst of a large cemetery.

Like some huge, silent dragonfly, the ship hovered a few feet above the gravestones. Something drew me from the ship's location, down a long row of dark tombstones. I knelt and felt one. It was completely blank.

There was no name or epitaph inscribed upon it. I tried again and again, but with the same results. It was as though all these stones were in some mysterious limbo, patiently awaiting the names of my men to be carved upon them.

It seemed as though I wandered endlessly through that huge cemetery, when suddenly the light began to gradually change from the pitch black of night to the initial gray glints of first light.

At this point, I could make out that not only were the stones blank, but each was made of coal-black marble. I turned and wandered back once again to the vicinity of the C&C ship, still hovering patiently as though awaiting the end of my inspection tour.

When I came to within thirty or forty feet, the ship began to slowly rise. Little by little, up it went. Horrified at the thought of being left behind, I ran toward it, but it was one of those awful foot-tied nightmares where you strain and heave, but can only run in very slow motion.

I tripped over a gravestone and fell, losing my helmet. As I regained my feet, I saw that the light of dawn was highlighting the face of Whisky Six.

Stirring, as though miraculously reincarnated, he turned in his seat until he was facing out the chopper's door at me. A kind, gentle smile played about his eyes and lips as he raised his right hand and waved to me in farewell. As the ship glided silently away I tried to follow it, but couldn't.

"Come back, Whisky Six," I cried, "oh, please come back, sir!"

My cries were in vain, and the ship slowly faded into the rays of the rising sun until it was completely gone.

As I reached for my steel helmet, my eye was caught by the large heart-shaped tombstone where I had knocked it flat. Like all the others, it was black. Unlike the others, however, it contained an inscription:

TED G. ARTHURS 1929–1967
MARLENE K. ARTHURS 1931–
SWEETHEARTS ALWAYS

As I stood there looking at the gravestone, contemplating its portentous message, I suddenly became conscious of a weak, distant voice crying to me.

"Top! Top! Wake up, sergeant major!"

It was Mac, the colonel's radio operator and he was shaking me.

"You've been screaming 'Come back, Whisky Six, come back.'"

Two hundred and four days away—the last of January 1968 beckoned for my battalion—the battle for Cemetery Hill.

For Whisky Six and dozens of my troopers, the battle for Hill 830 had ended.

There were more to come.

Dedicated to the memory of Maj. Walter Douglas Williams

Myron's Cigar

"Where did you get Myron from?" the Pope asked as soon as he had jumped off the chopper in our fire support base in the mountains of the Central Highlands.

"Why? Didn't he do well?" I was worried about the promotion board as Myron Beach was one of our best and bravest platoon sergeants.

"Well?" echoed the Pope. "He maxed the board! By next month this time, we should be granted a promotion quota and if that happens, I guarantee you that he'll be our outfit's newest six striper!"

"That cottonpicker not only answered every question correctly, but it was his confident manner that helped to win the board. The average guy is in there, bowing and scraping in an obsequious manner trying to figure out what the board wants to hear—and you can't blame 'em—but, not your Sgt. Myron. He gave that lieutenant colonel who was running the board as good as he got and then some."

The Pope never swore. He was our outstanding brigade sergeant major, and everyone in the airborne infantry knew how religious he was. He was a damn fine soldier on top of all that.

"When that lieutenant colonel and the rest of us were quite satisfied that he was the absolute best candidate, the colonel dismissed him, but he wouldn't go."

"What do you mean, he wouldn't go?" I was amazed.

"He said he wasn't goin'. He said, 'No, sir, I ain't leavin' this here promotion board until at least one of you members can stump me. I am an expert in my job, in the art of warfare, and especially out in that jungle.'"

The Pope told me that the colonel had thrown his head back and just roared with laughter.

"I believe that you are," admitted the colonel, "and if you ever get tired of that 4th Bat, you come and see me, and I'll give you a good job. But time is the essence here, and we have a few more candidates to interview, so I'm asking you to please pretend that you have been stumped, and leave. Okay?"

"He told everybody how the cow ate the cabbage on that board," said the Pope admiringly.

Vince went on to tell me some of Myron's other antics before the board.

"When he first came into the room and reported to the lieutenant colonel, the colonel asked him what battalion he was from. You aren't going to believe what he told him."

"Myron threw his head back," said the Pope, "and rang the rafters with a wolf call. ALLLLRRRROOOOOOOOOOOLL," imitating the 4th Bat's wolf call.

My nickname, for many years as first sergeant and sergeant major, had been "The Wolf," and the troops picked up on this with the wolf call. It built up the spirit of the fighting troops.

Some people looked upon all this as a ploy on my part to build myself up, but the dyed-in-the-wool older paratroopers understood and approved of such things, because they understood troops better than anything—or anyone—else.

"Anyhow," admitted the Pope, "you told me he was one cottonpickin' fine soldier and he convinced us that he was the guy for the stripe."

He handed me a box of fine cigars and said to give them to Myron with his compliments.

Myron was a tough little guy who would put you in mind of a light-haired Robin Williams. He had one helluva great personality, and the troops loved him.

"This may surprise you, Vince," I told the Pope, "But Myron's nickname is 'The Fox'!"

The Pope got a big kick out of that one. Of Flemish or Belgian extraction on his father's side, I guess it was natural that he was a pretty neat guy. He really looked after us jungle troopers because he had been one himself before becoming our 173rd Brigade sergeant major.

He was lucky. He had been the 2nd Bat sergeant major when one of their companies had been overrun when we first arrived in the Dakto area.

His colonel's C&C ship had taken enemy fire, and a rifle bullet came through the bottom of the chopper, up through Vince's canvas seat, slightly brushing his tailbone and backbone, and exiting his jacket without putting a scratch on him.

They might start calling anybody "The Pope" if that happened to them. Might change a fellow's point of view with a stronger slant toward religion.

I told the Pope that in Korea, when I was first sergeant of a rifle company, a Chinese 76mm direct fire high explosive round landed less than two feet from my company clerk as we were trying to dig in one night. His foxhole was only about three inches deep when the round hit him, picking him up and throwing him down the hill.

When I found him on the dark slope, from the sound of his moaning, he had screamed for me to please not touch him, but to let him die. He thought both arms and legs were gone, and so did I.

When I picked him up, I was completely sure that it was hopeless and that he'd surely die.

"He did not have one scratch on him, Vince. The next day, he was sore all over, and a huge bruise the size of a dinner plate welled up in the very center of his back. Paddy was from Brooklyn, and he told me, 'I am a believer, Top. I will never so much as miss Sunday school for the rest of my life.'"

Then you see a round land yards away, and everybody gets hit or killed. As the young folks say, "Go figure."

The Pope wouldn't accept payment for the cigars and as I walked him to the chopper pad, he told me to be sure and tell the Fox congratulations on his fine board appearance.

Several hours later, our column was ambushed at Hill 830, with the battle raging until dusk. At that time, the most horrible thing which can happen to a bunch of badly wounded troops took place. Thick fog rolled in, engulfing Hill 830 and the next hill to it where our reserve force had labored to fell the trees and create an LZ big enough for one dustoff chopper at a time to get in.

I have no training in meteorology, but my private opinion is that there are two kinds of fog in the mountains. There is ground fog, the same as in lowlands, created by the combination of humidity and temperature, and there is the situation where a plain, good old-fashioned thick cloud just lowers itself down over where you are, with layers of the same following it.

It happens so swiftly, that it would have to be a cloud. Whatever it was, it effectively trapped all those wounded because no helicopter can fly in and land in a small hole among those thick, two-hundred-foot-tall trees.

Our C Company was guarding the artillery fire support base four miles from Hill 830. During the battle, D Company had been able to reach A and B and support them.

When the fog rolled in the remnants of the NVA force withdrew. At this point, Capt. Alan B. Phillips, senior officer present, oversaw the consolidation of a perimeter around the hill containing the LZ, coordinating protective fires for the artillery defensive concentrations in case the enemy tried to overrun what was left of our troops that night.

It was a miserable night, with the unwounded troops caring for the wounded, blowing up air mattresses for them to rest on, trying to keep them dry and warm in order to prevent shock. We had lost some of our medics during the battle, but the troops were in good hands with Captain Phillips looking after them. The troops had done the best they could before dark, felling the thick timber with chainsaws and axes, but the end result was a miserably small LZ with trees lying hither and yon across it where they had fallen like huge jackstraws with bark.

The colonel was eager to get into that LZ the first thing in the morning when the fog burned off, or the cloud moved on, but of course, the priority went to the dustoff medevac ships to get the wounded out. When it came our turn to go in there, I marveled at Pete's piloting. Settling a Huey from two hundred feet up in thick timber, dropping through a small hole when it looked like the rotor was missing thick tree trunks by inches, is no task for the faint of heart. Neither is it easier on the passengers' nerves. My toes were curled up inside my jungle boots.

Pete balanced one skid expertly on a log as we jumped off and ran to the clearing's edge. As it was now time to begin evacuating the dead, Pete took out the first load of dead troopers. Our battalion commander, Lt. Col. Lawrence W. Jackley, told Pete to return in eight hours to pick us up.

While Colonel Jackley got with the commanders, I got with the first sergeants. I had provided each of my first sergeants with one of these green ledger books which you see in the finance offices, to carry in their rucksack. I had the master copy for the whole battalion in my own green book.

The first order of business was the information regarding the soldiers who were killed in action. Each soldier is issued two dogtags with appropriate data concerning name and serial number, blood type, religion and date of birth. The first tag is worn on the big loop of chain around the neck of the wearer. A second, much smaller loop, hanging from the bottom of the chain, contains the second dogtag.

When a man is killed, the tag and the large loop remains with him always, while the small one is plucked off and turned into the first sergeant to assist in accurate tabulation. Accordingly, A Company's first sergeant, "Pappy," gave me a loop of commo wire containing the tags of his dead.

"Before I forget, Pap," I said, handing him the Pope's box of cigars, "these are from the brigade sergeant major as a present for Myron. He might get promoted next month."

"Ummmm," said Pap ominously, as he accepted the box. "I'll give 'em to his guys, Ted. He didn't make it."

Pap, as Owen Schroeder was fondly called by his troopers, was the oldest man in our Fourth Bat, and shouldn't even be out with a rifle company like Alpha, humping an eighty-pound ruck while keeping up with those nineteen year old troopers. In fact, their medic had cut a spent AK-47 bullet out of his back and he continued humping that ruck as though nothing had happened. Captain Phillips had emerged unscathed.

It was a sad scene as I sat beside Pap on that log and we went through the still blood-stained dogtags. Tears welled in the old soldier's eyes and we hugged each other and had a good cry—not only for Myron, but for every guy we had ever seen die needlessly, before their time. After I had entered all the information into my book and tucked the wad of bloody dogtags into my jungle fatigue jacket pocket, it was Bravo Company's First Sergeant's turn.

It got worse and worse. He was missing two, a private first class and a platoon sergeant. I had practically raised the platoon sergeant from a pup, having been his first sergeant for about ten years in different paratrooper rifle companies.

No one had seen either one of them since the column was initially ambushed.

He knew without asking that I held him personally responsible to lead a search element for their bodies. I just stared at him.

"I can't ask anyone to go back there. It's eight hundred yards of thick mud and shit, with snipers thick as fleas. To risk more lives when Scully and Smith are probably dead would be criminal."

He took a deep breath and looked at the ground. He couldn't look me in the eye.

I finished tabulating all the dead and wounded and went and saw the colonel. I told him that I was going to take two men and go and find Scully and Smith.

"Take at least five men," said Captain Phillips. "Two for each poncho if you find them, and that leaves two of you to watch while you're on the move. Be careful," he added.

The colonel knew how I felt about such things.

I asked for five unwounded volunteers from Scully's platoon and, taking two ponchos and plenty of grenades and ammo with us, we set out down the steep LZ hill, to cross the valley and go up on Hill 830.

The first sergeant who wouldn't go for his own men, pursed his lips and shook his head, and then looked away as we left the perimeter.

It was about nine o'clock in the morning of July 11, 1967.

Dedicated to the memory of
Platoon Sgt. Myron Stanley Beach, Jr.

and to
Col. Lawrence Winfield Jackley (Retired)
Col. Alan Burgess Phillips (Retired)
First Sgt. Owen Schroeder (Retired)

Scully

As our small group of six warily made our way down the steep hill, the mud from the monsoon sucked at our feet and caused us to slip and slide. At one point, the trail wended its way by a rocky prometory extending out over the valley below, providing us with a chilling view of what was still to come.

I could see several places which would have been a natural vantage point for us to be ambushed and annihilated, but our honor to our dead buddies stood in the way of any retreat on our part. Beyond the valley, we could clearly see our forebidding goal, Hill 830, stretching in a long sweeping slope to our right and then disappearing from view. Like some giant ogre, waiting to devour yet another group of our troopers, it silently waited.

Traversing the slick downhill slope without falling seemed to be priority one. A small group of men, no matter how careful they are, will still make noise under these circumstances, so we were gambling that the enemy had either completely left the area, or, like us, would only be sending small searching parties to retrieve their bodies.

I didn't want to die, nor did any of my five men, but we lived by a set of mores. We didn't fight for money, we fought for one another, and alive or dead, we stuck together.

Countless American soldiers and Marines in Vietnam were astounded to find no bodies after a battle, and they knew better, but couldn't figure it out. Our "Kit Carson Scout," turncoat now working for the U.S., explained it to me. According to him, each NVA rifle company maintains its own squad of grave diggers. If the unit's objective is to assault point "A" at midnight, for example, the grave diggers are sent there a couple of hours in advance, with the mission of silently scraping out shallow graves for their buddies in the assault element.

Each was equipped with two miniature meathooks. When one of the assault force was killed, this guy would crawl forward, insert the point of the hook beneath his comrade's chin, then he'd hook another body in the same fashion, and drag two at a time back to their final resting place. They now had the body and the soul in the grave. I don't know if a priest later visited the site, or what, but you cannot apply logic to everything we saw going on in that jungle.

The going was slow and my mind wandered to the targets of this slight, but heavily armed expedition; Scully and Private Smith. Scully meant a lot to me. I had spent many years in the paratroops and had known him a long time.

The airborne infantry is a young man's game, and I was pushing thirty-nine years old. Two of the platoon sergeants in my 4th Bat were Chingo and Scully. Chingo was a brave pineapple from Hawaii, with his own story coming up later. We had been friends for years and I had been his first sergeant during peacetime.

Scully was a small Negro with slate gray hair of late and renowned as some soldier. He had an unshakable personality, coupled with enough humor and restraint to make him a favorite among his troops.

I had been pleasantly surprised to have arrived in the 4th Bat and found them once again to be platoon sergeants in my outfit. It was a good sign I felt.

Chingo and I always thought that the sun rose and set on Scully—he was just a pleasure to soldier with. He had nineteen and a half years of service and we knew that his goal had always been to retire on twenty and to open a small auto repair shop.

When the 4th Bat had kicked off its mission it had been to find and to destroy a battalion of enemy soldiers who were known to be operating in the area. The bad thing about such an operation is Dakto's geographic location, near the confluence of Vietnam's borders with Laos and Cambodia.

That entire area is part of the nine hundred mile long Chaine Annamitique Mountain Range which extends deep into China. The word "Annam" in one Chinese dialect translates to "Vietnam."

The Vietnamese portion of these mountains is inhabited by about thirty main Montagnard Tribes, which have never been conquered by anyone, including the Vietnamese. They are disdained by the Vietnamese, and the feeling is mutual. They are shielded by the same bulwark which the British ran into during their original encroachment into India some three hundred and fifty years ago: severe differences in the many native dialects. If you can't communicate, you cannot govern!

The Brits combated the Indians' eighty-five separate languages by making teaching English compulsory in every school in India. Their first hundred years were the hardest.

British patience paid off during the following three hundred years until India gained its independence in 1947 as a result of accords previously agreed upon by America and her allies during World War II.

What did the trick for the British was overcoming the language barrier—something which has never been done with the

Montagnard Tribes. This simple fact, plus their remote location from civilization has prevented any outside element from ever governing them. The various tribes communicate by drumming on hollow logs, mostly at night, their fascinating rhythm a sure bet to lull the listener to sleep.

Less than twenty four hours before, after our artillery and airstrikes had caused the withdrawal of the enemy's main force, our survivors had to carry our casualties down the steep slope of Hill 830 and up the equally steep slope which we were now slipping and sliding down, in our quest for our dead comrades. Most of my soldiers had themselves been wounded by shrapnel or bullet. One has to see to believe the grueling effort expended by exhausted troops in order to carry just one man eight hundred yards through thick bamboo in four inches of mud created by a month of relentless rain.

Now, as my small group was part way down the hill, I heard a sudden snapping sound from the last man in our little column, and glancing behind, I saw that he was pointing uphill. To our vast relief, Captain Phillips was leading his Alpha Company and Colonel Jackley down the hill to re-occupy the dangerous Hill 830. Our fears evaporated as we awaited this welcome panacea to our previous problem of NVA lurking on Hill 830. We all felt like cheering.

Colonel Jackley shook hands with each of my volunteers, and as Alpha Company rapidly approached the spot where they had fought so valiantly a day earlier, Captain Phillips narrated for us what they had faced; meanwhile, the telltale signs of yesterday's battle began evidencing itself where the thick vegetation had been blasted apart by the thousands of rifle bullets passing to and fro.

Aside from the noise made by our troops passing through the thick jungle, not one sound was heard from the denizens of what had been their paradise of thick, beautiful trees, clumbs of bamboo, ferns, and other flora of the age-old forest before it had all become ruined the day before by modern man.

This is typical of the birds and beasts, once their habitation has been disturbed by the sound and fury of such a terrible battle. Not one chirp from a bird, nor a single cheery sound from the howler monkeys addressing one another from near and far. It was as though everyone and everything had withdrawn and hidden in silent protest against the pillage of their Garden of Eden, where now the hundreds of trees showed bullet holes and splintered trunks or missing bark.

Soon we began seeing the detritus of scattered spent cartridges and accordion-shaped unexploded M-79 grenades where they had struck a tree. For the grenadier's protection, a grenade round, once it left the M-79's barrel, would not arm unless it made a set number of revolutions and had travelled approximately seven or eight yards. In that thick jungle, many of them had not travelled that far before striking a tree or branch.

The light showing through the trees ahead where an airstrike had been placed, disclosed some bad news. Enemy bodies were still in the area, which meant that the enemy carrying parties were still in the process of working the area.

"Look at the size of that gook over there, sergeant major," pointed one of my riflemen. "He has to be six foot two. He's a Mongolian or somethin'. You ever seen an NVA that size before?"

None of us had. Once Captain Phillips' men had secured the area, my guys and I searched for the bodies of our two missing comrades.

As I was thinking over the situation, we heard a shout nearby. Our two missing comrades had been found lying in a small ravine.

"Tree snipers," explained their finder.

Cursory examination proved him right. Each had been shot through the head from above. One of the other men found a dead enemy sniper hanging down the trunk of a nearby tree, from a rope tied to his ankle.

"They all do that," observed the finder, "in case they fall asleep and fall out of the tree."

We quickly placed each body in its own poncho and with a man on each end, two to a poncho, we eagerly started to "didimoww" out of that vicinity—per suggestion—before bad trouble arrived in the form of NVA carrying parties.

No more misery for poor Scully—just for his wife and kids. The private was a big fellow, who outweighed Scully by a hundred pounds. Accordingly, I decided after the first short rest stop, to carry Scully myself, place two on the larger man, and leave three riflemen to perform security.

Carrying those heavily-laden ponchos up that hill was a torturous task but we were grateful, once again, not to be shot at. Slipping and sliding, our hands bleeding from slivers of sharp bamboo grasped to keep from falling, we finally reached the summit of the hill containing the evacuation LZ.

Chingo was waiting at the small LZ which was only big enough for one chopper to land and take off at a time. He was just watching the last of the dead go out as I approached carrying Scully in my arms, still wrapped in the poncho.

After Bravo's squad had headed back toward Hill 830, leaving me at the LZ with the two poncho-shrouded bodies, I saw that Chingo and his two-man detail had just finished loading an out-bound Huey, which was just taking off. When he turned around and saw me, our eyes locked, and he shook his head sadly. He still didn't want to believe that it was his pal Scully all wrapped up in one of the two ponchos at my feet.

Chingo was a man of iron nerve, and when you see what obdurate acts he was capable of when we fought together later on during the battle for Hill 823, you might be inclined, as I was, to think him to be completely fearless. Fearless, but not heartless.

It started to rain again, and while we awaited the next incoming chopper, Chingo and I knelt beside our dead friend. Not a word was said as he gulped and hung his head to avoid my eyes as he ran his hands over Scully's body, smoothing the folds and wrinkles of the poncho where the rainwater collected upon him in small pools.

Finally, our ears detected the distant rotor of an incoming Huey. As it slowly descended down the 200 feet of narrow trough carved out between those huge trees, Chingo and I picked up the poncho and then tenderly loaded Scully's body on the Huey for his last trip from the jungle. The rain increased its tempo as though to sympathetically wash away the tears of two senior sergeants before the troops could see.

The pilot swiftly swung the ship about as we expertly dodged the vicious small tail-rotor and squinted to avoid the flying raindrops, twigs, leaves, and other debris as the pilot expertly poured the power to the ship in order to negotiate the dangerous egress from the small LZ. The ship lifted, wheeled, and canted, and with one sudden extra burst of power, Scully's hearse was gone.

Still silent, Chingo and I turned and trudged down the muddy trail to his platoon's portion of the perimeter in the dark, formidable jungle to prepare for the enemy attack which we knew could attempt to overrun our small perimeter that night.

For Scully, the battles of Dakto had ended. There were more to come.

In memory of
Platoon Sgt. William A. Scott
Maj. Douglas Walter Williams
Sp4 Joel Michael Sabel
First Lt. Daniel Walter Jordan
Platoon Sgt. Myron Stanley Beach, Jr.
Sgt. William Joseph Douerling
PFC John C. Borowski
Sp4 Franklin S. Shephard
Sp4 Oris Lamar Poole
PFC Arthur Albert Erwin
Sp4 Walter A. Samans, Jr.
PFC David Harold Johnson
Sp4 Roger William Clark
Sgt. David Paul Crozier
Sgt. Jesus M. Torres
PFC Jimmy Earl Darby
PFC Frazier Daniel Huggins

PFC Harry Diwain Spier
PFC Malton Gene Shores
PFC James Fabrizio
Sp4 Larry Allen Doring
Sgt. Siegfried Koffler
First Lt. Arthur C. Retzlaff
Sgt. Michael S. Mitchell
Sgt. Kenneth Lloyd Brown

Old Dog Company

As an aftermath to Scully's sudden death, my subconscious mind took me, in a very vivid dream, back to old Dog Company. Probably because Scully and Chingo had spent six years together in that fine rifle company with me as their first sergeant, I found myself re-living those days.

I had fallen into a fitful sleep, mindful of the pressures of many months of combat, and very worried about my men.

Old Dog Company had been part of the 501st Airborne Infantry of the 101st Airborne Division at Fort Campbell, Kentucky. The 501st was later redesignated to become the 173rd's Fourth Bat.

During our first two years together in old Dog Company, we had been very fortunate to have Captain Harold L. Barber as CO. He had been a USMC rifleman during WWII and he was the greatest leader in the world.

One Christmas, the new colonel had called Captain Barber and me into his office and said that our outfit had been detailed to provide the Santa Claus for the 101st Airborne Division. He would land by chopper at the huge sports arena, and be host—one at a time—to some four thousand eager kiddies.

The colonel stated that it would be his hide if the detail got fouled up, so he asked me if I'd "volunteer." Sure. Did the detail get fouled up? Ask the military police.

Every few seconds I had a child on my knee—sometimes a kid on each knee—flashbulbs popping. Say "HO HO HO" about a zillion times and you'll get the picture!

It was great, really, seeing those fascinated kids' eyes light up as they actually talked to the real McCoy. All went perfectly well until one smart alecky teen-aged boy sauntered out onto that stage and practically caused a riot.

This kid was a real rat fink. First, he plops into my lap and snatches my beard off, exposing Santa to be the fraud that some folks thought him to be anyway.

To the gasps of hundreds of little kids in the audience, awaiting their turn with Santa, he marches to the edge of the stage, hands on hip and then pointed back at ME!

"There ain't no Santa Claus," he pronounced loudly, "and he is an imposter because he's wearing jump boots and my daddy is a 'straight-leg' (non-jumper) so Santa Claus is prejudiced against non-jumpers."

I had spent hours, laboriously spit-shining my Corcoran Jumpboots until they shone like mirrors! I was putting my beard back on, trying to maintain some semblance of applomb, when this big, overgrown kid romps back over to me and quick as a wink, he scuffs his shoe across each of my boot toes.

I could have killed him. I lost my mind. I don't even remember grabbing him and soundly spanking him across my knee while hundreds and hundreds of aghast little kids watched.

Santa was beatin' up kids. When is it my turn?!

It goes without saying that Captain Barber and I got reeled into the colonel's office bright and early the next morning and expertly raked over the coals.

"When," said the irate colonel, "that little bastard's father jumped up on that stage and tried to stop you from spanking him to death, you didn't have to elbow his dad in the face, Top," he pointed out.

"And, did you," he continued unkindly, "know that he is a warrant officer in the CID? The Criminal Investigation Division, no less. They're talking about court martialing you, but even if that doesn't happen, every M.P. in the 101st Airborne Division is going to be gunning for anyone whose pass indicates that he's in our outfit. They'll write us up for even spitting on the sidewalk."

He had me sweating. He leaned back in his chair and looked back and forth from Captain Barber to me. Then he hit us with the hammer.

"Twenty percent of this division is black, and you beat up on a black kid and elbow his daddy in the chops, Top."

"I hadn't noticed, sir," I defended myself, but I hope an Irishman or a Jew doesn't scuff my boots, 'cause he's in for an ass beatin'—I don't care who he is. My black troops will tell you that I ain't prejudiced against anyone, sir."

Now, it's not too smart for a master sergeant to sass a colonel, but I had reached the end of my rope on the Santa Connection.

He dismissed us with dire warnings of things to come. The commanding general's sergeant major later told me that the C.G. had thought it was funny as hell. Chalk one up for me.

The following year, the same colonel gave us the detail again, reminding us that I had beaten up a black kid and his dad.

Well, we solved that problem. On the way back to Dog Company, Captain Barber and I hashed it out. We had a 6'4" black NCO named Manuel and you should have heard the applause he got from all those parents and kids when he stepped off that chopper at the sports arena in his Santa Claus costume. It was great.

That same colonel called us in one day and pointed to his beautiful Irish Setter, cowering in the corner with freshly painted six inch letters on each side announcing "DOG!"

Actually, it happened on two separate occasions and during neither session with him could we convince him that it was not necessarily a member of our Dog Company who had done the Leonardo da Vinci on the hound.

We were finally rescued from hounds and Santas when he and the dog were reassigned to another post.

The new colonel wanted our troops to make up songs to sing while they made their daily six mile run. His other most notable idiosyncrasy was a devout aversion to letters of indebtedness being forwarded to him from higher headquarters.

Captain Barber and I ended up in his office on both counts.

Airborne troops chant during runs. They echo whatever their leader shouts. For example, if he shouts "AIRBORNE," the entire formation will echo "AIRBORNE," etc. But, this colonel wanted songs and the troops thought this to be sissified and were very uncooperative! So, I penned a song more to their liking.

"IF IT'S FIGHTIN' YOU WANT DONE—
SEND FOR DELTA, FIVE OH ONE—
WE'RE ROMPIN', STOMPIN' AIRBORNE HELL
THAT'S WHAT MAKES US FIGHT SO WELL!"

All went real well until one morning when one of our more spirited, ornery young sergeants was running his troops through the senior officers' quarters housing area, and he substituted a sexual word for "FIGHTIN" and the same word for "FIGHT," and it didn't take a genius to ascertain which unit they were from, so Captain Barber and I got to hear the new colonel's learned opinion of singing such pernicious bawdy songs to awaken the slumbering wives of senior officers! He turned out to possess absolutely no sense of humor whatsoever.

Win some, lose some.

If you think about it, dreams are really weird, aren't they? Many are so realistic that one can awaken with one's heart pounding fearfully, experiencing unspeakable terror.

My dream about old Dog Company was a pleasant one, however, and it went on and on—ad infinitum, it seemed.

Dedicated to
Maj. Harold LaMance Barber (Retired)

CHAPTER 6

Hill 823

With a start, I suddenly awakened from my vivid dream about Old Dog Company. Feeling my rifle where it lay across my stomach, I was instantly brought back to reality.

A scant few hours had passed since Chingo and I had sadly loaded Scully's remains onto the evac chopper to begin the long trip home to his grieving family.

The rain stopped at first light and the raucous sounds of the awakening jungle around us were starting to be heard.

I told Chingo what had actually happened to Scully as we made "C" ration coffee in our canteen cups. He looked by my ear at something in the past.

"Ain't this a helluva way to make a livin', Ted," he softly agonized. "Chingo"—Lawrence Okendo—had been master sergeant since 1952. As we sipped our coffee, I thought about Scully's nineteen and a half years of service to the Infantry— how he'd almost made it to retirement, but not quite. I thought about Chingo. He and I each could have retired years before. Neither of us could know what lay in store for us. Were we going to eventually end up like Scully?

My mind was suddenly jogged back to the present by the sound of my colonel's chopper approaching the LZ. I said some temporary goodbyes to Chingo and went to join the colonel.

That's very wild jungle up around the Dakto area. One night our troopers wounded a tiger and we could hear its nearby roars and cries of pain and rage.

During that same time frame, an eleven foot four hundred pounder made off with a hapless rifleman, one dark night, in another outfit and they never found hide nor hair of him.

One night my guys opened up during an ambush patrol, only to find that they had killed several large primates about the size of an orangutan.

We never ran into any cobras. Our trouble was with the smaller bamboo vipers and huge rock pythons. The Vietnamese called the vipers "seven steps," ostensibly to describe how far one could get after being bitten.

This was a big lie, though, because each of my guys who was bitten survived with flying colors. These vipers had a nasty habit of buddying up with sleeping soldiers, and the fun began upon discovery of the unwelcome partner.

Of course, the poor Montagnards didn't have the luxury of medevac to a coastal hospital when they were bitten, so we lengthened their seven step lore somewhat!

Now, rock python is another subject! Two of our bravest pointmen were black guys; one feared nothing and the second feared nothing except snakes. He shot one one day which took four men to carry. I have the picture.

Another day, he was on point, froze and began making sounds like someone choking to death. I rushed up there to him expecting the worst.

"S-s-sarge," he stammered, pointing to our left where you could see the foliage still moving, "a f-freight train came through here . . . as b-big as a snake!" He wasn't shaken too badly.

I told him to veer around to the right.

According to my recollections, it was just about sixty days later when we were extracted from Dakto and sent to Tuy Hoa. We operated there chasing V.C. for six weeks, enjoying Tuy Hoa's version of the monsoons. The mountain version in Dakto was colder at night, so our troops welcomed the warmth of the lowlands.

Unexpectedly, the bony finger of fate once again beckoned from Dakto to meet a massive buildup right across the border, as confirmed by our intelligence folks. We had to return to Dakto.

Having had previous experience in this area, the powers that be earmarked us for the forthcoming conflict, along with the Fourth Infantry Division, to which we became OPCON. We just didn't seem to be able to shake Dakto because that's where the fiercest action of the war would be fought, time and again.

Our 4th Bat was the first battalion into the jungle. After an extensive briefing and short wait, we were committed a few miles northwest of the Dakto airstrip. We established Fire Support Base Savage around a naked area being bulldozed from the huge trees which comprised the terrible thick jungle in the Dakto Province. Dozers were out as far as we were normally concerned, due to thick jungle, but the nearby road made the use of them possible this solitary time.

Ostensibly, these large enemy forces intended to sweep through the area, gobble up this neophyte base of ours and then add the Dakto Special Forces Camp and airstrip as scalps to their belts.

Before it was over, the enemy did succeed in destroying a couple of C-130 troop transport aircraft on the strip, also in setting off the Dakto ammunition dump with mortars. It blew periodically for well over twelve hours, partially destroying the adjacent SF Camp. They messed up a whole bunch of us rifle troopers in the bargain, though, before we finally succeeded in decimating their ranks.

From the sixth of November through the twenty third, there was almost continuous contact with the enemy. It got much worse at times, of course, and then would subside, but in the long run something ferocious was usually going on because the NVA Regiments practically saturated the area with rifle troops.

Clyde never actually succeeded in stringing any of the scalps he had set out to do and by the time he was through tangling with elements of the Fourth Infantry Division and the 173rd Airborne Brigade, he would have been much better off if he hadn't tried.

It cost the enemy much more than it cost us, but it cost us too.

The real battle started on the sixth of November with the advent of what came to be known as the battle of Hill 823— although there were several hills involved. They finally gave up, what was left of them, seventeen days later, after my battalion and our 2nd Bat finally took Hill 875 on the twenty third of November, Thanksgiving Day. This ultimately spelled the defeat of their Dakto Campaign.

On the fourth of November, Colonel Johnnie had spread our Fourth Bat to sweep generally southwest of FSB Savage and deny the enemy this approach. Bravo Company stayed dug in around the FSB to protect the artillery while Alpha, Charlie and Dog made the sweep. "Dog" was Delta's nickname and callsign. This probe proved initially uneventful.

Now, you must take into account that those steep hills were covered in triple canopy jungle, ranging in trees over two hundred feet tall, down to clusters of thick bamboo. You had to see it to believe it.

Our general's theory was that he would have jets to triangulate three large bombs into the top of Hill 823, knocking down all these huge trees and forming a LZ large enough for several ships to assault at once. Oh yeah?

To my surprise and Colonel Johnnie's consternation, we sat up there at a thousand feet in our C&C ship and watched while the Airforce flew sortie after sortie, trying to put three of those bombs together.

It must be much harder than a layman could imagine, so we finally had to settle for an LZ composed of two adjoining strikes.

While our Bravo Company sat on choppers at the FSB, ready to buzz in onto Hill 823, the colonel wasn't satisfied. We were accompanied by Captain Ronald R. Leonard, our S-2, Major Richard M. Scott, our XO and Captain Shirley W. Draper, our Artillery LNO.

Along about this time, the uneventful started becoming the eventful. With three rifle companies probing on the ground and one on the rubber, all Hell suddenly broke loose!

In one second, Dog Company made massive contact with the NVA. In accordance with plan, Dog immediately pulled into a protective perimeter and started fighting for its life. Colonel Johnnie diverted the triangulating aircraft and used that air to neutralize what he could of the large force currently attempting to overrun Dog Company.

Dog C.O., Capt. Thomas H. Baird, was seriously wounded at this time and First Sgt. William A. Collins, who would be killed twelve days later, was doing his utmost to control the company by radio. Dog was having its hands full. At this time, a lot depended upon Colonel Johnnie bringing in definitive air strikes upon the enemy.

Air strikes really get furry. If you miscalculate from the air and put a bomb or some napalm on your own troops, it's all over with for them. Colonel Johnnie concentrated on the safest avenues of approach without endangering our own troops and then called in gunships which can deliver ordnance a lot closer to your troops without killing them in the bargain.

All through this, Bravo sat on their ships in the FSB, chomping at the bit, monitoring the fight by radio. As their proximity to the bombed LZ on Hill 823 was close enough to Dog's fight to make good sense, Colonel Johnnie committed Bravo to go. This, they did.

Simultaneously, Capt. Alan Philips's Alpha and Capt. Bill Connolly's Charlie Companies were converging on Dog from two different directions in order to support Dog and try to cut off the enemy and bottle him up. On the way, both of them made massive contact. The entire area was saturated with NVA soldiers. As there were several different hills involved in this fierce battle, the entire battle area is referred to as the battle for Hill 823.

While our Bravo Company was currently making its difficult landings—one ship at a time—on the bombed area of Hill 823, Dog Company was still in a very precarious position as they were confronted by a very large NVA force, bellied up to their perimeter, many of whom could not be reached by our artillery and air without killing Dog's troopers. Bad situation all the way around.

Almost immediately, Bravo's Captain Baldridge started reporting to Colonel Johnson in our overhead-hovering C&C ship that signs indicated that our initial bomb bursts had landed within a large force of enemy on Hill 823.

Many pieces of people and equipment were found while Bravo began to enlarge the LZ and to dig in simultaneously.

First Sgt. Jerry Babb, the former first sergeant of the famous Golden Knights Army Skydiving Team, had grabbed a chainsaw and was busily gnawing away at a huge tree, completely impervious to what was happening around him, when he suddenly was bombarded by large chips of the tree. An enemy machine gun was chewing the tree down around him. He threw down the saw and, finally seeing that everyone else had taken cover, joined them.

"Hey, six," he shouted at Captain Baldridge. "What in the hell are you cats tryna do, let me saw my way into hell?"

"We thought you were too busy to quit, Top," replied Baldridge.

Zzzzzzzzuck—KaRROWW. An enemy mortar landed in the perimeter. Zzzzzzz—Zzz—ROW-ROWW. Two more landed nearer to where they lay in the small, open perimeter.

"Hey, captain," screamed Jerry, "they're walkin' 'em right into us!"

Bravo was in a bad way, as it was turning out—just like the other three companies which had been in massive contact. First, automatic weapons fire—now accurate mortars.

"Parablast Six," called Captain Baldridge, "this is Bravo Six, over."

Colonel Johnnie answered him as the captain tried to explain Bravo's situation.

"Six, this is Bravo, we're takin' a lot of casualties from—" Zzzuck—zzuck—KROW ROWWW. Then silence.

The colonel looked at me and shook his head and pressed his transmitter and kept trying to re-contact Captain Baldridge, but no dice.

"Look at the map," he beckoned me and the others, "I believe mortars got Bravo's C.P. group." He pointed at the map and then out the door at the ground.

"See this steep cliff here on the northeast side of Hill 830?" We did. "O.K. Marry it up on the ground. See the two bomb craters together right near the cliff? I'm going to have Pete, our Pilot, to buzz up the side of that cliff, come in over its edge and plop down in the vicinity of Bravo's C.P."

He told Captain Leonard to take over Bravo's command and for Major Scott to go in with him and Captain Shirley Draper, our great Arty Liaison Officer, to coordinate air strikes and other fire to assist the besieged Bravo Company.

"I was first sergeant for thirteen years, sir," I told him. "I'll replace the first sergeant."

When the colonel briefed the pilot, Pete laughed philosophically. I thought to myself how Pete had been shot down before and was probably figuring he was ripe for an encore, as close as the enemy was to where we'd be landing.

It was a risky chance, but it had to be taken in view of the circumstances. Pete wheeled about and headed for the deck. He brought us in from an angle well below the clifftop where we were partially obscured from the enemy's view—popped up and swiftly landed!

We all jumped off and jogged up the slight slope to where the C.P. was located, where Colonel Johnnie's worst suspicions were confirmed. The entire C.P. group had been wounded and the radio operator seemed dying. As we quickly loaded them all onto the chopper to go out with Colonel Johnnie, the first sergeant pointed down a slope and quickly told me that an entire squad, struck by machine gun fire, lay scattered down there, in danger of becoming overrun and headshot by the NVA.

"No sweat, Jerry," I assured him, "we'll go get 'em."

As Pete wheeled the C&C ship about and rushed the edge of the cliff with his heavy load, some Clyde cut down on them with an AK-47 from a knoll just outside our perimeter. Luckily none of the slugs hit the men.

Colonel Johnnie told me later that it sounded like someone smacking the bottom of the ship with a sledge hammer and that stuff like confetti filled the inside of the ship! Pete was gone.

We had our own problems at that point. Several of us returned fire to the area where the enemy had cut down on the ship and then snaked up the slight incline to the C.P. area.

Captain Leonard sent for the platoon leaders. One young lieutenant was already dead, along with several of his men, and a bunch of them wounded. These were the ones that Jerry had told me about being scattered down the one slope, in danger of being overrun.

As the major and two captains moved their C.P. into one of the bomb craters, I located two unwounded riflemen and asked them if they'd volunteer to go down that slope with me after those wounded. One looked at the other and they both looked at me! It was clear that they considered this to be a probable death sentence.

"We'll go," softly conceded one, "anywhere you go, sergeant major!" The other nodded. They weren't any more afraid than I was, I can tell you.

Our first trip wasn't so bad. We located casualties within thirty or forty feet of the perimeter and got two of them back O.K. On the second trip, we learned to take advantage of the incoming jets making the run across our hill, and when this happened, we'd get up and run down the slope while we could hear NVA soldiers on both sides of us firing their AK-47s on full automatic, blindly up through the canopy of trees, hoping to hit each jet.

On each subsequent trip, we had to go further and further until we found Smiddy, the platoon sergeant and two more wounded, all huddled together in a little dip in the ground. All had been hit by rifle slugs and had patched each other up.

"Sergeant major," he said, "get this man out first. He's very bad. The slug busted my leg. There are two more wounded below us. You had better bring at least a squad to rescue them with as the NVA are all over the place."

As if to punctuate his remarks an AK-47 rattled nearby to our right and below us. His fire was answered by two of the wounded to our below left. I mentally marked where their fire was coming from and I knew they didn't have long to go unless we got some help to them soon.

It took all three of us to crawl up out of there dragging the poor unconscious kid, a black PFC who had been shot through the neck. When we got to the top of the hill we found Ness—

one of the platoon medics—working on some other wounded and he immediately went to work on our guy.

We went back down that hill—our fifth trip—but this time with a twelve man squad. When we got to where the two farthest were they were both pretty bad. One had taken two slugs; one down through the eye and bridge of the nose from the same slug—and one through the leg.

The squad killed two enemy soldiers nearby and put some more to flight. Coming back up the hill half the squad provided suppressive covering fire while the other half assisted me and my two riflemen in evacuating the wounded from their exposed positions.

I carried a small guy piggy-back after the area had been cleared of enemy soldiers. In spite of the possible loss of the eye, he was in great spirits at the advent of having suddenly become snatched from the jaws of certain death.

"What's your name buddy?"

"Just call me 'Sweet Peas' sergeant major. Boy, am I glad to get outta there. We was doin' pretty good until that bastard got us from the side an' done this to my eye an' shot off most of Bill's lower jaw. Ya think Bill'll make it? I done all I could for him as he was bleedin' like a stuck hawg. I stuffed my bandanna in his neck an' tied it. Will he make it?"

"Sure, Sweet Pea. You did fine. Don't worry."

We got to the top of the hill along about the time the rest of the squad brought Sweet Pea's terribly wounded pal, Bill, up.

Ness immediately grabbed Bill and unwrapped the bandanna and started to give him mouth to mouth resuscitation. I'd seen many badly wounded humans in my time but none of them sickened me more than looking at poor Bill's gaping wound where his jaw used to be.

Ness got him breathing again after he sucked out a blood clot the size of a marshmallow and spat it onto the ground. I know I turned green at that one and one of Bravo's men heaved his guts all over the ground when that big clod of blood landed on his boot.

At Captain Ron's direction, our portion of the perimeter opened up with suppressive fire to keep Clyde from shooting at an incoming medevac ship coming up over the cliff.

Ness asked me if he could go out on this dustoff to try and give Bill the breath of life until they could get him to the hospital and said that he'd be back on the very next available chopper.

The troops nearest the LZ already knew the order of priority in which the outgoing wounded would be loaded and soon the dustoff was taking off over that cliff. I silently prayed for poor Bill and the others to make it out alive.

The very next chopper to land disgorged Chingo.

In memory of
First Sgt. William A. Collins

and to
Lt. Col. Thomas Heritage Baird (Retired)
Col. Ronald R. Leonard (Retired)
Col. Richard M. Scott (Retired)
Maj. Shirley W. Draper
Lt. Col. George Baldridge (Deceased)
Command Sgt. Maj. Jerry M. Babb (Deceased)
Col. William Connolly (Retired)
First Sgt. Eddie Crook (Deceased)
Col. James Muldoon (Retired)
First Sgt. Ray Irwin Fraser (Deceased)

Chingo

Chingo's nickname derived from the fact that he called everyone else Chingo. The word translates to "friend" in one of his pineapple dialects, as I recall.

"What's the matter with you, Chingo? You got rocks in your head? You are supposed to be on your way to Cam Ranh Bay to go on R&R!"

He grinned, but then sobered up after I told him about the dead lieutenant and all the others, and I suggested to him that he take over that platoon, while I continued as first sergeant.

"Roger, Top, I'm on my way," he cheerily announced as he took off for that portion of the perimeter which would be his.

What was left of that platoon needed a good head to run it and Chingo was it.

The two bomb craters near the edge of the cliff overlapped each other like a figure eight. I scudded down the steep side of the one housing our C.P. group and had a long talk with Capt. Ron Leonard. I told him what I had done with Chingo and he heartily approved. We climbed the side of the bomb crater and began to take a tour of the re-consolidated perimeter.

Shortly before Chingo's arrival, I had taken six men down to act as a recovery party to retrieve the dead lieutenant and the rest who had been killed with him.

With sadness, I had remembered a few weeks before when the young lieutenant had initially joined the Fourth Bat. He was a tall, husky and good-looking fellow with short black hair.

As he waited for Colonel Johnnie to brief him, he had showed me his wife's picture. She was holding their small child, as I recall.

Then, after Colonel Johnnie had briefed him, we had watched him walking back down the hill to where he would catch the chopper to Bravo Company.

"Boy," I remembered Colonel Johnnie's words, "I sure wouldn't want to wrestle with that fellow, would you, Top?"

That had been the last time I had seen him until now, as we wrapped his mutilated body in one of our ponchos. Like all the other dead, he had been dispatched with a rifle shot to the head. Each had been stripped and some mutilated with machetes.

To this day, every time I see one of our high ranking officers on TV, over in Vietnam, currently hugging their former enemy and counterpart, I wonder if they could be doing such a thing if they had helped me to carry our mutilated dead up that slope.

I'm not going to try and tell you what a high powered rifle does when pressed to a human being's head, but it's enough to sicken a seasoned undertaker and sometimes no one could recognize the victim, believe me.

So, all you politicians go ahead and hug 'em. I owe it to my dead troopers to hate their cruel enemy until my last, dying breath. Believe me.

Now, as Captain Ron and I started to check our small perimeter, we ducked to avoid the landing skids of another incoming dustoff. Off jumped Ness, the medic. Captain Ron and one door gunner helped us to load up all the rest of our dead.

I gave the aircraft commander thumbs up and the three of us ducked to avoid the pieces of hard, red laterite clay which swirled about us as the chopper took off.

"How's Bill, Ness?" I asked, "The lad with no jaw?"

"He died on the chopper, Top," he admitted softly. "but I think the others'll be fine."

"Thanks. Damn fine job," I smacked his back. "Meet your new company commander."

Captain Ron and I talked with him for a few minutes and then the captain sent him to Chingo's platoon as their medic had been evacuated.

"Too bad about poor Bill, Ness," I told him, "but you did your damnest for him, God rest his soul—along with the others' also."

The captain then briefed our outstanding Weapons Platoon Sergeant Johnny Riley, our great "can do" super intelligent black trooper.

Together they decided to move the 81mm mortars into the bomb crater adjacent to the C.P. crater. Soon they began the dangerous job of registering their fire around our perimeter in preparation for what was obviously going to be a bad night ahead.

"Bring those concentrations in to within twenty five yards of our perimeter," Captain Ron told the astonished Johnnie.

"The enemy's going to belly up to us in the dark, Johnnie," I explained, "and feed us beaucoup hand grenades. We might end up wounding some of our own men, but there's no other way. We are surrounded, except for the cliff's side, and bringing your mortars in so close may save us from being overrun."

He nodded, as Captain Leonard told us that Major Dick Scott was also coordinating for the Airforce to provide us with mini-gun fire from their "Spookey" C-47 aircraft.

"Captain Draper," Ron went on, "is providing us with a ring of artillery steel tonight, too, but of course it will be striking way outside this close, narrow band where your mortars can protect us."

No Vegas gambler who knew our situation, would bet on us surviving the night, and within a few thousand feet of us, our other three companies faced our exact same situation. That whole area was saturated with thousands of NVA, thirsting for our blood! Nor could anyone know that during the next three weeks, Captain Leonard would earn the Silver Star and the Distinguished Service Cross for his actions in Bravo Company.

As Captain Ron and I continued around the already darkening perimeter, Captain Shirley's artillery commenced splattering Hell out of the probable enemy avenues of approach to our perimeter.

As Major Dick Scott was in contact with Colonel Johnnie, he had told Captain Ron that Dog and Alpha Companies had joined up for the night, but that Charlie Company was cut off—just like we were—and had formed a solitary perimeter for the night.

Chingo's decimated platoon occupied the last portion of the perimeter. We found Chingo in one position all by himself.

"Chingo!" exclaimed Ron as they shook hands, "are you going to play rifleman tonight all by yourself?"

"I gotta, sir," Chingo's eyes danced, "this big-hearted wolf here, conned me into takin' over a forty-eight man platoon, but it's only got eighteen men in it. We've got an area the size o' Los Angeles to plug up an' defend."

"Well, Chingo, you can make that twenty one fighters, old buddy." I told him. "I'm bringing Vicki and Jeff with me, soon as I can chase 'em down."

"Who in Hell's Vicki and Jeff?" Captain Leonard puzzled.

"Jeff's Vicki's handler, sir," answered Chingo for me. "She's a beautiful German Shepherd."

Captain Leonard told us that the C.P. had received a message that we were being surrounded by crack elements of the NVA. The captain explained that when he returned to the C.P., he would warn the troops to cease digging because the enemy would belly up to us at dusk, and toss hand grenades in onto any sound of digging.

"Hmm," I said. "So, we have to make do with the shallow holes they already have and the small amount of sandbags already filled, to lie behind? What about mortars?"

"I predict," said Chingo, "that they'll drop in a few mortars at dusk—which ain't far off. While we're in a tizzy from that, they'll move their troops up quickly to belly up to us. They won't mortar us after that for fear of hittin' their own troops, plus our Airforce C-47 'Spookey' would spot the flashes from their mortar tubes an' bring screamin' death on 'em with her mini-guns.

Captain Ron and I returned to the C.P. in the bomb crater and he radioed all leaders. Sure enough, we were mortared just at dusk. All rounds fell short except one which exploded right in the very center of the perimeter, doing no harm.

Soon thereafter the troops around the perimeter began calling in reports of sounds of movement. They were instructed to use only grenades—no rifles for the muzzle blasts would give away our exact location and positions.

"Chingo prediction number one holds water," exclaimed Captain Ron. "For number two, it should soon be raining grenades." I told him I was going to hunt up Jeff and Vicky and go and join Chingo on the perimeter, which I did.

I knew that his new platoon would have very low morale, having lost their leaders and many of their buddies and when they found out that I was with them, they'd figure that the situation wasn't all that bad.

The second reason that I wanted to be with the decimated platoon was because the enemy had seen that portion of our perimeter during daylight and I figured that it was most likely to become heavily probed that night.

"Just one more thing, Top," I cautioned Captain Ron. You probably know this already, but just in case. They're already starting to move in."

"So?"

"So, you must put the word out for our troops to put a grenade onto anything that moves and that translates to no movement around our perimeter by our troops. None. We're in bad danger of being overrun. No one shoots his weapon until the enemy gets so close that they have to."

"Fair enough, sir. Thanks and good luck."

I policed up Vicki and Jeff and we crawled out to where Chingo's position was. We hadn't been there thirty seconds when we got our first grenade in. They must have heard us getting into position.

"CCHHHT" went its fuse, "clackity-clack" bouncing off the bamboo it came and with a "BLALAM" it exploded to our left front, sending its shards of red hot steel everywhere.

Chingo whispered to me that his old platoon had loaned him one squad to fill in his gaps.

"You think it's gonna matter by morning, Chingo?" I whispered back.

All communications had to be in whispers for obvious reasons.

"I sure hope we're still around to find out, Ted." "CCHHT-clackity-clackity-clack-DDDBLLLAAM" one landed nearly in our lap.

"Bingo," whispered Jeff. "Say, what's them Chink fuses sound like to you when they pull 'em?"

"Like rusty casket hinges," said Chingo, "lookin' for someone to clang a lid on."

Actually, they sound like tabs being pulled on beer or soda cans. I offered this as my version.

"Exactly," agreed Jeff. "and me with just a few weeks to go until R&R."

"Oohh," groaned Chingo. "R&R your infantry ass. That's where I'm supposed to be right now if I wasn't such a dumb-ass."

There never was a more gungho guy than Chingo.

They probed the entire perimeter with grenades for hours. Other portions of the perimeter were probed during the evening by squad-sized NVA units, but we were spared until about 0130 hours in the morning when our portion sustained a heavy probe by at least two squads physically assaulting our perimeter.

One of Chingo's men from his old platoon killed a bunch of them with a Claymore Mine and I was pumping out M-79 flechette rounds as fast as I could load them.

The rifle and machinegun fire was deafening. The fat was in the fire and every weapon we had opened up. All in all, Chingo's platoon accounted for about two squads of NVA and they left us alone for about an hour and a half.

The exception was the loud screaming of their nearby wounded, which our men settled with grenades. Along about then we were treated to a long period of weird taunts.

In perfect English and coming from two distinctive points to our left and right front, some very remarkably effective invectives were shouted at us.

"YEEEEEE. You die, G.I." Then his partner would chime in from the other side. This went on for about an hour. On the other side of those voices, perhaps seventy or eighty yards down the slope we could hear a seemingly unceasing chorus of horrible screams.

"It's their forward aid station," hissed Chingo. "I'll betcha they've dragged all their seriously wounded to that one point down there. Listen to those guys howl! They've been hit hard."

With several NVA Regiments in the immediate area, God alone knew the size of the enemy rifle force which surrounded us. Each of our other rifle companies was sustaining some sort of similar action, but none fiercer than Bravo's that night.

"YIIIIIII" Our pal gently reminded us of his presence. "Chop chop macheteeeee," echoed his partner!

We had a good chance, with under seventy men, of being overrun by the enemy. That's when all your friendly wounded get their brains blown out and they kill you to the last man, many times defacing each body with machetes.

Laurel and Hardy lay out to our front, not so subtly planting these thoughts in my men's minds—every last one of them.

In November, it gets much colder up there in those mountains than the uninitiated might expect. All night long, my troops had to roll over face-down on the ground in order to urinate. No one could move around to tend our wounded. The troops tended one another.

Usually if one was wounded on a position, all the others were too, due to the nature of grenades and automatic weapons.

I had no rucksack, but had inherited Jerry's. I had loosened four grenades from their carrying straps, and arranged them across the top of his rucksack, and was hugging Vicky with my left arm for warmth, and holding the radio's receiver with my right hand.

Jeff was using his steel helmet as a pillow, cocked back on his head and leaning it against the rucksack when it happened! It was a few minutes past three in the morning.

Vicky straightened up like a shot.

I had my ear on the radio and could hear nothing else due to the rushing noise of its receiver. I was huddled up to Vicki—to her soft, warm fur—when her back straightened and every hair on her body bristled like a shoebrush as she stared intently out into the darkness to our direct front.

I snatched the earphone away from my ear and listened intently as there was no use in trying to penetrate the inky black with my eyes. Nothing.

Then suddenly, a few yards away, I distinctly heard the sharp, raspy voice of what had to be an enemy squad leader trying to get his men up on line to make an assault. Evidently he didn't realize how close he really was.

"Here they come—" I screamed and opened up on full automatic with my M-16. During that instant before I pulled the trigger, I could hear the thump and scramble of bodies and the rattle of the equipment they carried and could see the sparks from at least twelve or fifteen grenade fuses being activated at once.

They had spread out and were charging into us.

"It's all over now," I remember thinking to myself as I pulled the trigger, "this is the end of my life."

On the screaming enemy came as the grenades thunked down around and behind us. Our whole perimeter opened fire and repulsed the attack, but not before they had killed a brave platoon sergeant a few yards to the right of us, and wounded several of his men.

When all this was going on, my world was suddenly shattered by a brilliant, blinding purple light coupled with hundreds of red hot icepicks simultaneously piercing my entire body!

"You were lucky that concussion didn't kill you," our surgeon told me later, "to have a grenade land that close and also, it should have taken Jeff's head off!"

One of those grenades had landed in Jerry's open rucksack! Jeff had been lying with his steel helmet propped against it! To this day, none of us know why it didn't detonate the four which I had placed around the top of the rucksack, but it had simply blown them off into the jungle.

Jeff was hit four times in the back of his head, you could cover all the wounds with a dollar bill, and it didn't kill him! The shrapnel was slowed down as it passed through his steel helmet and liner, and barely embedded itself in his skin and skull without penetrating the brain!

Most of the shrapnel blew out the top and sides of the rucksack, so Vicki and I got the brunt of it where we sat upright two feet away. We ended up with a couple of dozen pieces each.

Nine years later, my left eye began burning and burning, and the Fort Sam Houston eye doctor mined a chunk from my eye and dropped it—KLINK—into one of those little pans. Just like in the movies.

He said it had worked its way to the surface from its nine year resting place and told me to go and buy a lottery ticket with my luck in having not been blinded all those years!

Chingo was hit the least of the four of us and only got a couple of pieces in his back. God was with us. The next day during daylight, we found that one of the fifteen or eighteen grenades was a dud, nestled in a small copse of bamboo head high to where Vicki and I had been sitting, and about two feet to our left. It would have killed both of us for sure.

Just to our left, two of the assaulting Infantrymen had gotten into the perimeter, but our troops were cool and stayed still. Following previous orders, they killed anything that moved, without moving themselves. I was really proud of all our guys.

We were saturated with luck. I have heard GIs in two wars cuss and discuss their steel pots, calling them worthless, heavy, and cumbersome—you name it—but Jeff became a believer that morning, let me tell you.

No one could even think about sleeping during the rest of the night, and as the first inkling of false light filtered down through the thickly matted vegetation to the jungle floor, Chingo put me on the spot!

"Hey, Wolf," he nudged me, "let's crawl down and recon the area for maybe a hundred yards an' see what's up."

"Um-hum. Let's crawl to Hanoi and see what's up, Chingo."

I wouldn't go down there with less than a platoon of paratroopers. What's up would probably be a casket for two!"

"Me an' Vik will go along," whispered Jeff. "She puts the edge on our side."

"There ain't no edge, Jeff," I pointed out. "If they're still down there as thick as fleas they'll eat us alive. How's your thick head—with all those doggone holes in it—think we could get back up this hill?"

He convinced us that he felt all right. I felt trapped. Those two guys and that dog were nuts. Crawling down Hill 823 was last on my list of priorities, when we weren't even sure who the landlord for the property was yet.

"Come on, Ted. Where'd you get that nickname 'Wolf' from? A small force kin sneak down there and maybe get some wounded prisoners.

"Yeah," I scoffed. "With thirteen million insane Clydes down there, madder'n hell. They are liable to get some wounded prisoners. Us."

My pals were disgusted with me. I got on the radio and informed Captain Ron what the four of us intended to do and told him that he would probably never see any of us alive again.

"Tell the troops not to shoot anything bald-headed or furry out in front of the perimeter, Six," I reminded him.

As soon as he got the word out, we left our steel helmets behind and began crawling down the slope. I thought wryly to myself that this would be a half-dozen trips down this slope for me, counting the ones rescuing the wounded the day before.

Somewhere in there, the law of averages kicks in. Chingo went first, followed by me and then came Jeff and Vicki. We have been criticized for this strategy by Monday morning quarterbacks ever since.

The dog should have gone first. Plus, according to them, it was suicide under such conditions for three men and a dog to go down there. Hell, I knew that. I just couldn't chicken out in front of my pals and my mutt.

If I'd possessed any soothsaying proclivities, I wouldn't have been on Hill 823 to start with. Whoever said I was smart to get roped in on such a deal anyway.

God looks after dummies, I guess. As it worked out, one catastrophe followed another, but us bringing Vicki up last ended up saving Chingo's life and probably the rest of us, too.

We were crawling, around and over enemy bodies and weapons for the first few yards. There were quite a few of them until we got out about thirty yards. After that, we'd only run into an occasional one here and there, killed by our mortars or Spooky or artillery.

Not one sign of a live enemy until we crawled into a little clearing perhaps the size of your living room rug. It was littered with neatly arranged bodies of dead NVA, plus four who were barely still alive, for a total of eighteen.

Of course there were no weapons. It was still pretty dark when Jeff made the discovery that several who were missing an arm or a leg had been killed by their own medics by cutting their throats!

We figured out later on that all that screaming the night before had prompted this quiet action to keep their cries from attracting our mortar crews' attention.

"What a couple of real dummies you an' me are," Chingo told me later, "remember all that screechin' an' moanin' an 'howlin' we heard the night before an' then suddenly it'd cease? Those guys were outta their heads and makin' trouble for the rest of 'em, so their faithful comrades just up an' cut their throats for 'em—guaranteed to stop pain and noise!"

We had never run into this throat-cutting routine before but we figured that their medics had run out of morphine and considered the horribly wounded to be goners anyway, and just silently put them out of their misery. Later in daylight when we examined dozens and dozens of bodies prior to burying them in one of the bomb craters, we never found anymore with their throat cut, so it must have been a field expedient of the medics only.

The four horribly wounded, unarmed prisoners were of no use to us as they would surely soon die, so we left them and crawled further down the hill.

Chingo was so deaf, he couldn't hear anything! He had spent a quarter of a century in rifle companies. I was starting to find out why he was such a well decorated guy. He had his share of guts.

It was getting slightly lighter now, as we crawled on down the hill. I could see Chingo pretty plainly now, maybe fifteen feet in front of me. I had my M-79 grenade launcher slung across my back, loaded with a flechette round and was clutching my rifle.

We were perhaps a hundred and twenty or so yards outside our perimeter and had to skirt an area where one of our mortars had blasted the sharp bamboo into a jumbled mess when I heard it—a slight rustle. There was absolutely no breeze, yet I heard a slight rustle which seemed to have come from a tree about thirty feet to Chingo's left front. Jungle animals never stir for a long time after such a big battle as had just transpired.

I hissed to Chingo. Deaf as a post, he plodded on, crawling across the jungle floor toward the dangerous tree.

Jeff hissed at me, and as I turned my head I could see Vicki alerting toward the tree! Impervious, Chingo crawled on! He would have already been a dead man if the sniper had more light to see by. I figured he was tracking Chingo by sound, and could just barely make him out on the dark ground and was trying to get his sights on him.

I had the advantage because I sky-lighted him against the sky and squeezed the trigger, with my weapon on full automatic. It spat its six or seven word message to the sniper who tumbled a few feet, suspended by a rope tied to his ankle.

When I had notified Captain Ron about the aid station, he told us, by the radio which Jeff was carrying, that he was sending a squad down to support us. As the sniper bit the dust, Chingo heard that.

Jeff brought it to my attention that the squad had come through the enemy's aid station area and was rapidly approaching to our rear because of my shots.

"Vicki's alerting to our right, Wolf," Jeff warned me.

Because of the thick foliage, I never saw the soldiers that Chingo killed until after they were dead.

"I kin see one of 'em, Wolf," Chingo cried. "Flip me a grenade—quick!"

He deftly caught the grenade, pulled the pin and held it a lot longer than I would have after the fuse popped, and tossed it underhanded into the thick vegetation a few feet away, killing that soldier plus one more near him who Chingo hadn't even seen.

Turned out later that both the NVA wore bandages from previous wounds, which probably explains their lack of alertness, were out of grenades and had only a few rounds of rifle ammo left.

When Chingo's grenade blew, several more which I couldn't see, got up and ran off to the right, which put them in plain view of the approaching squad, which cut them all down.

We were rich. We joined the squad, which immediately placed Jeff and Vicki to their front as we all began encircling Hill 823.

By now, it was as light as it ever gets in that thick jungle.

In memory of:
First Lt. Robert G. Darling
Sp4 Louis Charles Miller
PFC Clarence A. Miller
PFC Rufus John Dowdy
PFC Robert John Bickel
PFC Linwood C. Corbett
PFC David Frank Burney
Sp4 James Lee Ellis, Jr.
Platoon Sgt. Joaquine Palacious Cabrera
Sgt. Willie A. Wright
PFC Sherman Lawrence Jones
PFC Dewain V. Dubb
Sgt. James Dudley Shafer
PFC Richard Francis Laird
Sp4 Emery Lee Jorgensen
Sp4 Richard Arlan Stone
PFC Edrick Kenneth Stevens

Chingo's Cave

The squad leader was a young staff sergeant who knew his job well. He told me that Captain Ron had told him that his mission was to rescue those four dummies before they got themselves killed!

The captain had said for us to link up and then to make a sweep completely around Hill 823. I told him that he was in charge and Chingo and I tagged onto the end while Jeff and Vicki took the point.

As we started our sweep I must have day-dreamed a bit. I thought more about my friendship with Chingo. It went back for many years. I had been his first sergeant in Airborne Rifle Companies in various units.

The first time I had ever met Chingo had been fourteen years before at the conclusion of the Korean War. I was first sergeant of a rifle company in one of our parachute regiments and Chingo got assigned as a new replacement. I had looked up from my desk and seen this sharp little broken-nosed master sergeant standing tall all decked out in his best uniform and I couldn't remember having ever seen anyone with more combat decorations on their uniform in my life.

The captain had looked out through the door adjoining our offices and done a double-take. He called me in and closed the door.

"Who in hell's that kid out there masquerading as a master sergeant with all those decorations on?"

They were all well earned decorations. Chingo had started out as a rifleman during World War II and earned some of his decorations fighting in the South Pacific. By the time that World War II ended, he had worked his way up to squad leader and established a reputation for being one of the better infantrymen around.

During the Korean War, he was platoon sergeant in a rifle company and soon earned the promotion to master sergeant. He was to wear those six stripes for the next fifteen years. During peacetime—just as in combat—Chingo was a fighting fool. He took good care of his family, but he couldn't completely tear himself away from his rifle troops either.

"Vik's alertin'!" shouted Jeff as the rest of us joined him in stooping to our knees, every eye straining to see what terror lay masked in the thick surrounding foliage.

Vicki's nose or eyes had detected the presence of something. Cautiously following her, Jeff discovered a camouflaged entrance to a small cave dug into the side of a steep gulley.

Rifles at the ready, the rest of the patrol surrounded its entrance.

"Chiue hoi," called the squad leader, "Chiue hoi!"

Nothing. The squad leader nodded to a member of the squad armed with an M-60 machine gun, who stepped in front of the entrance and gave the inside a good long blast.

Still nothing. Chingo got a white phosphorus grenade from one of the squad members and told everyone to get down. He pulled the pin and let the fuse pop, waiting forever before tossing it into the cave. He didn't want it coming back into our laps on a return ticket before it detonated.

When it blew, nothing happened for a couple of seconds. We figured that either the cave was empty, or all its occupants were dead. Suddenly, in a rushing flurry of sound, an enemy officer flushed from the hole, meeting a hail of fire from the M-60 gunner.

Chingo joyously took the pistol from the dead officer's hand, cocking it.

"Be a pretty good joke on these li'l rats if there's any more of 'em in that hole an' I shoot 'em with their own pistol, wouldn't it?"

He started to crawl into the cave, flourishing the pistol. I held him back and tossed in a fragmentation grenade instead. The grenade killed two enemy riflemen. After it cleared up, our guys dragged them out, along with some medical supplies. It took the squad several trips around the outside of the entire perimeter before they had policed up all the NVA weapons. We found fifty-six AK-47s, which was a very good sign that we had hurt their outfit very badly, as they place a premium on retrieving their own weapons whenever it was at all possible.

After we got off Hill 823, I was supposed to meet Marlene for R&R in Honolulu, but we got trapped and I couldn't get out, so she got to spend an extra week there with friends of ours who lived in government quarters.

How we got trapped was a story all by itself!

Chingo's Farewell

As I recall, there were sixty-four of us left standing when we were relieved on Hill 823 by Charlie Company of our First Bat. My guys had worked tirelessly to bury almost two hundred NVA in the one bomb crater. While carrying parties brought up the corpses, it kept two men busy, one on the legs and one on the arms, expertly flinging each body down into the pile of inter-twined corpses.

"Better'n they'd do for us, Wolf," observed Chingo as we watched this ignominious military funeral.

Jeff handed me Vicki's leash as he went to spell one of the two guys tossing corpses. She was a beautiful Alsatian, and I said so to Chingo.

"What's an 'Alsatian', Ted?"

I explained to him that during WWI, the British hate for the Germans was so great that they made it illegal to refer to the German Shepherd as such, changing its name to "Alsat-ian."

"They hated 'em like we hate these gooks."

"Yep. They're dirty little cockroaches to headshoot our wounded, Chingo, but that's how they're taught. They look at us as interlopers in what they construe to be a just cause."

Vik's alert eyes never missed a thing, her head following the progress of each body from the top of the crater's rim to its final resting place on the ever growing pile below.

We were joined by Stanley Jones, Col Johnnie's efficient radio operator, on loan to Captain Ron since the loss of Bravo Six's regular radio operator.

"Why didn't we just leave the little sons of bitches lay, Wolf, like they do ours?"

"'Cause we ain't them, Stan."

American troops serving in Vietnam operated under an edict by General Westmoreland which contained a long list of what was considered to be "war crimes." Any soldier who vio-lated these rules faced a trial by court martial.

We tried our best to enforce these rules, but the average nineteen or twenty year old American had been brought up to consider tit-for-tat. We had a simple method of enforcing the rules in the Fourth Bat. In our one particular incident, a shakedown was ordered to find the missing ears.

Of course, they were seldom found for various reasons. The men would be exhausted from battle and lack of sleep and here some dummie—usually a new man—pays Clyde back for what Clyde did to our dead, and now everyone is squatting down in column, emptying his rucksack out on the trail for leaders to verify its contents, and this stuff gets old real fast. The next time anyone sees someone even thinking of cutting off ears, about four guys hop on his case right on the spot.

When the last body had been tossed into the grave, our exhausted troops went halfway down into the crater and using their steel helmets as scoops, threw the crater's loose dirt over the huge pile of corpses until they were covered by six or eight inches of dirt. Walking across the top of the mass grave was just like walking over a huge quivering bowl of jello. You could just barely maintain your balance.

The nasty job finished, the troops thankfully settled down around the perimeter awaiting the relief force, which started landing, one chopper at a time, about an hour later. As their eight men would disembark, we had a guide to take them to their portion of our small perimeter while eight of our men got on the ship for the trip back to FSB Savage.

Chingo and I shook hands with Jeff and patted Vicki, as they had to remain on Hill 823, attached to the new unit until the 39th Scout Dog outfit could replace them and send them back to us.

The relieving element was at least twice our size, so their unit was in much better shape than we had been. If they thought that grave full of Clydes was the end of it, they were sadly mistaken, though. A few minutes before the last ship came in for Chingo and me and several others, we all heard 82mm mortars hit the tube on the hill across the valley from us.

They had that perimeter zeroed in. Charlie Company of our 1st Bat didn't even have all their men on the hill yet and they had wounded to contend with.

A few minutes after the last round had landed, our taxi arrived. As soon as Charlie Company's eight men were off, we piled gratefully on and were ferried to FSB Savage.

I spent that night with Colonel Johnnie in FSB Savage, regaling him with tales of Hill 823 and bright and early the next morning, he told me to fly back to the Dakto Airstrip and catch a C-130 out of there to An Khe for processing to go on R&R.

I reported to our adjutant, who briefed me about my forth-coming R&R. According to him, I'd be on one of the C-130s in about an hour, headed to An Khe, then a flight to Cam Rahn Bay, which was the R&R Center. I'd be issued uniforms, socks and underwear, as we didn't wear them in the jungle, and then on to Honolulu.

I was enjoying a cup of coffee with him and our battalion admin NCO, confidently eyeing the three lovely C-130 aircraft which sat parked several hundred yards from us, when right before our eyes, one of them exploded skyhigh.

Bracketed by six or eight 82mm mortars, at least one of the thirteen pound rounds hit the ship. The gas tanks did the rest of the job.

We saw two figures sprinting from the edge of the field toward one of the two remaining ships. We could see its props start up, and then watched as the ship started to turn around, with at least two or three mortars bracketing the spot where it had just been.

All my troops in the battalion rear were wildly cheering as that brave pilot headed down that strip, faster and faster with the NVA mortar gunners bracketing their elusive prey. With one sudden burst of speed, he was airborne and away.

Unfortunately, the third C-130 was destroyed like the first.

It was going to be a long walk for me to go on R&R.

It didn't matter, because that was just the beginning. Clyde was just getting started. He next concentrated his fire on our huge ammo dump located near one end of the strip, adjacent to the Dakto Special Forces Camp.

Now, ammo is stacked on pallets, box on top of box, with the average volume being about the size of a large refrigerator. Picture an area the size of a football field and every twenty feet you have a stack of highly explosive material consisting of mortar and artillery rounds, grenades and ammo, etc.

You don't want to be anywhere near this area when it starts exploding. You'd think an ammo dump would go up with one grand explosion, but it took about twelve hours for ours to go up; each explosion jarring the eyeteeth of anyone near, raining down shrapnel and debris from the sky above.

It was probably midnight of the day the aircraft blew up, and the ammo dump had been going up for hours. Clyde had ceased mortaring our vicinity, so, four or five of us were lying on top of the sandbagged roof of a bunker, for easy access to the bunker's inside when it happened.

Our APO—Army Post Office—was located in a CONEX container, nestled between two other CONEXs packed with C-4, the army's version of instant dynamite. A CONEX container is a solid metal shipping container about the size of your living room rug six feet tall, with two swinging doors on its front.

Picture two of those things loaded with dynamite, now add a U.S. Air Force tanker truck filled with thousands of gallons of fuel. Finally, add one of Clyde's thirteen pound 82mm mortars to the mix and you will see why people for miles around could have read a newspaper at midnight when she blew.

The blast knocked all of us off the bunker's top and flattened every tent around the Dakto Airstrip. I know what they mean about a mushroom cloud now.

Doc, our battalion surgeon, was meeting his wife in Honolulu too, and it took us another four or five days before the Airforce could get us out of Dakto and started on our way. We met the girls in Honolulu, jointly rented a Mazda and drove the four of us all over the island. We had a blast and all too soon it ended and we found ourselves back in Dakto.

While we had been on R&R, the Fourth Bat participated in the terrible Battle for Hill 875, with Chingo acting as Colonel

Johnnie's Fourth Bat Sergeant Major and doing a fine job. Not long after this, Chingo's house burned down in the states. They lost everything. I got the message by radio and informed him to grab his rucksack—he was going home.

I escorted poor Chingo down to the chopper pad, leading Vicki on her leash to say goodbye to him while we awaited the arrival of the next ship. He took it all philosophically.

"Hell, it could've been worse, Wolf," he reasoned, "at least none of the family got burned up."

He petted Vicki. I told him that Jeff had finally gotten his R&R and would be back in a week or so. We reminisced a bit about our pals, Jeff and Vickie.

"Did the colonel put you an' me an' Jeff in for anything, Wolf?"

"The Silver Star, Chingo." At that time, it was to be my first—but it would be Chingo's third.

"Well," he looked pleased, "too bad they can't put ole Vik in fer somethin'."

We looked proudly at Vicki. She lay there at our feet, tongue lolling, just as pleased as punch because she heard her name mentioned.

"But," he nodded at her, "you know what she's gonna eventually git, don'cha, Ted?"

I slowly nodded in acknowledgment of his prediction.

"Ya know," he went on, "I'll betcha ole Vicki knows, too—deep down in her heart, Ted—they got a way o' knowin' stuff like that. But it ain't gonna slow the ole girl down one inch, though, is it?"

"Well, you can't tell, Chingo. She might survive all this and die of old age somewhere."

"Um hum," he said unconvincingly, "but I've got a request to make. It involves my awards an' decorations. You know my record."

I did. Just like everyone else in the Airborne Infantry did. Counting only the combat awards, he had been awarded two Silver Stars—with a third one coming—several Bronze Stars for

Valor, a half dozen Purple Hearts, the Belgian Distinguished Service Cross, the Vietnamese Cross of Gallantry and three Combat Infantryman's Badges.

He told me that he had finally seen the light and was going to retire before he got killed. He said that he had hung around enough bars to know how to run one, and that was his ambition—to go to California and open one. He looked at me wistfully. He sure had me puzzled. I nodded for him to continue.

"I wanta build me a big glass case up on top of the bar mirror and I'm gonna put every one o' my medals inside there so that all them customers don't think they're dealin' with a REMF or somethin! I'm gonna keep me maybe four or five steel helmets under the bar. Whenever anyone starts tellin' any combat stories about wars they bin in, we are gonna all put on them pots and just let 'er rip, ole buddy." He laughed.

I allowed as how I thought that would be a fine drawing card for the local vets.

"O.K.," he continued, "now here's the hammer. Do you think that I'd ever put me a medal in that case which I hadn't been awarded?"

I told him to quit beating around the bush and tell me what he had in mind.

"Well," he shrugged, "we both know the regulation. Ya gotta keep yer nose clean for so many years in a row to git the Good Conduct Medal, right?"

He already had every medal except the Medal Of Honor and the Distinguished Service Cross. When he came up with that Good Conduct Medal, though, I just couldn't help it. I threw my head back and roared.

Vicki jumped up and danced around nervously and then lay back down again, tongue lolling. She looked from me to Chingo and back to me. She didn't get the joke.

"Chingo, you have been in the infantry over a quarter of a century and you are a Master Sergeant with over fifteen years in grade and you have never—not even once—been recommended for the award of a Good Conduct Medal?"

"Affirmative, Wolf, I just got in a little trouble here an' there an' now an' then an' once in a while an' it all seemed to keep me from gittin' that medal."

We heard the UH-1 Huey coming and saw a speck on the horizon. Chingo was about to depart. I tore a sheet out of my small notebook and scribbled a note.

"Give this note to our Admin NCO. He'll make it happen for you, Chingo. I'm counting your years in combat as years toward the Good Conduct Medal. When I visit your bar, I want to see it right up there with the rest of your medals."

Chingo shook my hand and nodded to Vik and me as he loaded his rucksack on the ship and followed it.

"Be careful," he screamed to us above the rotor's noise. Then, to the amazement of the door gunner on our side, he jumped back off the ship and gave me a tearful hug.

"Goodbye, Vicki." He dropped to one knee and hugged her and then swiftly climbed back onto the deck of the waiting chopper.

I nodded "yes" to the doorgunner, who gave the pilot a thumbs up while I squatted beside Vicki and covered her eyes against the flying sand.

She whined and pranced and pulled away from my grasp as the ship took off.

We watched it until it disappeared from view, and she never ceased whining. Somehow she must have sensed as I did that she would never see Chingo again.

For Chingo the battles of Dakto had ended. There were more to come.

Dedicated to
Master Sgt. Lawrence Okendo (Ret)
and to
Sgt. Jeffrey Dick and his dog, Vicki

4th Battalion rifle troopers dig in to protect our artillery troopers.

Lt. Col. Lawrence
W. Jackley
commanded 4th
Bat from February
to August 1967.

Lieutenant Colonel Jackley relaxes after Dakto July 10, 1967, battle for Hill 830.

Lt. Col. James H. Johnson is the new CO, who will command from August 1967 to February 1968.

The colonel's new quarters in the jungle at Dakto, August 1967.

Author (left) and Special Forces friend Mike Collins at Dakseang Special Forces Camp.

Some of Sgt. Maj. Mike Collins' Montagnards at Dakseang Special Forces Camp adjacent to Dakto area.

Mike's Montagnards incorporated fields of deadly punji stakes into Dakseang's defenses surrounding the camp.

Dakto Hotel's great bathroom.

A "three-man" snake, which the author's troops roasted and ate with gusto.

Brave Platoon Sgt. John Ponting (left) with author and Bravo Company's great 1st Sgt. Jerry Babb right before Ponting was killed in action on Hill 875, November 1967 at Dakto in the Central Highlands.

Direct hit by NVA 82mm mortar on USAF C-130 at Dakto, November 1967.

The colonel's great radio operator, Stan Jones (now deceased), and the author dig in at Dakto's airstrip.

Stan Jones examines author's M-79 grenade launcher, a very powerful and extremely accurate weapon.

Chinook delivering 105mm artillery piece in jungle fire support base.

The powerful Chinook blows troops away at Dakto.

Our great Bravo Battery troopers preparing a 105mm artillery piece.

Rifle troopers on "search-and-destroy" missions hump eighty-pound rucksacks everyday until late afternoon, then dig into a perimeter (laager site) for the night.

A hard rain or a stream or river was his only panacea.

Long Range Recon patrolman being extracted from the Dakto jungle.

After an all-day hump, it took two troopers three hours to dig their foxhole with overhead cover to protect them from mortar fire. Then they might go on ambush patrol, but either way, they would spend the night on 50 percent alert with little sleep.

Author with "Red," a very experienced door gunner.

Troops lived off "C" rations.

Author (left) observes enemy POW being interrogated.

New trooper ponders horrible sting of huge foxhole centipede (many longer than one foot!). Jungle troopers re-supplied with blank fatigues and no socks or underwear.

One of our powerful 81mm mortars dug into bomb crater at Dakto.

November 1967: NVA blows up Dakto Ammo Dump.

Buffalo Gals ponder passing riflemen.

Very close airstrike.

Stan Jones with unlucky trooper's helmet on Hill 875 at Dakto.

After the battle of Hill 823 (November 6–7, 1967) at Dakto.

M/Sgt. Boyette P. Findley looks through the horns of a huge prehistoric deer still found in the Central Highlands. (All Montagnard photos are courtesy of him.)

M/Sgt. Boyette P. Findley spent several Special Forces tours with the Montagnard troops.

Thousands of years have little changed thirty main Montagnard tribes.

Fish and rice, basic staples.

M/Sgt. Findley's troops with one ham.

Supper for M/Sgt. Findley's guys.

Lieutenant Colonel Johnson and SGM landing at hot spot with command and control ship.

Typical sampan. COURTESY BOYETTE FINDLEY

Lt. Col. James H. Johnson during Tuy Hoa rice paddy action. In mid-December 1967, three weeks after the terrible battle for Hill 875, the 4th Battalion was moved south to Tuy Hoa Province to protect the rice harvest from the NVA.

Very close airstrike on Cemetery Hill.

The beautiful province of Tuy Hoa was destined to soon become the setting for the terrible battle for Cemetery Hill during the infamous Tet Offensive.

One of our brave medics makes his way to a wounded trooper on Cemetery Hill.

After Cemetery Hill (Tet Offensive, January 1968, at Tuy Hoa).

Checking enemy bodies after Cemetery Hill battle.

Aftermath of Cemetery Hill's terrible battle.

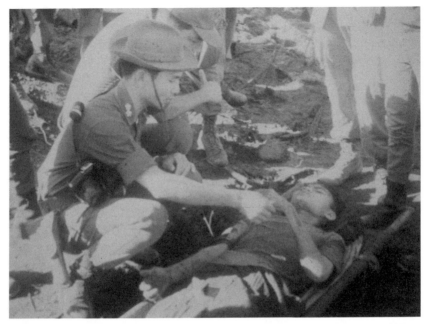

ARVN military intelligence analyst with POW from Cemetery Hill.

Concerned author, pensive over mass casualties.

Part of Cemetery Hill.

Farmers being re-located in Tuy Hoa Province, January 1968.

Shrines.

"To market, to market—"

A "five-man" inedible snake!

The rugged UH-1 "Huey" was the most versatile lifesaver and
workhorse for the combat troops.

A formidable flamethrower.

Our fine brigadier general, Leo H. Schweiter (now deceased), decorated Lt. Col. James H. Johnson.

Departing four days after the Cemetery Hill battle, Colonel Johnnie is congratulated by incoming CO David Buckner.

CHAPTER 7

The Grunts

The preponderance of my seven hundred jungle troopers were "grunts"—rifle soldiers. Each of them was serving a one year's sentence in the jungle. Many was the time that I felt like I was a city judge, rather than being the sergeant major of the 4th Rifle Battalion of the 173rd Airborne Brigade. There were so many life and death decisions to be rendered, due to the nature of our mission, which was "To close with and to destroy the enemy."

My grunts made it easier on me and my fine lieutenant colonel to do our jobs, because to a man, they were all brave volunteers, trained paratroopers who had a special *esprit de corps* going for them, because not everyone is capable of becoming a paratrooper.

One could easily pick out the grunts who had been in the deep jungle the longest, from their jailhouse pallor and the loss of fifteen or twenty pounds of weight from fighting that rucksack in heat sometimes reaching 120 degrees. Grunts do most of the dying. They get the most Purple Hearts per capita and the least amount of sleep. Most grunts don't last the full year in an outfit which never returns to the rear for rest, without eventually becoming introduced to a litter, or far worse, to a rubber body bag.

Try and drift from where you are as you read this, into the realm of the jungle grunt. A smart grunt can cut corners you'd never dream of. He must be the wiliest of his species in order to survive and he knows it. He practices his wiles every waking moment, which comprises the preponderance of his time, because of the complex nature of his duties. It is not at all unusual under these circumstances for a grunt to carry a rucksack well over eighty pounds all day long. During extreme heat, he must eat from six to twelve salt tablets per day, or he may start to see the little blue lights in front of his eyes, which are a prelude to heat exhaustion.

Such a rucksack is tantamount to you hoisting your living room's TV on your back, seven days a week. Sundays have no particular significance during jungle combat. Think about such a rucksack. Empty, it's light as a feather with tubular aluminum frame and nylon fabric. Loaded is something else again.

The average grunt is armed with an M-16 rifle. Each magazine for this rifle is designed to contain 20 rounds. In order to prevent jamming due to constant spring tension, most grunts back off two rounds of ammo. Most of my grunts carried 25 or 30 magazines, rather than to run out of ammo during a critical firefight. Some items of equipment, such as his entrenching tool, some ammo pouches, water, grenades and bayonet and first aid pouch are worn on the waist-belt of his "load-bearing" harness.

The outside of his ruck might contain a hanging machete and several quarts of drinking water. Inside would be the rest of his ammo, several more fragmentation and smoke grenades and a Claymore mine. Grunts were issued rubber air mattresses, but the ubiquitous thorns soon rendered them useless. Absolutely one of his most valued items of equipment was his camouflaged nylon poncho liner, along with the rainproof poncho itself. An added necessity was his mosquito netting and the meager toilet articles he is periodically issued. Next into that rucksack went enough "C" rations to sustain him for a five day period until an evening resupply by helicopter was arranged. On each man's steel helmet his camouflage elastic band secured one plastic bottle of mosquito lotion to help prevent malaria.

I want to once again stress that to my knowledge, the 173rd Airborne Brigade was the only outfit that I know of which spent over an entire year in the jungle without ever once returning to a rear area for rest, "stand-down" and training of replacements.

Our replacements were delivered directly into each rifle company by the supply fireflies which choppered in every fifth night with new "C" rations, ammo, water and other supplies as appropriate. At this time, every fifth night of his life, each trooper had the opportunity of eating a warm, fresh meal which was delivered in the rear mess's marmite cans. To prevent intestinal disorders, he was furnished with a paper plate and plastic eating utensils.

Just stop and think about going for a full year in such a situation, especially after I describe the things which happened to each grunt during one twenty-four hour period alone. Then you will see why they were all tired to death when they stopped for the night.

The preponderance of the Central Highlands area is covered by deep, dark, triple-canopied jungle. During the rainy season, the troops went for weeks at a time without ever becoming completely dry. More than one of my troopers was medevaced with pneumonia. Many of the troopers who had been there the longest suffered with huge ulcers of jungle rot on various parts of their body, although for some reason, some never contracted this terrible jungle malady.

These troopers went for months at a time without being exposed to a lengthy period of the bright sunlight constantly available to the majority serving within the open areas of Vietnam. That's why my troopers had nicknamed the Central Highlands as the "Land With No Sun," because to them, that's exactly what it was. These riflemen were serious grunts.

If anyone in jungle warfare had a more legitimate gripe than he, I'd sure like to hear it. Such a rifleman was faced with so many hazards and hardships that the cards were completely stacked against him to ever make it out of that jungle without becoming a casualty to some degree or other. To start with, even completely disregarding enemy action, life in that jungle on a daily basis consisted of a cruel pace of humping eight hours, digging for three and then getting only half a night's sleep.

The grunt is wise to the ways of the jungle and culls out all weight which he considers to be superfluous to the requirements of his rucksack. One complete case of "C" rations weighed about twenty-five pounds if he carried it all, so the grunt would keep his favorite cans of food, giving the rest to his buddies, or else puncturing the excess cans and burying them to deny them to the enemy. The average grunt carries a rucksack weighing more than eighty pounds—all day, every day. Sundays and holidays mean nothing in a combat situation. Tomorrow is the same as yesterday.

His rifle became an extension of himself, with thirty magazines weighing over a pound each. Most of my magnificent grunts willingly carried about thirty such magazines, rather than to run out of ammo during a firefight. These delicate magazines will immediately rust if not kept properly cleaned and oiled. Also, dust from helicopters or any kind of dirt contaminating the magazine or its ammo can cause a grunt to lose his life by jamming on him during a firefight.

Inside his ruck, he carried extra fragmentation and smoke grenades, a Claymore mine, all those extra magazines of ammo, his waterproof poncho and its camouflaged nylon liner, a mosquito net, meager toilet articles and five days' "C" rations. No clothing. We wore no socks or underwear—just the one set of jungle fatigues he was wearing—sometimes for thirty or forty days with no change.

In the weapons platoon, crewmen didn't carry nearly as much rifle ammo because they carried up to three 81mm mortar rounds at thirteen pounds each. Radiomen and medics didn't carry that much ammo because of the weight of that radio and medical aid kit. Hanging on the rucksack would be extra canteens of water and perhaps a machete, and fastened to its very top were fifteen empty sandbags—more about that later.

Each morning the grunt climbed into all this equipment, grabbed his weapon and donned his steel pot, ready to take his place in the column with his other squad members. Often in pouring rain, he could look forward to traversing rough, slippery and rock-strewn ground with vines to constantly trip him. These vines are real nightmares—especially the ones growing thorns, some of which are inches long with their own smaller thorns growing out their sides. Thorns with thorns. Down that trail he goes, carrying what amounts to be a TV set on his back. Try it for five minutes sometime. Then, multiply how that feels into months. Think what that would feel like for a year and think about this grunt. Mac was such a grunt.

Mac, a Grunt

I think of Mac often. Mac had put in many months as a jungle grunt in one of our rifle companies and I liked what I saw of him the first time that I ever laid eyes on him. I had to select a new RTO for Colonel Larry Jackley and Mac was one of the candidates. I asked him if he knew how to help to keep our colonel alive during a firefight.

"No, sergeant major," he shook his head honestly, "but I'd certainly be willing to learn. I know how to stay alive as a grunt but that's all. I know the proper procedure for a radio operator to follow when talking on the radio and I have a strong back. Other than that, you'd have to teach me."

"Well," I smiled, "when the slugs start flying, Mac, Clyde just looks around for our leaders to put a bullet into and the first thing that he spots is your big antenna waving around, advertising that you're tethered to the colonel. Charlie simply shoots you and me and the colonel. Get the picture."

I explained some tricks to Mac, such as the radio operator running the antenna down his pantsleg during a hot, close fight, and told him that in some situations he and I would double as bodyguards to protect the colonel, whose safety was critical to every member of the battalion. He already knew from past experience that snipers in the trees were formidable.

Mac was about my size—a bit more than 200 hard pounds, and his curly brown hair contrasted with what was left of mine after I shaved daily and just continued shaving my entire head.

During my interview of him, I guessed that Mac could easily hump the colonel's radio for him. Mac told me that he had already been wounded twice and that he had an eerie feeling if he stayed in Dog Company as a grunt, that it was probably in the cards that the third time was going to be "charm" for him! I thought that he was being pretty honest about everything and decided that he was the best man for the job.

I told Mac that he had the job. I explained to him that as I was the new kid on the block, having just recently arrived from the states, that my first order of business was to learn all about the hardships and disappointments facing my grunts daily, with the idea of looking out for their interests. I told him that I intended to write up some "combat tips" to hand out to other incoming personnel, stressing how to prevent the many horrible accidents which killed or maimed our own men, based upon my previous experience as a first sergeant of a rifle company in Korea during that war.

He knit his brow and thought for a minute and then told me that he would be more than glad to contribute his eight months of jungle knowledge and experience from a grunt's view.

It started raining. I had been digging a foxhole for the night as I was interviewing Mac and at this point, we spelled one another on the entrenching tool, filling sandbags for the overhead cover for the hole. As I took my turn digging, Mac held a sandbag for me to fill, expertly shifting the bag from side to side in order to make it easier for me to get the dirt in. I told him to tell me about some of the things which he had learned about the hard way when he had first been assigned to Dog Company as its newest grunt.

He decided that the easiest way would be to tell me from memory, all the things which had happened to him during his first twenty-four hours. I concentrated on his story and tried to visualize how it had been for Mac. Here's his story:

"I was scared to death as the firefly chopper stopped in mid-air and began settling down from several hundred feet, into a little ole postage stamp-sized hole in that dark, thick jungle below. It was just at dusk and raining and all of us new guys were watchin' that rotor as it seemed to come just scant inches from striking the surrounding trees which looked to be at least a couple of hundred feet tall."

Mac explained that there were six replacements counting himself and that they were met by Dog's First Sergeant, who squatted down in their midst and explained to them that they should all go through the chowline together. They did, and he had a runner to escort them to each of their new platoons. He said that it was almost completely dark when they arrived at the Third Platoon, which had no officer. The platoon sergeant shook his hand and told the runner to guide him to the first squad. The squad leader asked his name and showed him where to lay his poncho and bed down for the night.

Mac said that he hadn't realized it at the time, but this was to be the last time for an entire year, that he'd be able to get an entire night's sleep.

"The next thing I knew," he said, "I was shaken awake by a figure who said he was my fire team leader. 'Stand to', he had brusquely grunted into my ear as he scuttled off to the next rifleman on my left. It's my first morning in the jungle and at first I didn't know where I was. The drizzling rain brought me to reality and as I crawled out from beneath my warm poncho liner and the cold of the mountains of Dakto caused my bones to shiver, my morale was pretty low." I detected movement as the fellow on my left crawled over to me.

"Are you cold, buddy?" he whispered. When I acknowledged that I was, he laughed. "It's gonna get worse before it ever gets any better. At least you were dry last night. The rest of us have been wet for two weeks. You'll get used to it. After the sun warms those treetops it won't be bad at all. It's just at night and early in the mornin' You'll get used to it. Boy, I've got just two months more of this trash, then it's back to the world for me."

"What do you mean, back to 'the world?'" I puzzled.

"The world, man—the world!" He laughed again. "Where you just came from. Man, you don't think that this is part of the world, do ya? Man, you are green, aren't you? But then, that's to be expected as you're still peein' stateside water!"

It was pretty funny. I laughed too and then asked him about this 'stand to' business. He explained that Clyde has been known to overrun American perimeters in the period of first light. In a lax unit which was not on the stick, the enemy could wreak havoc. I was about to ask more questions but was interrupted by a voice on our right announcing that there would be a "turkey shoot"—on order—in about one minute, and to pass it along.

"Turkey shoot," my buddy announced to our left, and I could hear the order being relayed around the perimeter. He told me to slide a round into my rifle's chamber, put it on semi-automatic, and to be prepared to fire at will into the surrounding jungle. I nodded nervously because I didn't have the slightest idea what was going on, but my buddy seemed confident. He told me that Clyde had been known to erect large command detonated Claymore mines and decimate a large part of a perimeter just as everyone began stirring at daybreak. Suddenly, a voice far down the perimeter commanded "FIRE!" and in one instant, all hell broke loose as each of about 120 or more riflemen around our perimeter cut loose simultaneously firing outward, forming a 360 degree inferno of steel. As I ran out of ammo for my rifle and stopped to reinsert a fresh magazine, I noticed that the entire volume of fire had petered out a bit as others did the same; then once again the Turkey Shoot evolved into a thunderous crescendo of fire power.

Suddenly, the order came from the right to cease fire and soon the entire perimeter became quiet again. Very soon thereafter, I could see a squad of men down apiece from us, apparently departing the perimeter. I watched with interest as their tactical formation melted into the thick jungle.

"Screening patrol," explained my partner. "They'll sweep this entire perimeter all the way around for Clydes and Claymores. They do it each morning. One day they'll move out clockwise and the next it'll be counter-clockwise. Makes it harder for Clyde to second guess 'em and set up an ambush some mornin'."

"What's the story on Claymores? I thought those were our weapons."

"Well," he said, "we do have the original Claymore mine, I suppose, but Clyde has not complied with the patent, ya understand. He has, in fact, come up with some doozies of his own. One in particular is a command-detonated job which weighs in at about forty pounds. It's a long range, powerful weapon and very accurate. Clyde can shred targets—like people—at a fantastic distance an' I mean one o' those big ones can sprinkle hell an' damnation around a perimeter an' burn everyone a new ass who gits in its way. We are very vulnerable to 'em in such a static situation as we're in this mornin', although Clyde has used 'em on us before in ambushes while we were on the move too. One of our rifle platoon sergeants in this company carries over five hundred stitches in him from one of Clyde's big command-detonated Claymores."

"What's 'command' detonated mean?" I asked.

"Well, that simply means that he sets it off with little batteries and an electric wire an' he can sit way back over yonder— just as long as his wire is—an' maintain good visibility. Soon as he sees the largest number of us are in his killin' zone 'KAWHAM-KAWHAM', he starts to settin' 'em off an' yer in a big hurt."

He told me that the enemy fills the doggone things up with all sorts of stuff, that one kid in his squad had ended up with a big ole rusty nut and bolt blasted about two inches up into the guy's hind end. He said that the enemy sticks all sort of metal junk inside as shrapnel.

"I'll bet those surgeons could tell you some stories." I was learning. "Sure hope they never get the opportunity to use my carcass for a target."

"Listen, my name's Jerry," he offered his hand as I introduced myself. "They could be minin' rusty bolts outta yer ass by noon if ya don't climb down off those sandbags. If you keep a low silhouette you'll live longer." I quickly eased off the top of the fighting position. He told me that the first time he had been wounded, he had been violating that exact same rule and an enemy soldier had tossed a grenade at him.

"Two fragments just tickled me," he said, "I was sure lucky because one went about a half inch into my thigh an' the other 'un just skimmed the bottom o' my left nut enough for some iodine to do the trick, although some deep reflection on my part went into what had almost been."

He told me that the second time he had been wounded, that a mortar frag had put a furrow in his arm, once again not requiring evacuation. He showed me a long, still-pink scar which ran across a big tattooed Paratrooper's jumpboot on his arm, above which read "God Is My Jumpmaster".

"The first time," he explained, "the medic simply threw a tetanus shot into my hind end, swabbed off my balls with a cotton ball full of alcohol an' after I danced a little while, I was back in the squad, ploddin' along to greater things." He grinned.

At first I hadn't liked Jerry because he had razzed me so soundly about being new in the jungle but I was changing my mind. He told me that while I was new, that I should keep my eyes and ears open and my mouth shut and to listen to the guys who have been here the longest, no matter how low ranking they were, or how high they had been in school. He said that three of our riflemen had been to college and were just pulling their own load until it was time for them to return to the States.

I asked Jerry how many guys were in our squad and he replied that it was short three men, counting me as its ninth. He told me that we had less than an hour for us to shave, eat and empty the sandbags back into the foxhole and then to select "C" rations to go into our rucks for the next five days. I was curious as to why everyone didn't just let their beards grow? My logic being that who would know or care what we did in this God-forsaken jungle?

"If you git wounded in the face," he explained, "it cuts down on infection an' infection begets jungle rot." What a cheering thought. "You are gonna find out," he went on, "that ya git wounded fifteen or twenty times a day around here from thorns an' insects an' such along. Here, lemme show ya. Bein' as malaria control time's over now, we kin roll up our sleeves. Look at this stuff here. Some guys have bin here a long time an' have never caught jungle rot. Look."

I looked. It made me feel half sick to my stomach just to think of my own arms eventually becoming covered by such huge, oozing red and swollen ulcers. It was my first—but definitely not to be my last—encounter with the dreaded jungle rot. Jerry told me that he had it on his legs also.

"You don't shave," he warned, "an' thorn cuts kin transfer it to yer face, ya see? Nice, ain't it? The 'Bac se'—which is Vietnamese for 'medic'—gives us lotion to rub into the sores an' it helps a bit, but I don't think it cures 'em. If yer lucky an' don't aggravate 'em too much, they'll dry up an' blow away after a couple of months. Ya go fer months in this filthy jungle without washin' with soap an' ya also ketch it off all these bites from these huge leeches we keep runnin' into. Some areas are just crawlin' with 'em an' they'll eat ya up if you don't watch real careful."

"I was wondering to myself," Mac went on, "what other bad surprises were waiting for me in this awful place and I was soon to find out." It was my turn to hold the sandbags while Mac tried valiantly to hack out clods of the hard laterite clay with my entrenching tool. The rain had let up and it was just drizzling, but he held my interest as he cheerfully continued his story with a voice resonating with a pleasing West Virginia mountain twang which I can clearly remember to this day.

"Jerry explained to me," continued Mac "that in our battalion, everyone referred to our enemy as 'Clyde' rather than 'Charlie' when talking on the radio. He said that the enemy was not near as dumb as most Americans are prone to believe until they get the dubious opportunity of fighting him. They definitely knew who "Charlie" was, too.

We quickly emptied the dirt from the sandbags back into the foxhole and set them to one side to go on our rucks later. Jerry then helped me to select my next five days "C" rations puncturing any cans not used and he showed me how to tear up the empty foil-lined accessory packets to keep Clyde from unearthing and using them after we had left the area. He said that many G.I.s simply discarded such items without destroying or burying them.

"That's amazing," I told him, Mac went on with his story, "that we can be so dumb as to help to feed Clyde."

"Yeah" agreed Jerry, "an' to arm an' equip him, too. Many's the stupid jackass who threw away ammo an' grenades an' stuff to keep from carryin' it an' either ended up dead or with the medics pickin' his own stuff out of his hide after Clyde found it an' put it back on him later. 'Course Clyde captures a lot of our stuff back in the rear areas too. We was in one battle where Clyde used American M-79 grenade launchers on us. Ya oughtta hear one o' them projectiles comin' in straight atcha sometime, Mac. They're deadly, and very accurate."

Jerry explained to me that the enemy supplemented his supplies by living off the land, stealing rice and animals to eat from the farmers. He said that if they didn't cooperate, Clyde would just give 'em the business. He told me that out in the deep jungle, the enemy had organized parties which followed every American unit, unearthing discarded equipment and food. Jerry glanced at his watch and told me it was time for us to quickly clean our rifles and also to clean, oil and re-load the magazines which we had emptied during the Turkey Shoot. He showed me how he had wrapped his magazines in the poly-styrene covers, in which military radio batteries are stored and shipped.

"See," he explained, "keep this stuff wrapped around your excess magazines in your rucksack. Keeps the dust an' rain out, but the magazines sweat, so ya keep 'em wiped out clean an' they ain't hard to git to in a firefight if ya run outta the ammo from yer ammo pouches on yer belt. Keep 'em all cleaned up every chance ya git an' ya live longer that way."

Sounded reasonable to me. I asked Jerry what I should do if my rifle ever did jam in a firefight and he gave me a curious look and told me that I'd better be praying and un-jamming it real quick or I'd be dead. He picked up his M-16 rifle and showed me how he had already screwed his cleaning rod's sections together and carried the extended rod taped along the bottom of the rifle. I didn't see the connection until he explained that the best way to remove a stuck cartridge case was to ram the rod down the muzzle and bore until the faulty cartridge popped out. He unwound some excess tape he had wrapped around his rifle butt and gave to me while I rigged my rod just like his.

Mac and I switched places and he held the sandbags while I shovelled again as he continued to tell me about his first day in the jungle, eight months before. Neither of us knew at that time that the Army would eventually chrome plate the M-16's bullet chamber and change the composition of its cartridge powder as a successful panacea to the jamming which troops were experiencing with the earlier version of this fine rifle. Today, it's one of the best weapons in the world.

During my first few hours in Dog Company, I was making mental notes like a computer. I certainly didn't want to become an unnecessary casualty and it was beginning to look to me as though I didn't have a chance at survival with my meager knowledge of jungle warfare. We finished cleaning our weapons and our fire team leader came by and gave us each a pack of cigarettes and some candy to chew on. He had a "C" ration box full of assorted sundries and from this Jerry selected a tube of toothpaste and some razor blades also.

"These came from the 'goodie packs'" he explained. The real name is 'sundries' pack. It's the poor man's PX who is stuck in the jungle an' can't fend for himself. They come in periodically. Have you ever tried to eat a 'gorilla bar?'" It was a new experience for me as I tried and tried to bite into it and finally ended up with a small bite after giving my teeth the workout of their life.

Jerry howled with glee as I thought to myself, 'gorilla bars yet.'

The jungle was getting a bit lighter. The dark gray of false light had changed to a shade of green as the inklings of day-

light filtered down between the vines and trees. The rain had
petered out and Jerry was hunkered down heating what turned
out to be an innocuous liquid which passed fairly well for coffee. My eyes and ears and nostrils took in the jungle. I was to
learn later that the musty smell of the jungle and the sweet,
molded smell of the bamboo would permeate my very body.
This odor is something which takes much scrubbing to eliminate once one left the jungle. The birds and other jungle animals lent their welcoming voice to the impending full light of
day.

"ARROOP ARROP ARROOOOOOOOOLLLL," one very
loud voice in particular joined in with its beautiful, musically
vibrant effect.

"AARROOP ARROP ARROOOODOOOOLLL," echoed
an answering call from another part of the jungle.

"Pretty, ain't they?" Jerry noticed my intense interest.
"Howler Monkeys. What a beautiful sound. Ya know, I think I
may be turnin' into a Yard, I bin here so long. I hope I'm not
really gittin' to like the jungle. Probably only losin' my mind is
all." I didn't know what a 'yard' was and said so.

"A Yard. A Montagnard," he explained. "We'll see some of
their villages from time to time an' they are really somethin'!
The women never heard of a bra an' those little devils kin take
3 hunks o' bamboo an' some vines an' make an automobile or
somethin' outta it. You couldn't believe what they do. As their
name implies, they are mountaineers. They don't even speak
Vietnamese. They are fierce fighters and fight on the Americans' side because they don't like the VC or NVA any better
than we do because the enemy tries to shove 'em around an'
exploit them, but won't pay them like we do."

Jerry told me that one of the officers who had made a study
of them had explained that because of language difficulties
caused by extreme differences in dialects, that over the eons,
enemy invaders were never able to govern them and they have
always remained completely independent. The thirty some
main tribes can understand their own people, but have big dif-
ficulty in communicating with neighboring tribes. Sometimes

hollowed logs were used to drum out messages. Jerry said that if you heard the drums at night, they'd lull you to sleep.

Jerry had finished preparing the coffee and gave each of us a piping hot pecan roll from a can. I had watched with great interest as he had taken an empty cracker tin and manufactured a small oven out of it by punching holes in it here and there and then heating the cans of pecan rolls. After we had eaten that, he opened up two tins of less desirable rations which he had been heating while we had our coffee and rolls.

"Might as well live it up," he observed. "We go from rags to riches dependin' on the comings and goings of those doggone fireflies every fifth night." He gave me a piece of polystyrene to wrap my wallet in. He said it would rot in a week otherwise, and he told me to remind him to tell me about wallets later. I watched as he unwrapped what I thought to be his own wallet, but was surprised to see that it was six or eight lime flavored Kool Aid packs.

"Here," he tossed one to me, "pour the contents into yer 'fat rat' an' it'll kill the yukky taste of that chlorinated stuff in yer drinkin' water." It turned out that a 'fat rat' was a two quart soft plastic canteen worn on the outside of the rucksack. This pliable item of equipment is a life-saver, carried in a nylon holder to prevent puncturing by thorns, ruining its baloon-like skin. I did as he told me and took a swig and it wasn't bad. He told me that the lime aid did not come from goodie packs, but that his girlfriend and his mom always slipped one into a letter to him. He said that any other flavor was too sweet for the chlorine and only made one more thirsty.

I made another mental note for my letters home and Jerry stood up and told me to get into my rucksack for my first jungle trek.

First Trek and Last Trek

Mac expertly stacked our sandbags on either side of the foxhole and we started laying our freshly cut lengths of bamboo across them, so that we could stack the remaining sandbags on top to complete our overhead cover. I was finding his story of his first twenty-four hours in our Dog Company to be very interesting and informative. I urged him to continue as I mentally joined him on his first jungle trek eight months before. He continued:

"We're fixin' to move out shortly from the looks o' things up the line," Jerry cautioned. As it became our platoon's turn to filter into the column, I watched as our squad automatically melted in with the rest of the platoon and the entire column gradually became absorbed by the jungle due to the thick foliage. "Keep five yards between us," whispered Jerry as he took his place ahead and I followed him. You could tell that the sun must have risen as the jungle gradually turned from light gray to dark green. Before we had gone a hundred yards, I had trouble breathing and my back was killing me because of the ruck's weight. At our first break, I confided in Jerry that I was tired and kind of dizzy.

"In this heat an' until ya get used to that ruck, ya gotta eat four or five salt tablets each mornin' an' again in the afternoon because you're soakin' wet from sweat an' losin' all that salt. If ya don't, you'll start seein' little blue lights an' pass out an' it ain't even hot yet." I told Jerry that it was hotter'n the hinges of hell.

"Listen, Mac," he retorted, "that rucksack's killin' ya, is all. That sweat's because of yer ruck—not the heat. Hell, it gits a helluva lot hotter'n this when that sun gits high over this triple canopy. Believe me, you'll git used to it, soon as about fifteen pounds o' that fat melts off ya. You'll git in shape in a few days, remember I said it."

During that first break, I noticed that none of the old hands had removed their rucks, but were simply sitting in a fashion to shift the weight. I asked myself if I could make it a week? What would happen if I went month after month and then got killed? Wouldn't it be better for it to happen right now, if it was in the cards? I resolved to take this jungle one hour at a time and to put it out of my mind that I had over three hundred and sixty days of this torture to put up with.

The word came down the line in the form of troops getting to their feet, that we were moving out once again. As I hunched into my ruck's straps and re-shouldered it, it seemed to weigh twice as much as it had before the break.

Then, after a few yards on the trail, it seemed to lighten up a bit. What really gets to you is the continuous stopping and waiting, with that ruck's weight draining your strength while the area up ahead is scouted out to determine that it's safe to pass through, with no ambushes lurking. Then you move out again—then stop—then repeat. Move and wait—move and wait—over and over again. Suddenly we passed down a steep gully containing slippery lichen-covered rocks and quite a few of our troopers—to include me—ended up with their feet flying out from under them and taking a nasty spill. At this point, one poor guy went over backwards down the steepest portion of the gully. There was an unscheduled break while one of our medics looked him over and finally unstrapped a curious looking bundle of nylon off the top of his aid kit. A couple of riflemen looked at it and silently unsheathed their machetes and commenced cutting bamboo poles. I watched with interest as they helped the medic to slide the poles into one of the Army's new, portable nylon jungle litters. I shuddered selfishly as I thought that I could be one of the unlucky riflemen who would be saddled with the task of carryin the casualty and his rucksack in addition to their own until we could reach a dustoff point. He was in real pain and looked as though he'd weigh in to be at least 180 pounds or so. My worse suspicions were confirmed when my squad was the first one to carry him and after a few minutes, it was my turn. It was sheer torture, leaning down, grasping one of the bamboo handles, carrying this extra heavy load and with my own rucksack setting my back, shoulders and lungs on fire. I was dying on my feet and we hadn't gone fifty yards when I felt a hand tug my arm and Jerry—bless his heart—took my pole and gave me a break. After another few minutes, all four of those carrying him were replaced by fresh troopers and so it went, as they slowly passed the casualty up toward the head of the column as everyone took turns carrying him for a while. As we sat down for the second break of the morning, I discovered that I was bleeding from a few spots.

"Sure is hell," Jerry nodded sympathetically, "tryin' to dodge them sons of bitches of thorn-covered vines an' bushes an' what not while carryin' another trooper, buddy. They ain't nothin' we kin do about it. That guy's hurtin' for certain but at least he's gittin' outta this trash fer a while."

"Thanks, Jerry, for spelling me on that litter. I was about ready to conk out there."

"Don't fergit to take yer salt tablets regular, like I told ya," Jerry chewed his lip thoughtfully, "or you could make an enemy outta every trooper in the platoon—let alone in the entire company." He grinned cynically and nodded his head toward the nearby litter. "Git the picture? That guy is really humblin' ain't he? It ain't his fault we're carryin' him. But picture if that was you layin' there because you was all ate up with the dumb ass an' didn't eat yer salt tablets an' passed out as a heat casualty an' then all the guys had to pitch in an' work long, hard hours cuttin' down trees for the dustoff in case there was no clearings within reach. They'd all hate ya fer yer stupidity. They all do it willin'ly fer an honest casualty but not fer no ignorant deals."

The salt tablets took on an added importance for me with the impact of this lesson and I couldn't keep my eyes off the pathetic figure on the nearby litter. I involuntarily mashed a large spider which had crawled down the back of my neck and bitten me. Jerry looked at it and told me there was no sweat, that he was only half as poisonous as some. He told me the bite would swell up to about half the size of a pingpong ball and burn and itch like crazy and as these predictions started coming true, he told me some hair-raising stories about spiders and snakes.

"Once or twice," he assured me, "we've seen webs half the size of yer livin' room wall with a huge, mean-lookin' cuss bigger'n a man's hand with his fingers spread out. Now, that's in the doggone daytime an' ya could see it an' walk around it.

How'd ya like to walk face-first into such a web an' kiss such a feller as that in the pitchblack night aroun' here?"

He went on to tell me about one huge rock python that the guys had shot one time and he told me that the bamboo viper was not as deadly as we had been told. Rumor had it that they were nicknamed "seven step" vipers—ostensibly the maximum distance a victim could travel once bitten, but that swift mede-vac had saved every man so far. As nocturnal creatures, they travel at night we had been taught and coil lethargically during the daytime. I made up my mind to keep a sharp lookout for those little green buggers!

"When I see one," he warned, "I'll point out the big spider ya gotta watch out for. Once he bites ya, ya stay bitten!"

I could hardly wait. All this was just too much for me and I hadn't seen anything yet. I flinched at the thought of staying bitten. As it came time to move out again I gratefully watched as the litter and its heavy burden disappeared up the column. A warm rain dropped down between the trees stirring the gloomy jungle mists and my thoughts absent mindedly turned toward home. It must have been a half hour or more that I day-dreamed in that column when my reverie was interrupted by a loud shriek followed by much cursing and thrashing up ahead. I looked fearfully up the column to where the moaning sounds were coming from and I could see a group gathered around a figure which appeared to be writhing around on the ground. Jerry walked up a ways and then returned.

"That poor son of a bitch has had it for a while," he ventured as the column took a break until a medic arrived. I had kept my fear of snakes hidden and was secretly relieved not to find a cobra or something beneath each bush or clump of bamboo, lurking to take a bite of me.

"Fire ants got 'im. It happened to me once before I learned to watch fer their nests. He blundered into a big nest of 'em an' they all drop on ya at once an' start bitin' ya by the dog-gone numbers—like a hundred of 'em at once. Feels like a bunch o' white-hot ice picks all a-goin' on ya at once."

I almost got sick at my stomach. One more horror to add to my list. Jerry said that the guy was lucky and so were all the rest of us, because his eyelids had remained unstung. Had they swollen shut, we'd have had two litters to carry. While the medic was working on the poor guy, Jerry told me to never keep my wallet in my rucksack, because as soon as we would make contact, we'd skin out of the rucks and depending on the situation, we could find ourselves to be separated from them until dark. He said that a pal of his had once lost over a thousand dollars because everyone was fishing around in the rucks for ammo after dark and everyone's not one hundred percent honest. He went on to say that a postal clerk periodically came in with the fireflies to make money orders for us to send home. You keep the stubs until your folks verify that they got them.

As I philosophically got to my feet to re-join the column, I noticed to my amazement that I seemed to be getting used to the ruck's weight. The rain had stopped and then commenced again as the column plodded drearily along, stopping and moving. Suddenly I noticed that the jungle seemed to be getting lighter up ahead. Within about a half hour, I could see that we were coming out onto a big open area near a river. They were going to evacuate that poor guy and we wouldn't have to carry him any longer. As we fell out for the break to await the arrival of the dustoff chopper, I joined all the others as I heaved a sigh of relief and plopped wearily to the ground.

The earthen bank of the river, drenched only minutes before by the rain of the Monsoons, was warm to the touch and completely baked dry already by the rays of the hot sun. I thought to myself, 'What a crazy place! Hurry up and then wait. Rain and heat.' The hot sun began to immediately dry my jungle fatigues and I relaxed and enjoyed it while it lasted. Just about everyone else was doing the same thing—except Jerry, it seemed. He had slid completely out of his rucksack and was standing up stretching as I half-dozed in the pleasant sun and dreamily heard him counting the days before he'd get back to the world and to his girl and his loving family.

"Oh, man," he gloated, "I got just sixty days an- a wakeup to go in this here hell hole to do an' then—

Something warm splattered all over me from head to foot where I lay, still in my ruck, and simultaneously, a sound like someone kicking a watermelon interrupted Jerry's voice as his body pitched soundlessly forward onto the ground and his legs and one arm twitched violently before my horrified eyes. To this day, I can't remember having heard the crack of the sniper's rifle, but later on, other members of our platoon pinpointed it to have come from across the river, a hundred yards or so up near the thick jungle's edge. I must have become completely stunned out of my mind, for I don't remember anything for the first few minutes after Jerry's brains drenched me and I saw him die. The very first recollection I have of anything was the voice of our platoon sergeant, who suddenly appeared through my tears.

"I know, son, it's rough," he consoled me as he unwrapped my arms from around Jerry's lifeless body and I realized that I had been cradling him across my lap. In disbelief I stood and watched as the others wrapped Jerry's body into a poncho, shooing flies from his blood as they did.

"He only had two more months to go in this hell hole!"

"Sure, sure," he agreed, "it's awful. I know. I've seen 'em get it on their very last day prior to rotation. The sniper got away and you pulled a very dumb stunt and you must learn from this. When everyone else took cover and fired in the direction the shot came from, you stayed out there and held your buddy, right out in the open. You couldn't have helped him and that gave the sniper one more excellent chance to kill another soldier very quickly and then to be on his merry way. He may have been afraid that his second shot would have helped us to pinpoint him, but you can bet your boots that you were in his sights and then he had second thoughts and that's the only thing which saved you."

This instantly sobered me to the facts. He was talking sense and I would have to latch onto my emotions and control them for future reference or maybe lose my own life in a similar situation. I listened in earnest as his words began to sink in.

"Try," he went on, "and learn to react instantly to danger from now on. I know that you've only been in the company a few hours and your buddy gets killed. I know exactly what it's like but you've got to try and make your year over here and get out in one piece and you are not likely to do it, operating like that."

He left me to my thoughts and my fire team leader silently motioned for me to follow him to where we were to dig in for the night. About an hour or so later, our colonel and sergeant major flew into the perimeter, bringing two riflemen as replacements for our casualties. My squad leader asked me if I wanted to help one other man to load Jerry's body onto the chopper, which we did after gently placing the injured trooper's litter aboard.

I guess the two new guys were frightened at the sight of me tearfully arranging Jerry's poncho after we laid him tenderly aboard the Huey. The sergeant major had already boarded the ship and was waiting for our colonel who was off to one side, talking with our captain. He nodded somberly at me and pursed his lips sympathetically as I quietly patted my friend's still form and said goodbye to him. As I saw the colonel approaching, I stepped from beneath the whirling rotor and joined the two replacements, whose sympathetic, frightened eyes betrayed their cognizance of what they had just witnessed.

"Don't be afraid," I admonished, "and welcome to Dog Company. That was a good man who just left here. He taught me a lot and as you two are assigned to the same squad as I'm in, I have a lot of good tips for you on how to stay alive in this jungle and I'll pass them on to you as we go along."

"Well, Sergeant Major Arthurs," Mac's voice brought me back to reality, "that's the end of the story of my first day in the jungle."

I told him that it had been a very interesting and informative story and that I was looking forward to profiting from his experiences. I really learned to respect Mac in the forthcoming weeks. He taught me a lot about the jungle. He was one of the finest fellows I ever knew. He was right about his number being up, however. One hundred and fourteen days after he took the job as RTO, Mac was killed in action at Dakto—not long prior to his rotation date.

I wrote Marlene shortly thereafter and told her that when Mac died, I died a little bit with him.

For Mac the battles of Dakto had ended. There were more to come.

Dedicated to the memory of Sp-4 Richard Dale McGhee

CHAPTER 8

Lieutenant Numbnuts and the Pothead

Unfortunately, we had some fine lieutenants killed in my battalion in Vietnam. I'd say that every one of them was a brave, topnotch leader. Of these who remained, I would rate them the same, except for one who turned out to be a fabulous dud. He caused trouble with his know-it-all attitude and just about everything he was in charge of turned into some kind of horrible catastrophe. The first night he joined my battalion, he hadn't been off that chopper a half hour before I had a personal confrontation with him because he absolutely refused to roll down his sleeves at suppertime.

This is considered to be a cardinal sin in the Central Highlands of the Chaine Annamitique mountains where we were operating. The mosquitoes here are nocturnal night-biters, which, like all the others in Vietnam, carry Vivax, the mildest form of malaria. The catch to this situation is that they also carry the much deadlier Falciparum strain of malaria which can easily kill a soldier or can cause brain damage. It's nothing to fool with and to prevent needless casualties, our malaria control measures dictated that at dusk each evening, all the troops must roll down and button sleeves, apply mosquito ointment and button the collar of the fatigue jacket in order to minimize bites.

Everyone has to eat, so to simplify this control measure, Colonel Johnnie had issued an order that our cooks would not feed anyone who appeared in the chowline who had not complied. Now, Johnnie was one savvy Lieutenant Colonel who had many years of experience in the Infantry and didn't enjoy "thinkers" who tried to outsmart him or circumvent any of his well-considered orders. Our cooks knew to address our riflemen in a very respectful manner, because there are some tough customers in an Airborne Rifle Battalion, believe me.

So, this new lieutenant, who immediately earned himself the sobriquet of "Lieutenant Numbnuts", upon being respectfully reminded by the chowline serving cook, not only refused to comply, but ordered the poor cook to feed him or else to suffer a court-martial for disobeying an officer. With that turn of events, the mess sergeant notified me and pointed him out where he was eating nearby with his sleeves still rolled, in plain sight of the rest of my troops who were all obeying the order to the letter. This is very bad for discipline when the very leader who should be enforcing rules and orders disobeys them blatantly in person! I strolled over to him.

"Sir," I introduced myself because I wore no chevrons, "I am the Fourth Rifle Battalion's Sergeant Major. You have been told that you are violating Colonel Johnnie's orders. Please stop eating and comply right now, sir."

"I want you to know, sergeant major, that if the colonel wants to give me any orders he can do so in person rather than doing it through you or the cooks or any other enlisted personnel." He continued chewing and looked down at his food, completely ignoring me.

"Sir," I finally said, "believe me when I tell you that our colonel has a lot more to do than to run around all day and all night long giving personal orders to over seven hundred riflemen. Either roll down and button up or I can guarantee a personal interview for you with that colonel in just about sixty seconds and I am confident that you are not going to enjoy the outcome, sir."

He rolled them, but only after he had taken the trouble to personally make a fool of himself in front of all the troops. He and two other newly arrived lieutenants—who had immediately complied with the cook's reminder—were to be briefed by Colonel Johnnie following their supper, at which time he would assign them to their new rifle companies. I briefed the colonel on the incident and he didn't seem too happy with the prospect of getting a new lieutenant whose head was obviously as thick as a mahogany stump.

"Hmmm. Well, what do you think about it, Top?"

"I think he's some kind of nut, colonel—and I ain't kiddin' either, sir. He's a first class jerk, who uses about as much common sense and logic as our family dachshund, Schatzie, and I really pity the poor platoon sergeant who gets stuck with him in the jungle, sir."

"O.K., Top," he laughed, "you never steered me wrong before. I'll brief those lieutenants one at a time and in his case I'm going to let him know that I have your account of this fiasco and I'll give him a very strong commercial on taking the advice and guidance of his platoon sergeant in that rifle platoon. If he's got any kind of horse sense at all, he'll shape up."

"Well, I'm not from Missouri, sir, but you've still got to show me on this character."

"Bring him in first," he chuckled.

I did as directed and the next morning the three were choppered to their new units. About two weeks later Alpha Company sent a message to the effect that something very weird had happened to a rifleman assigned to Lieutenant Numbnuts' platoon. I still can't believe that it happened, and I know that it did. This was late at night, and one of Alpha's men had disappeared into the jungle. Immediately following first light the next morning, our command and control chopper flew in from the rear area where such Hueys were required to spend the night. None were permitted to stay in the jungle. The colonel told me to fly down there to Alpha's position and to get to the bottom of the case of the missing man.

Pete, our pilot, expertly landed the C&C ship in Alpha's small perimeter and I told him to shut it down, because I couldn't know how long we'd be there. Our "C" Company was dug in, providing security around our artillery fire support base, while Alpha, Bravo and Dog were operating a few kliks in the jungle, not too far from the rich coastal plains surrounding the city of Tuy Hoa, pronounced "Tooy Waw".

This jungle isn't as thick as the triple canopied stuff we had been used to deep in the Central Highlands, but it was thick enough. Pap, the first sergeant of Alpha, and Dave, the missing man's Platoon Sergeant, invited me for a cup of "C" ration coffee while they took turns telling me what a meathead this new lieutenant was. I told them about the mosquito control incident and they nodded knowingly.

Both were straight shooters and Dave began to tell me about the entire stupid incident.

"Well," he began, "the long and short of it is that this terrible fiasco would never have happened if this pompous ass I got foisted off on me as a platoon leader had kept his doggone nose out of it. If he had, PFC Rone would still be here, awaiting medevac." Pap nodded in agreement with Dave. "As it is," Dave continued sorrowfully, there ain't no tellin' what's gonna happen to Rone, out there wanderin' around by himself in the jungle, but I predict he's gonna end up cold, stone dead."

Pap and Dave took turns telling me that when the firefly had flown in the night before, Rone had popped off it, returning from his R&R in Hong Kong. No one noticed at first that he was acting kind of peculiar until his squad leader reported to Dave that Rone had suddenly gone off his nut and charged out into the jungle swinging his entrenching shovel, screaming about how he was going to kill Clyde for being responsible for him having to return to this God-forsaken hole from Hong Kong.

We all could see his point there. Dave said that two of Rone's squad members took off after him and tackled him and got him back into the perimeter after Rone had put a dent in the one guy's helmet that would have killed a horse if he hadn't been wearing it. He said that Rone is a pretty big boy and it took about six of the guys to hogtie him lengthwise to a log so that he couldn't do it again.

"Well," continued Dave, "I made my way up to the CP to tell Pap, here, that we'd have to medevac Rone the first thing in the mornin', but while I was gone, that lame-brained lieutenant of mine turned Rone loose. 'Cordin' to him, he had talked his fancy trash to Rone an' Rone come out of it and acted normal an' promised to shape up an' get aholt of himself if only they'd untie him."

Dave said that within five minutes, Rone went into his act again, snatching up a rifle, plus an M-79 grenade launcher and a sandbag full of grenade projectiles to fire from it. He said that Rone got out there a ways and fired a flechet round back toward the perimeter to discourage anyone from following him, which there was no danger of when the troops heard that overgrown shotgun pattern of darts whizzing through the bamboo. Dave said that no one in his right mind would have chased after Rone out there in the pitch black jungle and him being off his nut and loaded for bear.

"Then," continued Dave, "you should've seen my illustrious leader when that happened. I thought we was gonna have to tie him to the dadblamed log. He come runnin' to me, wantin' me to send someone after Rone again. I told him that he was the one that turned him loose, so that he should go an' ketch him an' bring him back in again."

"We could hear his shots out there," Pap added to the story, "for a couple of hours, with the sounds getting fainter and fainter. He was definitely makin' tracks out of this area." Both of them agreed that it had sounded like he had gone to the southeast, which was generally in the direction of Tuy Hoa's rice paddies.

They told me that their irate captain had torn the lieutenant's buns up over the incident and the lieutenant had staunchly defended his decision. He said that he was a psychology major and that it was obvious to him that Rone was faking to get out of the jungle on the psycho bit.

"If he was fakin'," declared Dave, "he sure oughtta get an Oscar for best actin' or for his originality in my book."

Pap walked me back to the chopper and I told him that the best thing that lieutenant could do would be to go roaring out into the jungle himself and never come back, because Colonel Johnnie was going to be fit to be tied himself over this deal.

Pete cranked the C&C ship and we took off for the fire support base in the jungle a couple of miles away. It was the monsoon season, which is really hard to get used to, flying around up there. Sometimes the rain hangs in the air in long, foggy-looking ribbons. You fly along for a few hundred yards in fairly clear sky and suddenly run smack into one of those long ribbons and become inundated by rain. You fly blind a ways with the rain obliterating everything and in one second, you are back in the clear again! I could never quite overcome the deep conviction that another helicopter could be flying dead at us, blind as we seemed to be, from the other end of the ribbon of rain and that the last sound I would ever hear some day would be a loud one—right in the middle of one of those blind spots in the sky.

The jungle foliage lay below us, its beauty enhanced by the spotty fog, lacing and draping itself among the treetops. Through the ribbons of fog and rain ahead, suddenly I saw the large horseshoe-like outlines of the dug-in 105mm artillery pieces from our support element, the 3rd Battalion of the 319th Airborne Field Artillery Battalion. Those guys had a tough job too, performing fire missions day and night, coupled with all that digging and sandbagging when we moved. The troops would wade in that ankle-deep water for a couple of weeks before we moved to another location and set up anew, a never-ending situation, the way we were forced to operate.

Pete circled the 400 yard FSB and landed. He looked at me questioningly and I gave him the cutthroat sign with my finger and as he closed down the ship, I ran up the slope and found the colonel. I told him the whole story and he gritted his teeth and stoically added Rone to the long list which he, as a typical combat commander, had worrying him. He told me that he hoped we found Rone before Clyde did and shook his head silently at the lieutenant's antics. Then he asked me to find Pete and his crew and tell them we were going on recon. I found them preparing to enjoy a cup of coffee at the cooks' messtent.

Colonel Johnnie brought our S-3 operations officer and artillery liaison officer and had us airborne once again into the sky which was still thickly beribboned with the crazy rain and patches of beautiful dark blue sky showing here and there. The reconnaissance flight lasted about an hour, during which time the major and captain gave expert advice to Colonel Johnnie on the selection of the new fire support base for our next operation. After Colonel Johnnie had marked his map appropriately, he had Pete to set out for our FSB again. We hadn't been on the ground fifteen minutes when the colonel sent for me to come to the TOC—Tactical Operations Center.

"Top," he indicated on his map, "see this little hamlet here? We just got word from the province chief that a South Vietnamese Army unit has picked up our boy Rone, down there. How about you flying down in the C&C ship and get that pothead from those ARVNs and bring him back here for Doc to look at?" I took another look at that map and mentioned that from the looks of things, Rone had travelled a couple of kliks of thick jungle the night before and a little over three thousand meters of rice paddies to get to that point! Colonel Johnnie nodded grimly in agreement.

"Roger, Top. Maybe Rone was flying so high on that dope that he evaded all the normal obstacles that the rest of us have to put up with in that jungle. Anyway, please go and police him up and bring him back here. O.K.?" I picked up Pete and the crew of the C&C ship at the chowline where they were trying to finally enjoy a cup of coffee and we once again headed for the ship.

"Hey, Top," prompted Pete, "what is it with you? Are you all of a sudden buckin' for a whole bunch of clusters on your Air Medal or something? Crank it up. Fly it around. Land it. Cut its throat. Crank it up. Don't you ever get tired of flying with us?" He laughed. He had an outstanding crew and we were always harassing one another.

"What time's the crash scheduled for?" I grinned.

"Don't say those things," he effaced mock horror.

"Well, I wouldn't want to miss it," I pursued him, "are we gonna lose the main rotor off this pigiron mutt at about a thousand feet or are you gonna let Clyde shoot this black cat jinx out of the sky with you drivin' it on Friday the Thirteenth as a grand finale?"

He shook his head at such blasphemy and we boarded the ship as the one door gunner whipped the tether from the great rotor of the parked ship, and I showed him on the map where the little hamlet which was our destination, was located and we soon took off. In our final approach to the hamlet, we could see a couple of hundred ARVN troops sprawled on the ground taking a break. They didn't seem too worried about the enemy. Pete circled and landed far enough away as to not disturb the closest elements and I told him to keep the ship running because it wouldn't take me too long to pick up Rone. How wrong I was.

As I approached where the soldiers were gathered, I kept looking for Rone's tall figure to detach itself from the group and come toward the ship but it didn't. When I finally found the ARVN Captain, the large body, wrapped in a poncho at his feet, spoke volumes toward solving that mystery. He shook his head in the negative in answer to my halting Vietnamese question if he spoke English or not. I knew that this situation was going to take some exploration, so I motioned for Pete to shut down the ship and he and the crew joined me in curiosity as to what was happening.

We rolled Rone out of the bloody poncho and took a look at him. He had been stripped but was still wearing his dogtags. He was not wearing his ears however as some ghoulish Clyde had lopped them off with a knife or machete as souvenirs. It didn't take long for us to surmise that something unusual and amazing had happened to this big private first class to cause his demise. He had been shot a half-dozen times in the chest and you could have covered the entire shot group with a steel helmet. That kind of stuff just doesn't happen. He should have had stray wounds all over him if that many rounds hit him.

Finally, they came up with one ARVN soldier who spoke about as much English as I did Vietnamese, and along with some of Pete's high school French between him and the captain, they finally told their version of the story and we told ours, of how our dead rifleman had come to be in that poncho. It took a lot of pantomiming and gesticulating and the murder of three languages and when I showed them on that map where Rone had run off from in the dark the previous night, the ARVN Captain looked very skeptical until I crossed my heart and held up my hand like I was swearing to it in court and they all laughed uproariously.

They told us that the farmers had told them that Rone still had his M-79 and rifle when the enemy soldiers had caught him early that morning, out of ammo and docile as a sheep. The enemy officer in charge had assembled all the villagers into a big horseshoe, at the open end of which they had tied PFC Rone to a tree. The officer had lectured his audience on the virtues of not looking to the Americans as their saviors and in very short order, he had placed a half-dozen riflemen about ten feet from the hapless paratrooper and dispatched him by firing squad.

The ARVNs were all in agreement that they thought Rone was lucky to have gotten off with such a merciful death as opposed to some they had seen this particular outfit to impose upon ARVN stragglers. As you'll see later on, the enemy laced some of the pot which was sold to our gullible troops, with much stronger stuff. I couldn't help but wondering, looking at poor Rone, what the exponents of pot-smoking back in the States would have thought, had they been there with us, looking at Rone there on the ground—hands still tied—no ears and having been used as a shooting gallery. Some of our troops didn't know what they were letting themselves in for, experimenting with drugs in Vietnam.

We thanked the ARVNs and loaded Rone aboard the ship and took off. I adjusted my headset and flipped the butterfly on the console in order to chat with Pete on the intercom. We made small talk about such situations as Rone's. In general, when a soldier got himself killed in such a stupid incident, the Army, in order to spare the family's feelings back home, carried the deceased as 'killed in action'. The trouble with this, as Pete pointed out, was when some idiot undertaker or someone like that thoughtlessly flapped his gums to the family back home, or more likely, some guy in the outfit knows the family and lets the cat out of the bag. In most cases then, some big politician would get in the act and try and fry the Army's hide for not telling the family 'the truth'—and for what? Sometimes it's far better not to know that their loved one got himself needlessly killed.

When the truth comes out in some bad cases like Rone's, then the finger-pointing starts. Instead of everyone honestly owning up to the fact that the kid was always a trouble-maker, they put the shoe on the other foot. To hear the politicians and the news media tell it, the deceased was certainly no meatball who caused his own demise. It always comes out that the guy was of sterling character before the good old Army corrupted him out of his impending ordination to the cloth. It never comes out that the guy was a rat fink to start off with in civilian life and was just showing his true colors.

"What nobody realizes, Pete," I pointed out, "is that some of this pot is laced with heroin. The stuff sold in this particular area we're in now is noted for running a smoker out of his tree in short order. You can't convince anyone of it, though. All they know is that they smoked pot in L.A. and nothing horrible ever happened, so why not do it now? Then, by the time they find out we've been givin' 'em the straight scoop, it's too late—like with poor Rone, here. His squad said his rucksack was loaded with the stuff."

Pete told me that he had a carbon copy of an investigation in his aviation unit that he wanted me to read. He said they had a dud who got all gooned up one night and took his rifle and went to a local Tuy Hoa whorehouse where he found this other dud in bed with our hero's virtuous girlfriend. He said that they found out later that the dead guy had even tried to submit paperwork to try and marry this whore.

"So," said Pete, "to make a long story short, our guy threatened to let the other dud have it with his rifle, but that slick cat had a loaded forty five caliber pistol beneath his pillow and he blew our meatball away with about five slugs before one could say 'Jack Robinson.' The army is carrying him as 'killed in action'. Now, is the family better off to know the truth, or to think of the guy as a hero who died for his country?"

Through the wisping ribbons of fog and rain, we could discern the FSB's horseshoe-shaped artillery positions up ahead, as Pete expertly wheeled the Huey into a wide circle of the base and finally settled us onto the area designated as the landing pad. The two door gunners carried Rone's body over to the S-4 supply chopper pad for evacuation to Graves Registration on the next ship out and I went and informed the colonel that Doc wouldn't be talking to Rone.

"Hell, Sergeant Major Arthurs," snorted the colonel, "we've missed our calling. If we could film some of the trash that goes on around here, we could probably sell the movie rights and both retire comfortably. Another pothead who probably turned a deaf ear to his folks' teachings and look where he ends up. Now we get back to that idiotic lieutenant who helped to aggravate this incident. First good lieutenant who arrives on the scene as a replacement, I'm gonna ricochet that dud back to the rear someplace with an efficiency report that's gonna sound original in the annals of modern warfare."

Then, Colonel Johnnie told me that he had a surprise for me.

Lieutenant Beartrap

Colonel Johnnie asked me if I wanted to accompany our Alpha Company on an experimental mission, suggested by our general. I was to be an observer and to give him a first-hand account of an interesting combat patrol. As a general rule, U.S. units didn't move around in the jungle at night, other than each rifle company routinely posting ambush patrols at dusk with the mission of interdicting enemy units at likely avenues of approach to friendly positions. Once they set up, they stayed in position for the night and didn't move. This patrol was to be different.

Well, I didn't realize how different. The plan called for an entire rifle company to take off under cover of darkness and to travel a couple of thousand yards through very thick jungle to its destination; a river crossing recently teeming with enemy activity. The unit would catch the enemy unawares by setting up a night ambush and then pouring it to him in broad daylight.

If the enemy hears you coming and sets up his own ambush, he could make it very hot for you. Accordingly, strict stealth and noise and light discipline are the order of the day—or night. One guy lighting a cigarette or coughing could easily do everyone in. It's serious business and it is one Helluva lot harder to accomplish in that rugged, triple-canopied jungle of the Central Highlands.

All four of our rifle companies were outstanding and Alpha was no exception. Captain Alan and Pap, the First Sergeant, were quite a team and their leaders, like Dave, Lieutenant Numbnuts' Platoon Sergeant, were all hard to beat, with the exception being Numbnuts himself! But then, how could one dud lieutenant screw up an operation of this magnitude?

Pete landed me in Alpha's perimeter early in the afternoon and I told Pap that I was going to accompany Dave's platoon and maybe keep an eye on Lieutenant Numbnuts and he got a big charge out of that one. He definitely needed a keeper. During the afternoon, I wandered from platoon to platoon noting the expert preparation of the young troopers by their ever-vigilant squad and fireteam leaders as they supervised taping of equipment to soundproof the column maintaining stealth and security for the forthcoming event. Adjusting and wrapping rations within rucksacks to prevent un-necessary rattling and that sort of thing culminating with one last cleaning of each weapon completed the preparation phase of the operation.

Dave welcomed me as an additional rifle with his platoon. We talked over old times of years before when I had been first sergeant of what was now our Dog Company and Dave had joined the unit as a buck private. What great times we had. At that time our 4th Bat was still the 1st of the 501st Airborne Infantry of the 101st Airborne Division at Fort Campbell Kentucky. Then it had been reorganized to become part of the 101st's 2nd Brigade.

Finally, the 501st had been redesignated in 1966 to become the 4th Battalion, 503rd Airborne Infantry, of the 173rd Airborne Brigade. Dave said that things had not changed one bit after our meatball lieutenant had contributed to Rone's loss. He was pretty comical and I had to laugh!

"Top, honest to goodness I'm serious. The man's a menace. If I die, I want to be reincarnated as a NVA sniper so I could legally assassinate that moron. Pray we don't git lost Top. With this jackass in charge, we'd probably wander into the wilds of Laos somewhere—git interned an' spend the rest of this here looney war eatin' rice an' puttin' up with our illustrious leader, Lieutenant Fuzz Numbnuts."

He was cracking me up.

"One little skanky platoon in the midst of eight million Clydes in the black o' night! If we git separated from the rest o' the company, we'll be wanderin' around in ever-diminishin' circles—with a madman at the helm."

I could hardly wait. Just at dusk, the head of the column began to move out toward our destination. The canopy was very thick in this area. Under these conditions, it's pretty dark during daylight hours. At night, especially on such a moonless, cloudy night, it's unspeakably dark. As we wended our way into the jungle, full darkness set in. I thought to myself that you get the feeling that you are wading in a tar-pit and you must hold to the ruck of the man in front of you in the file or else become lost and all those behind you be lost with you. This is a sobering fact, especially to the last man in the file.

Dave and I were about mid-way in the platoon's column. It was coal black. In some places the bamboo was so thick that we had to get down on our bellies and crawl through—some places at a half-crouch. All in all, it was hell. Sometimes going downhill, the momentum of the column would make you lose your grip on the guy in front. Then you flail silently about you like kids playing blindman's buff, trying to find your buddy to the front. It gets furry. I could see why policy prevented such moves.

Everyone was trying their best to maintain as much quiet as they could. Imagine our surprise when suddenly we all heard the animal-like anguished scream from further up our column, where the lieutenant was located. It was immediately followed by a piercing, heart-rending plea!

"God help me! I'm in a bear trap!"

Of course, these screams had compromised the entire mission. My guts churned as Dave and I hurriedly made our way up the column. Both of us had seen the horrible bone-mangling bear traps used by the Montagnards, also recently adapted by some VC units to cripple American soldiers. With this nagging thought in mind, we reached the prostrate, sobbing figure of what proved to be Dave's lieutenant. What puzzled us were the voices of other men in the dark, all of them seemed to be coaxing, as one might to convince a small child to stop crying.

"Come onnnnn, let him goooo now," soothed one voice.

I grabbed the lieutenant's leg and ran my hands down to the ankle, fully expecting the worse to be a mangled, half-severed ankle with mashed, protruding bones—certainly crippling the lieutenant. My searching hands found—instead of a bear trap—the jaws of our huge German Shepherd scout-dog, Buddha. He had a death-grip on that lieutenant's ankle and he was not letting go for love nor money. His teeth had closed tightly around that ankle portion which included the Achilles heel.

I shuddered in sympathy with the poor guy's plight. I didn't know what the huge dog had against that lieutenant but I was hoping that there wouldn't be an epidemic of it in the area when we finally pried those jaws off. When, in his agony, it finally dawned upon the lieutenant what was actually happening, he ordered everyone to shoot the dog. None of us were about to shoot that dog! Dave got on the radio and notified the captain that there would be a short delay in the operation while we either un-dogged the lieutenant or un-lieutenant'd the dog—whichever way it came out.

We finally got the medic up there, who knew just what to do. He ran two lengths of bandages through Buddha's mouth, back at the hinge of his jaws and we had to pull up and down at the same time to get him to turn loose. It wasn't as easy as it sounds and the dog fought for every inch of that lieutenant's ankle and got a new grip or two before we finally got him away from his victim.

All that screaming and hollering didn't help much and it may not surprise you to learn that it put a serious crimp in this stealthy operation.

The lieutenant was evacuated the next morning and spent several weeks in the hospital. No one ever knew what the lieutenant had pulled on old Buddha—probably kicked him at one time or another—but from that day on whenever anyone in Alpha referred to the lieutenant, he was known as Lieutenant Beartrap. Alpha's troops fed Buddha the choicest tidbits and morsels of chow that they had from that time on. I suspect it was out of a dual motive on the part of the troopers—"thanks for ridding us of that dud lieutenant, and also please don't ever get mad at me, Buddha."

I had almost forgotten about Lieutenant Numbnuts-Beartrap until he popped off a chopper one evening, came straight to me and told me he wanted to speak to the colonel. Colonel Johnnie had a small field tent which could be packed on one man's back, with bamboo poles being cut for immediate erection. I went to the tent and told him that Lieutenant Beartrap was back and that he had fire in his eye and wanted to speak to the colonel. He grinned and told me to bring him on in, which I did. The young lieutenant glared at me like I was the one who had bitten his ankle and not Buddha. He said that he'd like it much better if only the two officers talked and I started to leave.

"The sergeant major will stay," Colonel Johnnie shrugged, "now what's on your mind, lieutenant?"

"Simply this, sir. You shoot the dog and I'll stay. Otherwise it's your responsibility if I'm mauled again, sir."

The colonel got a perplexed look on his face. He looked at me and he looked at the lieutenant and I almost expected him to explode. He scratched his face, which I had learned to recognize as a danger sign that he was getting angry, then he bit his lip like he does when he's almost to the end of his rope and is trying to control his temper. He finally shook his head as if

he had arrived at an agonizing decision and looked the lieutenant squarely in the eye.

"Lieutenant," he said evenly, "go and get your rucksack. You
are being transferred and have a long trip to make."

The lieutenant saluted, did an about-face and ducked
through the tent flap.

"Whew," I said after his departure, "damn, colonel, there for
a minute I thought you were gonna shoot the lieutenant and
transfer the dog. What made you take so long to make such a
simple decision as that?"

"Not a chance," he grinned, "that I'd ever shoot a valuable
contributor to this battalion's mission like old Buddha, Top,"
and with a twinkle in his eye he added, "but, how would that
ever have looked if I'd made up my mind in one instant—on
an important swap like that?"

He had a point.

Runnin' Berserk

Not long after the beartrap incident, we suddenly received
orders to move to the Tuy Hoa North Airstrip, where USAF
C-130s flew us to Komtum for further movement back to Dakto
by truck. During the month of November, the Fourth Bat participated in several fierce battles against the numerically superior NVA forces arrayed around Dakto, culminating in the
terrible battle for Hill 875 involving the Second and Fourth
Bats during the week of Thanksgiving, 1967.

This is the story of one of those heroic leaders who survived Hill 875. Capt. Ron Leonard was one tough trooper. He
was one of my best friends in the outfit and he was just as
straight as a pulled string. He and I were together in Bravo
Company during the battle for Hill 823 when I was acting first
sergeant, after which he stayed on as Bravo's commander, end-
ing up with a well-deserved Distinguished Service Cross for his
exploits on Hill 875. Ron was about as husky and good-looking
as a fellow could get and still not get signed up for the movies.
He was one rugged individual and I'd bet that anyone who

ever tangled with him physically would have known he'd been in a scrap. At the same time, he was a kind, fair and understanding commander and his troops thought the world of him.

I only saw Ron get riled up enough to go into his act one time and even though I was a semi-participant and semi-spectator in this free-for-all fracas, I was sure glad it wasn't me that he was working on. I'll tell you the story and you be the judge. First of all, you must understand the setting. Immediately following Hill 875, my entire battalion was very short of riflemen and what was left of the outfit was permitted to move into tents around the Dakto airstrip for about three days while we awaited the arrival by C-130 of 335 replacements. It was the good life for my poor troopers, some of whom were getting their first shower in six months. Our cooks were preparing three meals of hot "A" rations daily, and my troopers had access to an outdoor movie each night. They were in heaven. Colonel Johnnie authorized the consumption of two cold beers per man per day and the troops had full access to ice cold cokes and ice cream.

Our cooks stayed in the rear all the time, where it wasn't hard to find pot and harder drugs. We had a strict policy to move any user from his good deal in the rear area, directly into a rifle platoon in the jungle and this put the brakes on drug use as a general rule. One brand new cook found out the hard way when he was hauled in front of Colonel Johnnie for disciplinary action. He had threatened another cook with his rifle and the mess sergeant had found a lot of marijuana when they shook down his gear. He had to be the biggest guy in our battalion—six or seven inches over six feet and perhaps 275 pounds, with no fat visible.

He put the dog-eye on Colonel Johnnie and me when the colonel informed him that he was not going to court-martial him for this first offense, but was sending him to Bravo Company. He wanted to go and complain to the Inspector General that he was a cook, not a rifleman, but I explained to him that anyone who had completed basic training was qualified to perform as a rifleman. He accused Colonel Johnnie of trying to murder him as punishment for using a little pot and the colonel told him that he was getting this free second chance to make a man of himself and dismissed him.

When we got outside Johnnie's little tent, I escorted the big cook—who reminded me of a big tree—to Bravo Company to see Captain Ron. It was Bravo's turn at the airstrip's showers and no one was left at the company's CP except Captain Ron and the company's runner. He didn't impress Captain Ron one bit when he started whining to him that we were all commit-ting legal murder as punishment for a little pot use. He tried the same song and dance on Ron about not knowing how to be a rifleman.

"Look," says Ron, "I need pot-smokin' cooks out in the jun-gle like I need more holes in my head. It tickles me to see you come to Bravo Company about as much as it does you. You are being weaned off that pot, so get that chip off your shoulder and you are starting out in Bravo with a clean slate. You can go up or down—it's all up to you. You're lucky the colonel didn't throw you in jail."

"Captain," he pouted, "I'd rather be in that nice, safe stock-ade than to be out there in that jungle as a rifleman and to lose my life."

"You haven't lost it yet," Ron pointed out, "so be a man and pull your duty. You might surprise yourself and become proud."

"Um-hmm. Well, I ain't in that jungle yet, captain, an' nei-ther are either of you two." He eyed us both ominously.

"See me the day after tomorrow," Ron laughed, "and tell me if you think that you are in the jungle then or not."

He started to sound off to Ron again and Ron told him that he had heard enough of his insubordinate mouth and to follow the runner to the first rifle platoon. As he started to fol-low the runner, the huge ex-cook turned back to me and told me that he knew that it was my recommendation which had landed him in a rifle company and that he didn't intend to for-get that fact.

"Like I said," he sneered, "none o' the three of us is out in that jungle yet."

I made my way back to my tent, which was only about thirty yards from Ron's CP tent and was busily brushing the dust from my rifle about a half hour later when suddenly, Bravo's runner came barreling around the side of the tent screaming that the new replacement was trying to kill Captain Ron. I threw a magazine into my rifle and followed him on the run. I didn't know exactly what to expect as we sailed around the corner of Bravo's CP tent and pulled up short at the sight which confronted me. That crazy cook had Ron backed up against a sandbagged bunker, holding his M-16 rifle one handed with the muzzle shoved into Ron's chest while he held a razor sharp machete up against Ron's neck with his other hammy hand.

I jacked a round into my rifle's chamber and quickly jammed the muzzle of my rifle strongly up beneath the cook's left armpit. From my position I couldn't tell if the cook's weapon was off safety or not, but it looked to me as though Ron was about one inch from finding out what it's like to be zipped into a rubber body bag. After all the combat he'd been through, he was just on the verge of being done in by a pot head.

The cook had a crazy look on his face and he was shaking and breathing real hard and his face was as red as blood. I just knew that he was going to shoot Ron. It was a real 'Mexican standoff'—the cook had Ron sewed up tight and I had that doggone cook by the short hairs. He shoots Ron; I shoot him. We all three knew this, but that cook couldn't have been thinking too clearly. The company runner had rushed off and gotten his rifle and he was standing to the rear of the three of is, backing me up.

Ron is definitely a hard man to bluff. He had to know that even if I shot the pot head first, that Ron was going to get a burst in the chest. If I had been in Ron's position, I would have been bowing and scraping in an obsequious manner in an attempt to talk that nut into putting that rifle down. Not our Ron. He doesn't slow down one bit and he wasn't backing down one inch.

"O.K. you pot head," Ron said. "You scummy, yellow-bellied rear echelon son of a bitch, you. Smoke your way out of this fix. You are in a bad way now, asshole. Shoot me, and Top'll kill you dead as a doornail. If you don't shoot me, I am gonna court-martial your worthless ass and stick you in jail for about 300 years just as a start—so take your choice," he sneered up into the huge cook's face.

On top of everything else, Ron had a bunch of stitches in both his legs where the medics had recently sewed him up from Hill 875. I shook my head and frowned and made faces at Ron to keep his mouth shut. I started talking fast, too. I told the pot head to lay his rifle down and that there wouldn't be one word said about this incident and that I would get him transferred out of Vietnam. I knew that this nut would be evacuated and I couldn't see Ron helping him to get worked up into enough of a frenzy to where he'd pull that trigger and it looked like to me that he was very close to it. As hepped up as he was, he could easily have pulled that trigger accidentally, holding that rifle up one-handedly as he was doing.

I would have told that nut that we were going to promote him to brigadier general if I thought it would make him let Ron go. When he threw back his head and laughed in an insane manner, I almost shot him right then and there because I thought it was all over for poor Ron at that particular point.

"I wish I could kill both of ya," he shrieked insanely, "an' that chicken shit fuckin' colonel too. You bastards are tryna kill me."

At this point, I was getting worked up into a frenzy too and I had had enough of his shit. I jammed my rifle muzzle up a lot harder into his tender left armpit, causing him to lift the machete from Ron's throat.

"Listen, pal," I told him, "I'm going to give you one last chance. Lay down that rifle and there won't be one word said. Now, I just gave you an I.Q. test to see how smart you are. There's your way out. I'm countin' to three and then I'm gonna blast your ass with this whole magazine. One . . . two . . ."

He cursed and threw the rifle to the ground and Ron hit him and then wrapped him in a bearhug as the nut tried to cut the back of Ron's neck with the machete he was still clutching in his left hand. I quickly wrapped my left arm around the nut's neck and grasped his machete hand and quickly bent one of his fingers back, breaking it and releasing the machete. The nutty cook outweighed Ron by about fifty pounds and was a raving, slobbering nut at this point, gibbering some unintelligible stuff and he threw me and Ron around like we were a couple of limp rag dolls. I guess I was hindering Ron, as he kept hollering for me to back off and to let him have the guy, so I let go and they went at it some more.

I looked behind me and the rifleman had all three of our weapons so that the nut couldn't get his hands on one again! I told him to run and get the medics and to bring two litters and some commo wire or rope and he took off on the double. Good old standby for psychos—the nut is the weenie and the litters are the bun, then you wrap him up like a cocoon. I had learned this trick the hard way one night in Korea and it worked like a charm. I took charge of the three rifles while the runner made his sprint to the medics' tent.

As they rolled on the ground, I saw that the cook was trying to gouge one of Ron's eyes out and then I noticed that both of Ron's legs were dripping blood from where his stitches had broken loose. Poor Ron was on the bottom and I dove onto the cook and threw a choking neck lock on him from behind. That cook had arms like a woodcutter, but everyone has to breathe and I was definitely getting to him with the neck lock and I poured it on as strong as I could as two medics ran up with the litters.

That nut was about ready for the transfer that I had promised him. It took all five of us to keep him between those two canvas litters and wrap that commo wire around him. He was still slobbering and screaming and those litters were just throbbing as he struggled to break out. One of the medics gave him a shot of something which took about ten minutes to quiet him and they carried him away.

Ron's one eye was all red where the nut had almost done a job on it. He was squinting and gulping and I know he was hurting. He licked his lips and grinned at me and shook my hand.

"Quick, Watson, the needle," he laughed. "Man, you were right on time, Top. Thanks a lot."

"No sweat, sir," I told him, "you would've sweet-talked him out of it, using psychology along with those soothing phrases you were whipping on him. Has it occurred to you that some of these cats hate to go to the jungle more than some others." I told him that he had better go and have the surgeon re-stitch his wounds and I thanked him for backing me up and this puzzled him quite a bit!

"Sure," I explained, "I promised that nut that if he'd drop that rifle, not a word would be said, an' you just silently knocked the shit out of him when he dropped it." We laughed.

"You sure know how to get a rifle and machete off a nut," he grinned, "when the chips are down, Top. It was music to my ears when you busted that big rat's finger before he could cut my throat, too. He won't be playin' the violin with that paw for a while."

He patted me on the back and limped off to the aid station for more stitches. Colonel Johnnie just shook his head when I briefed him on the incident.

"I'm tellin' you, Top, we could sell all this stuff to the *Saturday Evening Post* or somebody. Can you believe that this is a typical rifle battalion with all this crap we've had going on?"

At this writing, Ron is a retired full bull colonel with a steel pot full of medals. He made it through all that action and the nutty REMF trying to kill him, and I'll bet he never forgets any of us.

I'm sure never going to forget him.

Dedicated to Col. Ronald R. Leonard (Retired)

CHAPTER 9

Top Sergeant

Every unit in the U.S. Army has a commanding officer—usually a captain and a first sergeant, who is usually a six striper E-8 wearing the "lozenge" or diamond in the center of his chevrons. They must be the big team and each must know his limitations. In essence, the first sergeant organizes things and runs the company while the commander is the final decision maker in garrison and is in charge tactically during combat or field exercises.

Top was our first sergeant of Dog Company. He always pronounced it "DAWG" Company. Top was a born hillbilly, about six four, with a homely, weather beaten face that resembled a map of the backwoods of North Carolina and Georgia, where he had spent most of his formative years. Top could peer at a trooper through his fierce bush of thick, black eyebrows and those eyes would burn the truth right out of a private who had never really intended to tell it at all: Top understood privates more than most because he had been one for about five years, years before. Until he married, he had been a happy-go-lucky hard-drinking private. He knew that a private had to be wily at his job, or else he'd get much more than his share of details.

On this day, Top was lecturing Dog Company's men, who were all sitting on the ground near the Dakto Airstrip, having just received over sixty new replacements who had just disembarked from an incoming C-130 a few minutes before. Top was laying down the law in that terrible attention-getting voice of his. He had recently completed his year's jungle tour and had extended it for six months and had just returned from a month's leave in the U.S. and he was giving them hell.

"I can't believe," he began, "that I've only been gone for thirty days and somehow you musicians have all went an' let your ha'r grow clean down over yer eyes. Some of ya have ha'r so long you'd have to stand on a stump to put your jungle boots on. Welllll, the great cat-daddy of all barbers is now back an' the voice o' the clippers is gonna git heard throughout the land an' that ain't a threat—it's a promise!"

The troops just howled. The older troopers knew Top to be a man of his word, who carried a set of hand clippers in his ruck. He told the men to go ahead and light 'em if they had 'em and he stood there with his hands on his hips and looked each of the new men in the eye as everyone took advantage of his smoke break. I noticed most of them to be looking him over rather keenly. Top told the troops that they had three choices; either get their hair cut that afternoon by one of the Vietnamese barbers plying their trade near the strip, or go to the jungle wearing a dog collar or carrying a fiddle on their rucksack. He knew just how to handle the men, and a little humor didn't hurt a thing to get his point across.

One of the old troopers made a sign with his hand and a sound like he was getting his own throat cut and the others all laughed good-naturedly because they knew that Top definitely meant business. Top cleared his throat and you could hear him for a country mile.

"While I was gone," he declared, "Ole Frank Franklyn got a delinquency report as thick as the Gutenberg Bible for punchin' out a MP. Now, Frank got caught. He didn't have sense enough to do it an' then to escape and evade the authorities. No, sir! Not our Frank. He had to wait until the MP reinforcements come an' then threaten to do 'em all in an' the result is that our C.O. has to answer to the colonel now."

He searched the semi-circle of seated troops until he locked eyes with Frank, who knew that he was next on the agenda. He got a look on his face like a bear which has just stepped on a punji stake. Top told the troops that through Frank's stupidity, Dog's Captain's neck was on the block. Frank closed his eyes and shuddered. He knew it was coming.

"Stand up here, Frank," commanded Top, "an' take a bow an' tell all these jump troopers here how ya couldn't stand prosperity bein' back in the rear area as our supply rep with a big, fat racket an' not havin' to hump a eighty pound ruck anymore, gittin' shot at an hit an shit at an' missed fer a livin'. Come on."

Frank was a big, good-looking, and good-natured black soldier from Chicago, about twenty years old, who had done well in the field and after two wounds, was given a good job in the rear. He sheepishly stood up and smiled and told everyone that Top was right, that he had ruined his own good deal through drinking and he was ready to return to the field. He shrugged philosophically and sat back down.

"Yep," Top bore down, "Frank's one of our best jungle fighters. He fought his way out of the dang jungle and then he just went an' fought his way back in ag'in."

The troops just roared. It had to be the funniest thing in the whole world to listen to Top reading the riot act. Even so, the troopers knew that he meant every word. He chewed on his lower lip and looked around through those thick black eyebrows.

"Don't git me wrong, now," he admonished, "I would expect none o' my rough an' tough paratroopers to take nothin' off of them rear echelon mother fuckers back there in the rear. Nossir. Those REMFs back there ain't got no idee of what you combat troopers do fer a livin' out in the jungle an' I wouldn't even want a soldier in this here lashup who didn't do a little serious drinkin' when he had the chance to. You just gotta use yer head an' don't git our good captain in trouble, see?"

I had personally been first sergeant of Airborne rifle companies for over thirteen years and I knew that it paid off to get the troops together periodically and give them the whys and wherefores. One certainly didn't get this opportunity very often in a combat area, because of the danger of enemy mortar rounds falling on a concentrated group of men. At this particular time, we had driven the NVA back across the border and the area where we were congregated was fairly safe, for the moment anyway.

"Next subject is nitwits. How's that sound fer a subject: Nitwits. Well, they is several kind o' nitwits but the two worse kinds is the ones who accidentally commits murder an' then the ones which commits suicide. It happens every day an' don't you kid yerself. They is both kinds of nitwits in this here company right now, 'specially you new replacements. Come up here, son. Yeah, I mean you!" Top singled out a new replacement—a big redheaded kid with freckles. The young private struggled to his feet, his eyes taking on the look of a rabbit which has just been cornered by a rock python. Top then told Gator to come up to the front. Gator was a sharp black corporal who hailed from Florida and he obediently made his way forward until he too, was standing in front of Top, while the rest of us watched with interest.

"O.K. Gator—as one of the oldest members of this here company who has survived almost yer whole year over here, I wantcha to tell the troops a few things fer me. The subject is hand grenades an' I wantcha to tell everyone about the first platoon's nitwit replacement while we was still down at Bien Hoa before we ever come to this here God-forsaken Central Highlands."

"Right, Top," answered Gator, "we got some replacements in an' they was all told how to wear their hand grenades, namely to carry them inside their extra canteen pouches which we carry for that purpose. The pins can't snag or nothin' an' drag out an' then activate the grenade. They are very handy to reach durin' a firefight an' yer regular canteens with water go into the ruck an' hangin' on the outside by their chain. Under NO circumstances do you ever run the retaining strap on yer ammo pouch through the ring on a hand grenade, where it kin snag an' accidentally pull the pin. This is the worse kind of nitwit trick." Gator looked around the group.

At this turn of events, the face of the redheaded replacement turned the color of his hair. It was then that I noted why Top had selected him to stand tall in front of everyone. The retaining strap on every one of his ammo pouches had been run through a grenade ring and then fastened. His knees began to tremble as it dawned on him that he was a walking tragedy, looking for a place to happen, as everyone in Dog Company stared at the offending items.

"Go on, Gator," urged Top, "tell everyone about the loud noise at Bien Hoa." At this point, we could all imagine what it had been, with a buildup like Gator had given us.

"Yes, sir. Well, one dark night—I mean you couldn't see nothin' an we was workin' this one area near a road an' a message come through that they was sendin' two trucks to pick up us guys in the first platoon an' take us down the road a few miles 'cause of some emergency down there."

"How come you never got there, Gator?"

"Because, Top, I woke up in the hospital. I was the first man on the truck in the dark. Guys kept pilin' on an' this brand new replacement—I never did learn his name—got on an' was about in the center of the truck when it happened."

Everyone looked at our redheaded hapless replacement with the glaring grenades, as though he was purposefully planning on executing each one of them. I could see the purpose of Top's strategy in employing Gator and the redhead in this manner. It was definitely serious business that we were dealing with.

"We was all loaded up" Gator continued, "an' crowded together, rucksacks an' all an' the canvas top prevented anyone from jumpin' off the sides to escape what this dummy did. He had his straps through the grenade rings an' in the dark, crowded truck, one of those grenade pins got pulled accidentally."

A shudder ran through the large group of men, sitting there awaiting the horrid punch line.

"We all heard the fuse pop an' everyone was screamin' an' scramblin' to git off the back of the truck an' o' course, some of the luckier guys did make it off before it blew. All I remember is that suddenly the whole world turned bright purple an' I had this horrible achin' kinda feelin' in my mind an' I don't remember nothin' else 'til I woke up in the hospital and was told that the young kid killed hisself an' a whole bunch of my buddies an' wounded the rest of us. Some lost an arm or a leg or an eye. It was a terrible waste fer nothin', Top."

Gator stared around the semi-circle of troops. There was dead silence. They stared back. Not a sound was heard.

"All gone," he said softly, "blown away by a dumb, inexperienced kid. But, it was all of our faults, you see. We should have seen that he was messed up during daylight hours, an' made corrections on him." Gator's sad eyes told the story of the horror which he and the others had experienced.

"Thank ye, Gator," said Top kindly, "set down, please."

All eyes were on the replacement who was really the focal point of this portion of the safety lecture now. I know that he was expecting that Top would crucify him. Top turned and looked him right in the eye.

"You wouldn't want to kill yerself an' all yer buddies, would ya, son?"

"No, sir," breathed the redhead sincerely.

"O.K. Ya got about one minute to git right an' stay right." The young fellow was already undoing the straps from inside his grenade rings and I noticed that several other members of our audience were busily engaged in doing the same. Top had everyone's undivided attention now.

"The hand grenade," he announced, "the number one accidental killer of friendly troops. Who knows what the number two most dangerous weapon is in the hands of an inexperienced Infantryman?" Hands shot up and Top pointed to one husky blond haired trooper.

"The M-79 Grenade Launcher loaded with the flechet round, Top." "Why?"

"Because it's loaded with many tiny metal arrow-like darts which can tear up a whole squad of friendlies if it is accidentally discharged in a column or group of our soldiers."

"How do ya know?"

"Because, Top, right here at Dakto two months ago I saw my best friend get blown away by a brand new replacement with such a weapon."

"Thank ya," said Top, adding, "now, all of ye who are armed with that 'blooper', break it open an' hold it up. I wanta see some empty chambers. Keep it helt up there, son," he directed one grenadier who was furtively trying to lower his. I guessed rightly that this particular soldier's weapon was loaded. Top told the hapless private to come front and center and Top took the short shotgun-like weapon from him and opened it, removing the high explosive 40mm round, hefting it in his hand as he handed the weapon back to the man. This particular round looks almost exactly like a huge .22 caliber rifle bullet.

"The M-79 grenade launcher," announced Top, "probably the most versatile, accurate method of deliverin' a powerful grenade that there is. With correct range estimation, an expert with this terrible weapon kin put a high explosive projectile into a small window of a hut at 300 meters' distance." He hefted the round for emphasis and continued. "That's for long distance. Fer close combat, this round's sister—the flechet—will mow a whole bunch o' enemy down while those darts make 'em wish they was somewheres else."

He explained that while the grenade projectile had a safety feature requiring that it travel between seventeen and twenty-seven feet after leaving the weapon's muzzle, before it armed itself, that the flechet round had no such safety feature and could kill your buddy one foot away if discharged accidentally. He went on to say that violation of the rule prohibiting the loading of the M-79 unless in actual enemy contact, would eventually equal friendly deaths and that he would not tolerate such flagrant disregard for the rules.

"All right," Top waved both hands, "Now I want everyone to remember these things 'cause yer not gittin' a second chance in the jungle if I ketch ya. We need a big garbage sump to be dug every night in that jungle to git rid o' trash and "C" ration cans an' sech. I'm gonna give ye some more do's an' don'ts violation o' which kin cause ya to dig until yer paws drop off, so pay attention." Everyone looked alert at this point. They didn't want to be doing the digging.

"All right," Top stroked his chin and bit his lower lip in thought, "number three would be havin' a round in the chamber of a .45 pistol. Doc, tell 'em what kind o' hole such a slug makes in the human body an' how to prevent it, please."

"A big, hideous hole, Top," replied Doc, a nice-looking kid of Italian extraction, from New York. "To prevent accidents, you do not keep a round in the chamber. It only takes a second to jack one in there upon making contact."

"O.K., Doc," Top encouraged, "now, tell the troops what the number four accidental killer's slug does to flesh an' bones."

"Right, Top. A slug from our M-16 rifle tumbles when it hits and it's better if it happens to the enemy than to your best pal walkin' along in front of you in the column."

"Thank ya, Doc. Now, guys, we are authorized to keep a cartridge in our M-16 rifle's chamber. But the safety must be on. Every hour on the hour, the word passes down the column in the jungle, 'safety check,' at which time each man checks his safety an' passes the word on down the column. This is very important. You don't want to accidentally shoot yer buddies." Top looked around until he found a thin, pale looking lad and asked him to please front and center. His name was Eddy, and Top told him to give the guys the straight scoop on malaria.

"Right, Top. You old guys remember me. I've been in the hospital for months. I've lost a lot of weight and have been as weak as a kitten but I'm gettin' my strength back. When I first came to Vietnam, my folks and my girl were always writing to me to get the Hell outta here any way that I could and I ran into this smart guy who told me to just pretend to take my malaria pills and I'd get vivax malaria. He said he had spent a month and a half in a nice hospital with no enemy to worry about, watching TV and coolin' it and it all counts off as good time on your Vietnam tour the same as the suckers who stay in the jungle and get blown away. So, I listened to his shit, see? Well, it seems there are two kinds of malaria; the mild kind like he had and the killer type of Falciparum like I got hold of, which like to have killed me. You can't know how sick it makes you. So, if a smartass tells you this kind of shit, smack 'em in the teeth and take your chances in the jungle, believe me."

"Thanks for bein' honest with us, Eddy. Go on an' set down. Couple more don'ts I want to git across. First one is pot. Mary Jane. Marijuana. There is many different grades o' that stuff, plus if ya buy it from Clyde, he has learned to lace it with opium just to goof up us Americans, plus all the profits go to the VC to buy arms with. Take it from me an' stay off of it. We already had one man in this battalion to go into his wild man act an' lose his life over it, so listen to me while I'm talkin' to ya, an' let it soak in, fellas."

He came up for air and looked around at all the faces.

"Also, ya know, back on the block when somebody gits all gooned up he ain't carryin' six or eight frag grenades an a dog-gone M-16 rifle either. So, think about it. Next thing is rabies. Hydrophobia. They ain't no cure fer it if you ketch it an' it's 100 percent fatal. Do not try an' play around with these monkeys an' other furry li'l friends you see—dawgs an' sech. Plus, the jungle is crawlin' in some spots with rats and in some spots with bats. If ya git bit, turn into Doc immediately fer evacuation an' a shot a day fer two weeks to prevent rabies. Some guys is skeert o' shots, but the alternative is the undertaker. If ya git bit, own up an' quick"

These new troopers were getting an education that they didn't get in basic training and I could tell that they were impressed by Top's candid methods in getting his points across!

"Last thing. I'm proud to be yer first sergeant. If you do like your leaders tell ya to do, you'll not only survive to rotate back to the U.S. but probably with a couple of more stripes on yer arm. We git resupplied every fifth night, an' it kin git very furry in between times. For this reason, you will carry a mini-mum of six frag grenades, two smoke an' 600 rounds o' rifle ammo an' if I ever ketch anyone tossin' any of it away to lighten the load, he's gonna dig from now on out. I'm tryna save yer life fer ya. It's gonna be a rough year, but it don't have to be real bad if you follow my guidance. Keep yer eyes open fer everything I've told ya an' we'll all git through this together with flyin' colors."

Within two days, we were back in the jungle and I told Colonel Larry that I intended to hump with Dog Company for a few days. Colonel Larry had graduated from West Point seventeen years before and was a grand fellow who really looked after our troops. Battalion commanders only stayed with the troops for six months before they went to a staff assignment and we got a new one. For this reason, I ended up serving with three different lieutenant colonels during my year.

They all operated differently to a degree, but Colonel Larry liked for me to go out with the troops and look to their needs. So, I donned my rucksack and went out with Dog.

The Ghost of Ski

Larry Jackley was undoubtedly one of the finest officers I ever served with. A devoutly religious man with patriotic convictions, he loved his family above everything. This is the kind of leader that you can count on to watch over the troops. His career came second to his family and his soldiers. He sure wasn't a "ticket-puncher" just using this combat command as a stepping stone to the stars, like many others. Although he was a West Point Officer and a Lieutenant Colonel, he treated me as an equal partner in running our battalion insofar as all our troops were concerned. He never confided in me on matters concerning the officers, which is as it should be, but today was an exception as he walked to the chopper pad with me.

"The reason," he explained, "that I have assigned that brand new captain to Dog Company, is because he has never been in combat previously and as we both know, Dog's First Sergeant is undoubtedly one of the Army's finest rifle company first sergeants, who runs the troops as straight as a string."

"Right, sir. He sure won't be bashful about giving guidance if he sees things going astray, I'm convinced. You know, like it's my job to advise you to start getting some sleep, sir. You are looking haggard and it's not going to do any of us any good if you're killin' yourself through lack of sleep, sir."

"Take care of yourself out there with Dog," he grinned, playfully punching my shoulder.

While we waited for Pete to arrive with the C&C ship from its overnight stay on the Dakto Airstrip, I pulled my green clothbound record book out of my ruck and briefed him on the status of several projects vital to the interest of our troops. Ostensibly our battalion had moved from Bien Hoa into the Central Highlands only for a ninety day period, so the rear administrative functions stayed in Bien Hoa and anything which couldn't be resolved by radio had to be done by courier. I'd make a list of everything which our S-1 Adjutant needed to get done back there, and send it with the courier, keeping my handwritten carbon copy in my green book.

"See, sir," I showed him, "our rear Adjutant General Section still hasn't cut orders awarding over three hundred of our troops their Combat Infantryman's Badge, not to mention 150 Purple Hearts and some Air Medals and other things which I'm riding herd on."

I told him that the next time our brigade's one star flew into our FSB, that the colonel needed to tell him to put a boot in that AG Major's ass back there in the rear and to make him change his system.

"When everyone was together back there at Bien Hoa, sir, their system worked perfectly. When a man was rotating back to the States, an A.G. clerk would sit down with him and conduct a records check. He'd insert orders right on the spot and make records adjustments and the guy who had put his year in was sent home happy as a lark, wearing all his well-earned ribbons and badges and it was great."

I went on to explain that this system did not take into account our mass casualties incurred in the Central Highlands. In other words, the wounded guy was evacuated—how could he have a good records check? If he was seriously wounded and never returned, then A.G. simply forwarded those incorrect records to wherever the guy ended up and he got screwed out of his awards and decorations.

"It ain't hittin' on nothin' sir, like the troopers say. I recently got a letter from a sergeant who was one of these unlucky evacuees. He had reenlisted and was writing me from his unit in Germany. He said that his records contained no general order awarding him the Combat Infantryman's Badge. Accordingly, he wasn't permitted to wear it. The catch was that the Guy's records did reflect that he had been awarded the Silver Star, the Bronze Star For Valor and two Purple Hearts, so he was allowed to wear them, sir."

"What a rotten deal! Where in Hell'd they think he got all those medals for valor if he didn't also earn the CIB?"

"Well, that's Catch 22, sir. Only our A.G. back there in Bien Hoa has the authority to cut those CIB orders and they are as slow as Moses in getting all this stuff straightened out, sir. You have to explain all this to our general and sic him on that A.G. outfit back there, sir."

We could see a speck on the horizon gradually turning into our C&C ship as we gradually picked up the sound of its approaching rotor. We walked off the pad to avoid the churning maelstrom created by the rotor of the settling Huey and then approached the chopper as Colonel Larry wanted a word with Pete. He climbed into the ship for a chat with him while I settled my ruck on the ship's deck and sat in the canvas seat adjacent to Bobbie, the left door gunner. The congenial red-haired gunner was on his third tour in Vietnam. He cupped his hands and leaned into my ear to override the noise of the whirling rotor.

"Pete loves flyin' for your Colonel Larry, there," he nodded his head toward the front of the chopper. "The other C&C pilots think he's a cowboy an' are skeert to fly with 'im but Pete's the world's original cowboy, so that's why we always come to the 4th Bat."

I laughed my head off, because I remembered the incident, several weeks before, when one of the less daring pilots had been assigned to fly the C&C ship for us. On this particular morning, Colonel Larry had just put in a pretty rough 36 hour period with no sleep and he told the pilot to fly us down to Bravo Company's position, which was a very small perimeter in real thick jungle, requiring slow, expert maneuvering for the pilot to negotiate our dangerous journey downward into such a small LZ.

On the way down, Colonel Larry and I made small talk over the ship's intercom through our flight helmets' headsets and at one point, he suddenly broke off and I noticed that he was snoozing. As the ship settled to the ground, no one approached it and it dawned on me that Bravo had already departed the area.

"Son of a bitch, sir," came the excited voice of Richard, the pilot, "we're sittin' ducks here, sir! Bravo's gone." He was really bent out of shape.

"Vacate," answered Colonel Larry.

We flew back to the FSB and after landing, I noticed that the rotor hadn't quit turning when Richard unassed the ship and ran to the other side where I could see him busily engaged in losing his breakfast.

"He usually does that," said the one doorgunner, "before we ever leave the Dakto Airstrip if we're flyin' for Colonel Larry."

"Why?" I puzzled.

"'Cause he's in the wrong racket," he said knowingly as he tossed the line expertly over the now still rotor to tether it until its next trip.

Every vocation had their meatballs, I guess, but Richard was the only chopper pilot I ever met who wasn't a fire-breather.

I stayed with Dog Company in the jungle for the first week after all those new replacements had arrived. That was when I found out how soft-hearted that Top really was inside. We were still at Dakto where the hills are extra high and the jungle is extra thick and dark. About the second or third night, we were digging in the perimeter across and around the top of a ridge for the night and I was accompanying Top as he personally inspected each and every foxhole and talked with each of the men who were digging them. All around us in the dark could be heard the 'tun-tunk' digging sounds of entrenching tools as those poor guys tried to pierce the terrible cement-like red 'laterite' soil which abounds in those mountains.

Top was very close to the men. He knew most of their problems and tried to provide solutions when possible. As we made our way silently along the perimeter, the cloudy sky prevented even one ray of moonlight or starlight from filtering down through the dense growth. As we quietly approached one particular hole, we could hear the digging men discussing Top.

"Top gitcha yer R&R quota for meetin' yer wife in Hawaii yet?" asked a voice whose owner was obviously holding a sandbag for the digger to fill. We weren't three feet away in the pitchblack.

"Nope," replied the digger. 'Tunk-tunk-tunk' went his entrenching shovel.

"Think he will?" asked the bagholder.

"Fuckin' right he will," insisted the digger, 'SHOOSH' went the loosened laterite as the digger expertly found the neck of the outstretched sandbag.

"Double fuckin' right I will, Rogers," promised Top to the surprised diggers.

"An' the sergeant major an' I'll see to it that those REMFs don't git all the Hawaii quotas before the rifle troops do, won'tcha, Ted?"

Everyone laughed as I assured them that I would. Top told us that they went exactly and precisely by the R&R roster in Dog company. He said that they'd have to move Hell and half of Georgia before he'd ever let anyone go ahead of someone else when it wasn't their turn. On our way back to our hole, Top mentioned that you can hear some interesting stuff just by keeping your ears open in the black of the perimeter by night.

"Well, Top, you found out that the men trust you, anyway."

"Uh huh," he replied, lost in thought.

When we reached our hole, we had to dig for another hour to finish, spelling each other on the bags and shovel. Then, while Top got down into the hole and heated us some "C" ration coffee, I rigged our ponchos for us to sleep under. As we drank our coffee we talked about R&R quotas for the men and then I stretched out beneath the poncho to get two hours sleep while Top watched and then we switched turns. It might have been about midnight when Top was having a horrible nightmare, crying and sobbing.

"Ski. Ski. I'm sorry," he mumbled, "Oh, God, I didn't go to do it to ya, Ski—mumble mumble—Ski."

I shook and shook him and then he went into a deep sleep. Over a cup of coffee in the morning, I asked him who Ski was.

"Who?" he abruptly spilt some of his coffee, his eyes burning into mine. "Who'd ya say?" I told him what had happened.

"Yeah, Ted," he admitted reluctantly, "I see Ski quite often. Sometimes complete with wife an' kids to boot—sometimes jest by hisself."

I told him that I didn't want to pry. He gave me a hurt look and asked if I had ever been first sergeant in combat and I told him that I had during Korea.

"Good. Then ya understand. Ski an' me was friends for years in peacetime. Same company an' all that—wives an' kids all best friends—know what I mean?"

I nodded. I had a sneaky hunch that Ski was dead and that Top was holding himself to be responsible.

He continued sadly and told me that they had come to Vietnam together and pulled strings to get into Dog Company together.

"And Ski got killed," I finished for him.

"Yeah, only it wasn't that simple. See, Ski's wife an' kids occupied government quarters in Hawaii while he was over here an' to make a long story short, I just the same as kilt him messin' with that R&R roster."

He told me that it had been Ski's turn to go on R&R to Hawaii, but Ski had begged him to let Ski's young lieutenant go there first because the lieutenant's wife was due to accompany her folks on a trip there, which would save the young couple a lot of money, so Top had gone along with the request just to suit Ski.

"So, Ski got killed while his lieutenant was on R&R and you blame yourself, Top?"

"Yep. So now, I have nightmares about my pal—an' daymares too, if ya know what I mean." I did.

I told Top that you couldn't mess with fate, that if Ski's number was up, it didn't matter about the R&R roster, but I don't think I could convince him.

That was in July. In late October, the brigade conducted a promotion board to award one first sergeant's promotion. As Top was a five striper acting first sergeant. This was his golden opportunity to be promoted to be a six striper, grade E-8. Out of all the candidates, Top emerged as number one.

I had just finished congratulating him and he was waiting for our C&C ship to return him to Dog's position in the jungle when we got a radio message from the brigade adjutant that the promotion regulations permitted one waiver only, and that due to Top's lacking a highschool education, he was short one waiver and ineligible for his well-earned promotion.

Well, Top threw a fit and I didn't blame him. We both knew that due to his six month's extension, he was eligible for a good job, safely back in the rear.

We went and saw the colonel, who promised him that he would move Heaven and earth to try and get our general to get special permission to waive Top's requirements. The colonel told Top that the choice was his, that he could go to a safe job in the rear, or back to Dog and sweat out the possibility that the general could wield some influence.

"Fair enough, sir," thanked Top, "what with our captain leavin' to be the general's aide an' the Lord knows who we'll be gittin' in to replace him, somebody's gotta look after Dawg's troopers. I 'spose that's where I'd better be gittin' to. I know that you an' the sergeant major'll look after me an' that's all I could possibly ask for."

He saluted the colonel and left for Dog Company. I was proud of Top for that decision. I was proud of my own efforts and the colonel's for our part in keeping Top in the 4th Bat.

I escorted Top to the chopper pad and he gripped my hand in that huge paw of his.

"Me an' you are more than jest first sergeant an' sergeant major," he declared, "you're my friend an' hev went a way out on a limb for me. I hope I make you proud of me. I bin thinkin' a great deal about Ski an I wanna thank ya right smart fer settin' me right on Ski. He gripped my hand again.

I can still see his tough, honest and weather-beaten face as he looked at me through those thick eyebrows of his as the chopper lifted off with him aboard. I ought to. I see it in my nightmares often enough—and in my daymares.

At the time I thought I had been counselling Top honestly and correctly about Ski's fate. I wonder.

How could I have known when I had helped Top to stay in Dog that he'd be killed a couple of weeks later in Dakto's jungle? Top had his Ski; I've got my Top.

Top was promoted posthumously and is buried not too far from Lumberton, N.C. in a pleasant grove of trees on the top of a hill. One fall day in 1968, I made the trip with his widow to visit his grave in that peaceful old cemetery. The stone reflected that Top had been 38 years old when he was killed on the 18th of November, 1967 at Dakto.

A lot of strong paratroopers in Dog Company broke down and cried when we lost Top.

For Top, the battles of Dakto were over. There were more to come.

Dedicated to the memory of First Sgt. William A. Collins

CHAPTER 10

Wearing Chevrons in Combat

One time there was a big meeting for all the senior officers and NCOs and as another sergeant major and I walked up to the front entrance, two lieutenant colonels approached us from the opposite side.

"Good morning, sergeants major," said one, using the precise King's English, as we exchanged salutes.

"Good morning, lieutenants colonel," I retorted.

"Touche." He joined the other in laughter.

I want to tell you the story of what happened to two sergeant majors in fighting outfits in Vietnam. I knew each of them personally, so I'll give you some of their background as I tell the story.

First of all I'd like to mention that the average sergeant major in Vietnam was working on at least his second or third war. Most had started out as privates years ago and grown up in the type outfit they were fighting in and the great majority had been first sergeants for many years before becoming promoted to the top enlisted rank of sergeant major.

Now, when you are a first sergeant, you have your own little kingdom and if you surround yourself with experts in their own field, you can have a great unit and your troops will benefit from being in an outfit which runs like a well lubricated machine.

If you have any meatballs on your staff, you must immediately shape them up or your operation will suffer drastically, and your captain can get relieved, ruining his military career over the mistakes of just one dud.

For this reasons the first sergeant actually runs the machine, while the captain drives it. As long as everyone knows their place and does their duty accordingly, life can be beautiful in a rifle company, or any like unit.

Of course, it doesn't always work like that, and then there's hell to pay.

So now, the first sergeant, who is used to running things with an iron fist, and knows how to run a very efficient operation, finds himself as the outfit's sergeant major and when he starts making corrections, he finds that he is now butting heads with some staff officer, who considers that the sergeant major is intruding on his territory.

Now, a smart colonel or general will get his head together with his sergeant major and work out how they are going to operate. Once that's established, it helps if the sergeant major's boss tells all his officers that if the sergeant major tells them anything, it's the boss talking.

If the sergeant major doesn't get carried away, this works like a charm, and the entire unit will benefit.

Because the sergeant major has the top officer's ear, he is resented by some of the officers in the outfit, and that is where trouble can start.

Bear all this in mind when I tell you about the very serious trouble which each of these well-decorated, highly experienced sergeant majors got into while trying to do their duty once again in combat.

The catch is that their previous combat experience had been as first sergeants and platoon sergeants and so forth, where the highest ranking officer that they had to please was their own captain.

The great majority of the officers who fought in Vietnam were outstanding. As in any vocation, there were exceptions to the rule.

This was true with the NCOs who fought.

I started not to write the sad story of what happened to these two outstanding soldiers because I didn't want to convey the mistaken impression that the ratfinks they ran into were typical of the fine soldiers who fought in Vietnam.

I say again, they were one in a million meatballs.

The first one of the two to go to Vietnam had been Dirk. The second was Burke.

You'll see why I have changed their names when you see what happened to each of them.

The Hatchets

"This Silver Star Medal is awarded," read the citation, "for gallantry in action, above and beyond the call of duty."

It went on to describe Dirk's bravery in saving the lives of two of his soldiers in combat. Disregarding his own safety, he had made two hazardous trips under very heavy enemy fire, to rescue his comrades who had been wounded on a desolate hill in Korea.

He was promoted to be the rifle company's first sergeant. After returning to the states, he remained first sergeant of rifle companies for about ten years, when he was promoted to be sergeant major.

A couple of years later, his entire unit was sent to Vietnam. Think of the experience that this fine man had in rifle companies and rifle battalions. He had held just about every job from rifleman to sergeant major and he knew every trick in the book. Most of all, though, he knew troops and how to take care of them, especially in combat.

His unit soon tangled with the North Vietnamese Army and the mutual mauling took place which happens when two rifle outfits participate in a battle in the jungle.

After the battle, Dirk's lieutenant colonel's time was up, and something had happened to his incoming replacement. So until they could bring in a new commander, the brigade commander—a full colonel—gave the OK for the battalion's XO to take over temporarily. A battalion XO's job was to stay in the rear area and coordinate the battalion's staff sections for sup-

ply, mess, administration, and support duties. So on the day of
the lieutenant colonel's departure, a chopper was sent to the
first support base to get him, and the same helicopter brought
the major out to assume command. Dirk said that from the get-
go, there was absolutely no question about the major's aggres-
siveness.

"He un-assed that chopper, bringin' two burly privates with
him, who began unloading cases of brand new hatchets," said
the astounded Dirk.

"He told me that he had scrounged those four cases of
hatchets back in the rear and that they'd come in handy in the
jungle, when he introduced his 'new policies,'" Dirk shook his
head disgustedly.

He told Dirk to send the old colonel's radio operator to a
rifle company, that one of the burly privates would be his new
radio operator, while the other was his bodyguard.

Bodyguards in the Infantry? Guarding from what? Every
one of us carried a rifle and grenades in the jungle. We were
our own bodyguard.

"I lasted less than seventy-two hours with this nut, Ted," he
said sadly, "and I told him that he needed to think about getting himself a new sergeant major—right now."

Then Dirk told me one of the most unusual stories I had
ever heard.

Heads and Hatchets

Our rifle soldiers in the jungle, searching for the enemy NVA
Infantrymen, or for the local V.C., required close artillery support.

For this reason, our riflemen would conduct a heliborne
assault upon open terrain suitable for a battery of 105mm
artillery guns to be emplaced. After they secured the area, the
six huge guns would be choppered in.

While one rifle company of infantrymen dug in and
secured the perimeter, the Artillerymen dug in the howitzers
and began their fire support.

This was known as a jungle fire support base, and in most cases, the Infantry Battalion Commander had his staff to set up his command post inside this protected perimeter. He also moved the battalion's own 4.2 inch mortar platoon into the perimeter, giving the commander immediate control of all this firepower.

"He sent our chopper to get all four rifle company leaders," said Dirk "and had all four captains and first sergeants seated on the ground next to a big tree stump, with those four cases of new hatchets stacked up beside it. Then he went into his act."

Dirk said that the major laid down the law to the group, telling them that not only would they have the best battalion in Vietnam, they would be the most feared.

He said that the enemy soldiers had desecrated the last corpse with their machetes, that they were going to, that their battalion was going to beat the enemy to the punch.

"He worked himself into a kind of frenzy," said Dirk, his dark eyes mirroring his disbelief at the recollection, "and he took one of those hatchets and began whacking on that stump with it, while those first sergeants and captains eyed one another as if to say, 'is this guy for real?'"

"You should've seen him, Ted," he said, "wavin' that hatchet around like a wild man, and whackin' on that stump with it."

"What for?"

"He thought he was motivatin' 'em, I guess. He made a speech that'd curl your hair. His very words were 'We'll teach Charlie to carve up our troops. I want every fuckin' head chopped off every enemy corpse and displayed on top of a bamboo pole on the spot and left there to rot as an example for the dirty little bastards to see what they're gonna get from the best battalion in Vietnam.'"

Dirk told me that because the enemy had desecrated many of our corpses, that his troops would have gone wild with those hatchets if such an order had gone out into the jungle riflemen, but we couldn't lower ourselves to the cruel, uncivilized level of the enemy, no matter what he did.

"Did they do it, Dirk?"

"Hell no. Our troops'd be committin' war crimes. I jumped up there and tried to reason with him and he ordered me to sit down and to be at ease, and I wouldn't do it and neither would you have, Ted."

Dirk said that he told the four captains and first sergeants that this was an insane, illegal order and that every one of them would eventually be court martialled if he followed it.

That was when he told the new major to find himself a new sergeant major and jumped on a resupply chopper back to brigade HQ, where he and the brigade sergeant major took the story to the colonel in command of the brigade. The colonel immediately put a stop to Operation Hatchet. At the same time, Dirk told him that he'd get into big trouble if the colonel sent him back to be that major's sergeant major, so the colonel sent him to another battalion. Within weeks, the major was replaced with a new lieutenant colonel and was sent back to the rear to be the battalion's XO again.

Now just think about what could have happened in that outfit if Dirk had not been there to bring everything to a screeching halt at the right time. Any one of those four young captains could have done the same thing that Dirk did, but a number of factors must be considered. This happened a couple of years before the infamous My Lai Massacre, which caused many heads to roll even before the U.S. Army completed its investigation. Essentially the same situation had prevailed then as it did in this case: the wily local VC had been whittling away the troops everyday with mines, booby traps, and ambushes, while the troops contending with these attacks suspected that the local villagers either were VC or at least were assisting them.

We all know what happened to the villagers, many of whom were undoubtedly innocent of any wrongdoing, and when the terrible massacre came to light, the repercussions were heard and felt around the world. Of course, what the troops did to those civilians violated any number of articles of the Geneva Convention, as well as many directives published and promulgated by Gen. William Westmoreland and his staff.

Even so, when it comes right down to it, considering the myriad operations conducted by our U.S. armed forces during the ten years that we fought in Vietnam—and, for that matter, during the current Afghanistan and Iraq campaigns—it's a tribute to the overall discipline of our fighters that there were only two serious incidents such as these. I'd bed that such detrimental instances constitute far less than one percent of the total operations. For comparison, just look at the enemy's record.

I think the moral to the story is that Dirk was "Johnny on the spot" and prevented a serious incident. This speaks volumes about the inestimable value to a commander and his unit of the experience and savvy possessed by their command sergeant major.

Burke's Short Tour of Vietnam

Burke was an old soldier. He had fought in the Marine Corps as a private during World War II, working his way up to corporal before being discharged at war's end.

After a short stint in civilian life, he decided to make the military his career and joined the army. He was glad that he did, and he went right up the ladder to become first sergeant and eventually became a command sergeant major. When he received orders to Vietnam, I briefed him extensively on some of the pitfalls he would run into there as opposed to what we both had learned fighting in Korea. He was assigned to an Infantry Division to be the two star general's sergeant major.

The general was a good scout, and Burke really liked him. He, too, was a World War II veteran, having been a platoon leader in Europe and then commanded a rifle company during the Battle of the Bulge as a captain.

As a result of similar backgrounds, they both saw eye-to-eye on everything, to include the fact that there was the difference between day and night when comparing their jungle troopers and their daily existence with how the troops in the rear echelon lived.

Due to the nature of the beast, there was absolutely no equation of the two. The rifle soldiers had all the hardships and the rear area troops had it made. The rifle troops got all the purple hearts and the body bags while those in the rear slept on cots—and sometimes in beds—had showers and movies, not to mention clubs where they could drink at night, for very cheap prices.

Vietnamese prostitutes abounded—and so did dope.

The rifle troopers knew that the only way they would ever be sent to the rear to one of those luscious jobs was to be wounded the third time. The law of averages saw to it that most riflemen were killed before they ever received that third wound, so there wasn't much to look forward to in a jungle unit except to hope and pray that you wouldn't end up in a bodybag.

Some jungle troopers were so gungho that they wouldn't trade places with those REMFs in the rear, even if they could. In their vernacular, the acronym REMF spelt out to "Rear Echelon Mother Fucker." The jungle troopers looked down on the disdainful REMFs.

Burke had been in Vietnam about a week when his general told him that he was getting a lot of incident reports caused by the rear echelon clerks and jerks.

"They've got too much time on their hands," he told Burke, "so I want you to go back there and spend a couple of days and find out who the ringleaders are. Bring their asses out to the jungle and trade 'em for some good, deserving riflemen to go back and do their cushy jobs for 'em."

Their division's rear area was located in Tan Son Nhut, a huge military supply/operations/air base located very near Saigon.

Burke went back there and started poking around. One senior NCO tipped him off that one particular tent, which he showed to him, was the nightly gathering place for pot-heads and some who even used stronger stuff. He said that the joint'd be jumpin' by about eight that night.

Burke waited until about half past eight and sauntered into the tent, where the surprised group soon fell to stone silence.

Burke coughed as the strong, thick smoke assailed his lungs and eyes.

"I'm your new division sergeant major, he announced, "and I want to see some I.D. cards right now. You people are going to the jungle tomorrow, as "eleven bush" riflemen," he said, using the slang term for the 11.B connoting a rifleman's specialty.

One or two of the men obediently started digging for their I.D. cards.

"Hold it," commanded one of the smokers. "This mother fucker'll kill all of us 'less we frag his fuckin' ass about 'o dark thirty' tonight! Who's with me? A dead lifer don't cause no trouble."

Several loudly agreed.

"I ain't goin' to no jungle," agreed one.

"You'd better quit while you're ahead, sergeant major," softly suggested one who had been willing to cooperate and had been digging for his I.D. card.

Burke turned on his heel and quit while he was ahead.

Returning a few minutes later, he barged in among the jubilant revelers and fired a round through the roof of the tent.

"I've got a round in this rifle for each one of you sons of bitches who want to try and frag me, and I'll blow your asses away in an instant! Now, hand me some I.D. cards right now or you die on the spot."

He collected fifteen I.D. cards, and the dogtags from three who swore they had lost their cards and fell them outside in two ranks and started marching them to the M.P. Station when one of his prisoners took off on the run!

"Halt!" yelled Burke, then twice more, and then he shot the fleeing figure right in the buttocks, dumping him in front of one of the tents in the dimly lighted dirt street.

Two M.P. jeeps rolled around the corner in seconds, having been called for by a vigilant soldier a few minutes before when Burke had fired through the roof of the tent.

The M.P.s had to call for a truck and an ambulance for the wounded doper, and Burke spent half the night at the M.P. Station, making a statement for the C.I.D. Agent on duty, and answering all his questions.

"It was stupid to shoot the guy," a one star general told Burke as he stood in front of the general's desk a few hours later at the headquarters of the three star who commanded MACV.

Burke nodded in agreement.

"You had his I.D. card, according to this report, and the rascal was high as a kite."

"I dunno, general," said Burke, "they had all just threatened to kill me, sir—and that'll rattle your cage a little bit, and when he took off, my reflexes just ran away with themselves, I guess, sir!"

Tan Son Nhut was also the home of the huge airbase servicing international flights.

"The boss says you're out of here," said the one star not unkindly. "I don't blame you, I guess, but he says you should have called the military police to start off with. You'll be on a flight this afternoon for CONUS."

Continental United States.

The general told Burke that no charges were pending against him. He said that the three star had said that the best way to handle it would be to ship Burke.

"No sticky mess," he pointed out to Burke, "you're dismissed. The major in my outer office has all the details."

A few days later, my own phone rang at West Point and I was amazed to find Burke talking to me from Fort Hood, Texas, of all places. Of course, I thought he was still in Vietnam.

"You were right, Ted," said Burke. "Vietnam surely to hell is nothing like Korea was."

He went on to astonish me with what happened to him during his first week in Vietnam. He was pretty philosophical about it all and still couldn't see where he had done anything wrong in shooting that doper and I had to agree with him.

"You know, Billy Burke," I laughed, "hundreds of meatballs who goofed up stateside in the U.S. Army, found their asses to be shipped to Vietnam as a punitive measure, but you are the first one that I ever heard of who got tossed out of there."

We were both laughing when we hung up. Burke went on to much higher assignments up the chain of command and ended up being the command sergeant major for a four star general.

Well, those are the stories of what happened to two devoted, outstanding command sergeants major who found themselves to be in the wrong place at the wrong time in Vietnam.

Both are retired now, forgetting the few bad things and reflecting on the many good things that happened during their long, exciting military careers.

It's fitting.

Frank's Poker Hand

Frank had been known to get into some hind of devilment or other. He did a fine job in the jungle as a dependable rifleman, but he was guaranteed to get into some kind of trouble if he ever got back into the rear area. A big, nice-looking and clean-cut black soldier, he was quick with a smile, very easygoing and was well liked by just about everyone who knew him. For all these reasons, I was very surprised when "Doc," our battalion surgeon, approached me and Colonel Johnnie with a terrible problem concerning Frank.

We were still operating out of Dakto—pronounced "Doc Toe." For several important reasons, the troops considered Dakto to be the end of the world. Dakto proper consisted of a small airstrip with an equally small Special Forces Camp located at one end of the strip, while the other end stopped just a few hundred yards short of a medium sized Montagnard village occupied by members of the Dakto Tribe. All the rest was solid mountainous jungle as far as the eye could see in every direction.

The entire area gets very muddy during the monsoons and is soon baked when the hot sun comes out. Our troops said that

Dakto was the only place in the entire world where one could stand ass-deep in the mud with the wind blowing sand in your eyes, while being sniped at by snipers simultaneously.

There's not much in the way of entertainment there for the troops who found themselves waiting for a C-130 to ferry them out of Dakto for R&R or back to the world upon completion of their tour in the jungle. In addition, due to our heavy casualties in the jungle, my battalion had a turnover of over six hundred men coming and going in short order. Doc started getting suspicious when some of the new replacements started showing up with V.D. out in the jungle. This sort of thing can get out of hand if you take into consideration that helicopters were our only mode of transportation and you don't have to be a genius to realize that there is much more valuable cargo to consider than riflemen being sent back to the rear to be cured. Sometimes V.D. knocked a soldier out of action—sometimes not, depending upon the type. The most common forms in our area were gonorrhea, syphilis and chancroid. Ninety percent— the gonorrhea cases—could be treated right in the jungle with a shot or two, while other, more sophisticated treatment was required for more serious cases, necessitating the soldier's evacuation by chopper. These few cases still hurt the commander's fighting strength in the jungle.

A certain number of soldiers—which equally applies to civilians—will contract V.D. no matter where they go. The Dakto prostitutes for the most part, congregated in a little group of huts located across the airstrip from the village. This place came to be known by the troops as 'Dak Kok.' Needless to say, the medics were kept quite busy trying to police up known V.D. carriers and cure them, so the place was constantly patrolled by military police accompanied by medical personnel.

Colonel Johnnie was very concerned about the problem and had asked Doc to keep him personally appraised of the situation. It was during one of the times that we were sitting near the Dakto Airstrip awaiting replacements when this unusual episode took place. It started when Colonel Johnnie and I were standing by the strip talking and we were approached by our surgeon, Doc, who had brought Frank to see us. Frank was waiting about ten yards away and couldn't hear the captain's conversation with us.

Doc explained that Frank had come back from R&R in Bangkok and had been treated on the spot for gonorrhea. Then, he had been wounded and upon his return from the hospital, had spent several days on the Dakto strip, during which time he had contracted gonorrhea, chancroid and syphilis.

"Hmmm," said the lieutenant colonel, three of a kind, huh? He's a walkin' plague."

"Yeah," I chimed in, "one more PAIR and he'll have a full HOUSE!" Doc looked at us both like that's about what he had expected we'd come up with and calmly continued.

"Well, sir, Frank won't tell me who the girl is, but he kind of likes the sergeant major. I want you to go with Frank, sergeant major, find the girl who is responsible and bring her back to me so that we may treat her before she infects more soldiers."

"Can I trust you," the colonel grinned with eyebrows raised, "to come back without three of a kind, Top?"

"Ha," I retorted, "I'm a famous coward! You don't even have to worry about me havin' openers, sir."

Doc told us that in addition, until he had Frank completely cured, he suggested that I take Frank to the fire support base with me. The colonel agreed and told me that I could use Frank as an assistant, to dig foxholes, etc. He asked me if I'd have any trouble keeping Frank busy?

"Not at all, sir. He can prepare the colonel's chow for him also, and little things like that."

"Yuk," he replied, "that's not exactly what I had in mind. He could fill sandbags and dig sumps and so forth."

We looked over at Frank, who was looking at US! He was probably wondering what fate was in store for a man with three of a kind—which was taking a lieutenant colonel, a captain, and a sergeant major so long to devise. He looked pretty worried to me!

"Sure, sir," I agreed, "ole Frank's got natural pickaxe paws. I'll hold the bags and he can dig. It's a democracy, isn't it."

"You've adopted him, Top! Now tell Stanley to drive you and Frank after that girl with my jeep."

I got Stanley to crank up his jeep and told him how Frank was all eaten up by three different kinds of V.D. and what we had to do, plus that Frank would be working with me and Stanley from then on out.

"Wow, Top. Sounds to me like he's eaten up by three different kinds of the dumbass. Have you ever seen any of those hags who hang around down there? I wouldn't touch one of them witches with a ten foot pole."

"You ain't Frank, Stanley. Let's pick him up and get this show on the road."

We piled Frank into the back seat and I explained the deal to him and he looked at me like I was some kind of nut when I told Stan to run us down to Dak Kok. He told us that the girl was way on past Dak Kok, and at his direction, Stan wended our way around the strip until we ended up on the west side by the river. Frank told us to keep going and we went down a long slope and into a valley and around a big bend and then back up another steep hill. At this point I started sweating it out! Looking around apprehensively, I observed that we were way to hell and gone out in the middle of nowhere and ripe for an ambush. I could just hear the music around our house if Marlene got a notification that I had gotten killed hunting a gal with three different kinds of V.D. I passed on these observations to Stan and Frank.

"Naw," scoffed Frank. "Wait 'til you see this place. There's enough armed GIs out here to start their own war."

He directed us down a little trail off to the right and there must have been ten or twelve other government vehicles parked in a little clearing about a hundred yards back, none of which were visible from the road. We parked and followed Frank down a path into the jungle and before long the sound of revelry could be heard. There was a big clearing back in there and somebody had a portable radio turned up full blast and rock and roll was reverberating throughout the jungle.

Some GIs were sitting around on straw mats drinking 'Ba Mui Ba' Vietnamese beer which has been likened to formalde-hyde. Girls were sitting with them. There must have been at least twenty women that I could see and here and there a guy and gal were either slipping off into the jungle or just coming back.

"Hmmmm," I observed, "business as usual, huh, Frank?"

"Yeeaah," he replied enthusiastically, looking around the area to see where the action was.

I shook my head at the sight and told Frank to quickly point out the girl to us, so that we could get the heck out of there and take her to Doc. He replied that we needed a truck! Stan caught on quicker than I did.

"Go ahead, Frank," he cackled, "introduce the sergeant major to just any of these broads here that you have laid."

"O.K. Lemme see," Frank shrugged amiably, "there's Margie there, the li'l chubby job, with no upper teeth. Ummmummm, man, has she got it."

Stan laughed fit to kill and told Frank that Margie had probably given 'it' to Frank, too."

"Negative on that," frowned Frank, "Not Margie. She's my baby. She's clean as a whistle. No. Maybe Ginny there, did. She's the one-eyed one lookin' this way. Naw, that's her bad eye lookin' this way. I don't think she sees us." Both Margie and Ginny were real beauts. Stan looked at me and cocked his head and then we both looked at Frank in aghast awe. Along about that time, some of the unattached girls spotted Frank and made a beeline for our little group.

"Uh oh," warned Frank, "here comes Sandy an' Shirley. They ain't so bad, but they got 'The Vampire' with 'em. Now, she is probably the one which give me that V.D. Ya wanna watch her like a snake."

"Why?" Stan stepped back a pace. "What's she do—an' which one is she?" he added hastily.

"Third one back," advised Frank, "Bleached blonde. She's wavin' now. One with the gold tooth."

They were on us by then. Other beauties streamed in from the sidelines until they had us completely surrounded.

"Fuckey-suckey," cried the Vampire as she grabbed poor Stan and tried to kiss him, "bess in wess, G.I. cheap, too."

Stan winced and pushed her away as the rest of them continued jabbering at us in pidgin English, pulling on our fatigues and fondling us and giggling and carrying on, trying to get us to take them into the jungle.

"Well," breathed Frank, "we are in it now. We kin not hurt their feelin's an' make 'em lose face. We have to take some of 'em inta the jungle. Just don't take that Vampire, though, I'm warnin' ya, because I'm convinced she's the one which got me into this here fix."

"Fuckey-suckey," said the Vampire, again grabbing Stan by the lapels of his jungle fatigue jacket, trying to kiss him again!

"Git," threatened Stan as he tried to shake her off!

"You girls," Frank looked lovingly at the group, "you girls are number ten." He shook his finger at them as one would admonish a small child.

They all looked shocked and stopped pushing and giggling and looked up at big Frank in amazement. He nodded his head and grinned and grabbed up one that looked sixty and held her like a doll in his huge arms and hands while the girls crowded in closer as Stan and I looked at one another apprehensively. Frank hefted the old gal in his arms and she kissed him warmly on the mouth and I almost lost my lunch right there.

"Listen," Frank yelped, "somebody in this here outfit got V.D. 'cause I ketchee V.D. from somebody here." He swept his hand to illustrate his point. I didn't know if he meant just our girls, or those in the entire clearing! I couldn't tell which.

You never heard such a commotion in your life. Those girls were completely aghast at Frank's rude accusation. V.D.? V.D.? No, sir. Not from this crew. They couldn't believe that Frank could tell such a lie. They were pushing and shoving and murmuring angrily, looking up at Frank and then at Stanley and me. Frank had definitely said the magic word.

"Umm, Frank," I began, "how many of these bags did you . . .?"

"All of 'em, Top. Once or twice, Wolf. They are all damn nice. See, the G.I.s come here instead of to Dak Kok because they're broke. These gals all give us payday stakes. Love 'em now—pay for 'em payday, see?"

I looked all around. Never was a more motley looking, filthy bunch of bags gathered in such a small place before, I was sure of it. That clearing was filled with witches. They just had to be infected with everything in the book. I looked at Stanley. Stan gave a little guffaw and looked up into the trees as though he were afraid of a sniper lurking somewhere. I shook my head in disbelief.

"Frank! You couldn't possibly have all your marbles if you had sex with all these bags. Why, some of them must have leprosy, for heck's sake. Why, I'll bet you that you have that other pair of diseases to make that doggone full house and you and Doc don't even know it yet."

"What full house?" he wrinkled his brow in curiosity.

I explained to him that all these broads had obviously been run off by the Vietnamese authorities for having some kind of creeping, crawling crud and that was the reason why they were all out in this God-forsaken spot giving broke guys payday stakes and meanwhile infecting everyone in the process. I told him that I wouldn't doubt it if the V.C. was running the place.

Finally, I had enough. I took a deep breath and yelled at the top of my voice and hardly anyone paid any attention, so I told Stan to run over into the middle of the clearing and to turn off that loudly blaring radio. Well, that got everyone's attention—especially those who were dancing. When everyone looked at Stan like he was a killjoy and hollered for him to turn it back on, he just pointed at me. I took another deep breath.

"At ease!" I sounded off with my best parade-ground voice. "I am the 4th Rifle Battalion sergeant major and I have it on good authority," I glanced dramatically at my watch, "that this place is getting raided by the military police in exactly," I squinted at my watch, "ten minutes."

The big clearing exploded into running figures. That was the fastest I ever saw a bunch of GI's move. Some came from the jungle dressing on the run. One guy swooped down on the radio, scooped it up on the run and moved out on the double toward the parking area, the same as the rest of the exiting soldiers. The girls they had been with were all shrieking and wailing and chasing them, screaming for them to come back. It was really a sight to behold—a real riot. Stan was enjoying it all. He was looking around, laughing at the antics of the girls and the swiftly departing paratroopers. Frank, on the other hand, was looking at me in disgust and utter disbelief.

"Jeez, Top. I never would'a believed that you'd pull such a nasty trick on a bunch of pore ole combat troops. You sure ruined their fun. You know they ain't no MP's comin' to raid this place." He looked at me accusingly.

"The hell they ain't Frank. I can guarantee you that they'll be here today. And as far as the troops are concerned, I have probably saved some of them from the creepin', crawlin' crud, is all."

We looked around us. All the GI's were gone and we could hear the last of the truck engines as they roared up the hill toward the main highway. Just about all the girls had returned to us as we were the only potential customers left in the clearing. There must have been thirty whores ringed about us, all weeping and wailing at once. By this time it had dawned on all of them who the cause of all their misery was. They knew it was me, but they also understood that it was Frank who had brought me there, causing all their trouble. Stan still stood outside the ring of women, looking at me apprehensively. He cast his eyes and nodded his head suggestively toward our jeep where it still sat about a hundred yards away.

I had heard tales of troopers being slashed by razor blades for failure to pay some of those tough women back in rear areas and as I looked at those angry faces with flashing teeth and at those long, razorsharp fingernails, I was wondering about such things as knives and razorblades, and I'm sure that Stan was, because when I shook my head "yes" to him, he took off like a rabbit toward our jeep while I started to gingerly work my way out toward the edge of the crowd.

"Fraaaank," I called in an innocuous manner, "I think it's time for us to motor down the freeway, Frank." That crowd was in a very ugly mood and I was trying not to make our impending exit too obvious to all those mean women.

I almost got unscathed to the outer circle, and if it hadn't been for that stubborn Frank, I am sure I would have. But, instead of listening to me, Frank was standing his ground and arguing his case with the girls and trying to sweet-talk them. Well, it sure wasn't working. The girls were all crowding up to me, pushing and shoving me and shouting invectives in pidgin English, French and Vietnamese, with a little Montagnard thrown in for emphasis.

In their eyes, a sergeant major was rich as Croesus, and they wanted reimbursement—on-the-spot—for the loss of all that business which I had caused them. Finally, without hurting any of those little gals, I started wading through them, bulling my way toward the jeep, hoping that what I knew was going to happen wouldn't.

It all happened kind of spontaneously. I heard a shriek as one of them suddenly raked Frank's bare arm with a set of terrible fingernails which each girl was armed with. Stan was almost to the jeep. He was hollering, "Run, you guys, run!" Stan was definitely making hay while the sun shone.

I swiftly turned and looked to see if I could help Frank, but nobody could help Frank. They were on him in one second, like a horde of wild vengeance-bent alley cats! At about that same instant, a red hot iron seared my neck from behind. At first I feared that I had been cut by a straight razor, but later on, Stan informed me that one of those little gals had jumped straight up in the air and got me on the rebound with her nails. With a yelp and one tremendous burst of energy, I was free. I must have bowled over several and trampled one or two more in my mad attempt to escape those claws, but suddenly, I was loose.

I ran a few yards with about a dozen of them chasing me and chanced a quick, fearful backward glance. My worst fears were confirmed. Frank had been completely overrun by the enemy, lying helplessly on the ground. He was on his own. I turned on the speed, still heading toward our jeep. I could hear Frank's terrified whoops and yelps as the wildly screaming and shrieking women worked him over. I doubt if his whole ordeal lasted more than fifteen or twenty seconds, but it must have seemed like a lifetime to poor Frank.

My legs are much longer than those of the little Vietnamese gals and as I reached the jeep, which Stan had started and was backing rapidly toward me, I jumped in and quickly looked back toward Frank's group to see how the huge private was faring. At the same time, I could see my pursuers gathering rocks and empty Ba-Mui-Ba Beer bottles. They were hanging in there for the long siege.

Frank suddenly let out a horrendous rebel yell, surged back to his feet and I could see him, bowling on out through that big circle of milling, scratching, yelling undomesticated cats and suddenly he was loose and headed our way. He took the pressure off me and Stan as my pursuers unloaded their rocks and bottles on him as he passed through their midst at what appeared to be at least the speed of sound! By the time that Frank sailed into the rear of the jeep, Stan gunned it toward the exit and we all ducked as the women sallied out onto the edge of the trail en masse and threw bottles and rocks at us.

Missiles ricocheted off the jeep and whizzed by our heads as Stan frantically stomped the accelerator to the floor on the trail heading for the main road. Something bounced off my shoulder and Frank took a rock in the middle of his back and suddenly, we were out of range.

Frank was a mess. His jungle fatigues and boots had saved some parts of him from being scratched and bitten, but he was bleeding from dozens of places on his hands and arms and on his neck and face. We found later on that he had been bitten in many places on the legs and stomach and back and he was just a mess in general! He was out of breath and shaking like a leaf.

"Those filthy, ungrateful whores," he cried, his voice shaking emotionally, "an' after all I done fer 'em. Look at me. I sure hope to hell I don't ketch nothin' off of 'em from all these here bites an' wounds."

Stan and I laughed so hard at that prospect that I thought Stan was going to run us off the road into the ditch. Finally, even Frank saw the humor of the situation as he joined in and began to laugh. It had to be the funniest thing in the whole world. By then, we were approaching the Dakto Airstrip and Stan looked both ways and took a shortcut across the strip and as we pulled into the area, all of us still laughing our guts out, we surprised Colonel Johnnie, who was sitting on a sandbag outside his little tent, shaving. He looked up in surprise, stopping with the razor halfway to his face in midstroke.

We had to be a terrible sight. Stan and I were still in full uniform but Frank had lost his steel pot and his jacket was all snatched out of his pants and his trouser legs were unbloused, and he was bleeding from the crisscrossed wounds from his battle!

"What tha hell," began Johnnie, "did Frank fall out of the jeep?" That got the whole crew to laughing again and it had to be five minutes before I could tell the dumfounded colonel what had happened to the three of us.

"You definitely sent three boys to do a man's job, colonel," I explained, "let me run and call the military police and give them directions to go down there and raid that place."

Stan took Frank to see Doc, while I did that. After I had rejoined the colonel, Doc came up to see us. He shook his head and gave a kind of little laugh.

"Poor Frank comes to me and the only trouble he had was three cases of V.D. We were going to do some good and corral the chic who infected him and now—it took six yards of bandaids and a whole bottle of merthiolate to cauterize his wounds. HE looks like he got a direct hit with a mortar."

"Yes, sir, Doc, I replied, "Frank sure caught it."

I was telling Doc the whole story and along about that time, one of our squads brought in an eighteen- or twenty-foot rock python they had shot on patrol and everyone was so busy taking pictures and taking turns with four or five guys posing with it over their shoulders like firemen with a hose, that we just forgot about Frank.

Frank had his picture taken with it and all covered with bandages and I wonder to this day, what his folks back home thought when they got that picture. Frank told me that he had learned his lesson and would sooner tangle with a live python than to ever get mixed up with a batch of witches again. I wonder.

Dedicated to Sgt. Stanley Newman Jones,
November 19, 1940–March 7, 2005

On the Warpath

Most of the American Indians I served with in the USMC back in the forties and later on in the army's paratroops for about twenty-eight years, were outstanding, dependable riflemen. Each seemed to possess the same Achilles' heel—an adverse reaction to the consumption of alcohol. I only knew one American Indian who could have drunk ole Patrick and Rudolph under the table, and he is a hero who lost an arm and a leg in Vietnam, but he could still do it.

During the Korean War, two of my Indian pals and I were first sergeant of rifle companies and I want to tell you what happened to each of them after that war when we all three ended up in the airborne infantry at Fort Campbell, Kentucky.

"Tomahawk" outranked Ray and me and he was the first one to get busted. His outfit was sent to Camp Hale, Colorado for winter training and his soldiers swiftly discerned that a Paratrooper who could easily run six or eight miles in Kentucky, was hard pressed to run a mile up in those mountains without gasping for breath! After a few days, a runner's lungs became acclimatized to the rareness of oxygen at that altitude, and he could do his thing normally.

Well, the first night Tomahawk's troops visited the town, some hardy gold miners ganged up on two of the troops in this one big bar, breaking one guy's arm and the other had mucho cuts, dents and bruises. Tomahawk fell the entire company of over 200 troopers out of the barracks into the snow and told them to go back in and get their entrenching shovels, that it was open season on the people in that bar! He told them that he did not want to see one board, bottle or shingle left of the place. True to form, his troopers dismantled the building.

Well, the general dismantled the bottom chevron from each of Tomahawk's arms. He was one helluva guy. He retired, years later, as sergeant major, with a pot full of medals.

Now, Ray was the quiet one of the three, but he was definitely a man of his word. He earned three Silver Stars and nine Purple Hearts during Korea and Vietnam, and was absolutely one of the bravest soldiers I have known. Three or four years rocked by after Tomahawk's fiasco and it began to look as though both Ray and I were going to retain our first sergeant's chevrons, when fate beckoned for Ray's outfit to go to Little Rock, Arkansas in 1957 and confront the state's authorities and national guard in defense of the federal government's forceful integration of the state's schools.

This sounds innocuous, but it was on top of several very fierce riots that were some real lulus, so the general who headed that task force from the 101st Airborne Division's Screamin' Eagles, was careful to point out to all the senior officers that he wanted everything handled very cautiously, to ensure the fewest number of civilian casualties possible, in order not to exacerbate the political bombshell involved for all parties concerned, to include his own stars. Nobody bothered to tell Ray this.

Three hundred and some odd years prior to the birth of Christ, the "phalanx" was devised by Philip II of Macedonia and this military formation helped his son, Alexander The Great, to conquer much of Europe, Asia Minor and part of Asia. Most forms of the phalanx constitute a huge "vee" pointed at and marched into the face of the enemy. Alexander used shields and spears, but the modern version of the phalanx consists of rifle soldiers with fixed bayonets pointed out of each side and the front. Every time the soldier's left foot strikes the ground during the advance to break up a riot, he thrusts the bayonet outward while shouting a simultaneous resounding "Yuh!"

Ray told me later that some of those rednecks fomenting the strife were running around imbibing from pint-sized Atlas fruit jars of what the troops used to refer to as "sploe"—good old mountain dew. Well, the idiot who broke from the crowd and tried to wrestle the rifle from the man at the very tip of that spear, didn't know who he was messing with. Ray bayonetted his buns while the newsreel cameras rolled, recording the entire scene.

Well, outside of breaking up that riot in a great big hurry, once the message reached all those rednecks as to the versatility of the phalanx, some of us more militant observers hypothesized that the general was going to probably decorate Ray for meritorious achievement.

But, it was not to be. Summoned before the general that night, Ray soon surmised he had a rocky road facing him when the general advised him of his rights under Article 31 of the Uniform Code Of Military Justice—the civilian Fifth Amendment, and then the game began, with the general holding all four aces. He told Ray that what he had done was stupid, that Ray should have simply given the miscreant a vertical or horizontal butt stroke with his rifle instead of feeding him the steel. He explained that they had come to Arkansas to stop riots, not to start more of them.

"In view of your superb military record," the old general said, "I'm only taking one stripe off you. You made a bum decision and it's up to me to see to it that you pay for it. Do you have any questions before I dismiss you?"

"Yes, sir" Ray said, "I'd like to respectfully ask the general why you gave the order 'fix bayonets' if we weren't going to use them, sir?"

"You will have ample time in the future," replied the general, "to ponder the stupidity of that question. You are dismissed."

Sadly, after surviving all those battles in several wars, Ray finally ended up in Valhalla last year after a terrible bout with cancer. He was a fierce fighter to the last.

Well Tomahawk and Ray were two gutsy guys, but wait until you see the ordeal suffered by Chief Seven Fingers.

Chief Seven Fingers

His nickname was "Chief" because he was a full-blooded Chero-kee and he certainly looked it. Chief was a rifleman and a fine brave one. See if you think that you could ever have done what he had to do to preserve his own life.

He had lived through more than his share of calamities before he ever got to Vietnam, having been an orphan, adopted by other reservation Indians. He was shuttled back and forth between different families for over a dozen years and it must have made a patient person of him. Maybe God takes all these things into consideration because it was the stoicism he had acquired during those unfair, but formative years, which undoubtedly saved Chief's life at Tuy Hoa.

At this particular time, the enemy situation permitted our general to assign us the mission of setting up squad-sized ambushes. It was rice harvesting time at Tuy Hoa and the local VC were sending out small parties who would raid the farmers, steal their rice and then make them and their relatives carry the bundles of rice back to the VC unit's point of origin.

By virtue of the fact that the enemy was operating in fairly small groups, our ambushing tactics worked well. Each rifle company's nine rifle squads when spread out, could cover a very large area. The fly in this ointment was that if one of these twelve man squads ran into a numerically superior enemy, the going, could get furry very quickly.

That is exactly what happened to Chief's squad, which was itself ambushed by a company-sized force just as they were get-ting ready to get into position to set up their own ambush.

Chief had been shot in the head, a grazing wound, as it turned out, which knocked him unconscious and during the melee which followed, he was left behind. He doesn't know to this day whether it was this slug which knocked him unconscious or the many grenade fragments he still carries throughout his body bespeaking the culprit to have been concussion. The result was that his head and face were covered with blood, which led the enemy to believe him to be dead.

What he does know is that when he regained consciousness, it was nearing dusk and two Clydes were sitting on him, chattering their own lingo and eating what appeared to be rice balls. They had evidently taken one look at Chief, with blood congealing through his eyebrows and down his face and were convinced that he was beyond wasting a slug to the base of his skull.

The startled Chief lay perfectly still and scarcely breathed, silently congratulating himself for having not groaned or otherwise given himself away as he regained consciousness. At this point, Chief was in a bad way indeed. He could discern the waning light as the sun inexorably set—probably for the last time as far as he was concerned, he thought wryly.

When I first saw him the following day, he was buck naked and his body was criss-crossed by a plethora of thorn scratches and insect bites, his face appearing as previously described. He was also missing one of his fingers, the stub of which had been neatly tied off with a short length of bootlace as an improvised tourniquet. He had crawled all night through the jungle, using the sound of our mortars as a guide during his trek through the fearful black with the enemy who knew where?

That brave little lion refused morphine and vowed that he would also refuse his pending medevac and return to his unit. Doc couldn't let him do that, in his condition, of course, but he wanted to. While we awaited the dustoff, I fixed him some soup and coffee from my rations. While sipping the coffee, he told Doc and me his story. Doc never wanted to be referred to as "captain" or "sir." He was really entranced by Chief's story, as was I.

At this point, Chief didn't seem to possess a feeling of regret or of persecution. Rather, he was elated to have survived and considered the fortuitous fact that he was still alive to portend that he would soon rejoin his platoon and help to punish Clyde for his sins. I wish that you could have heard his story and seen the look in his eyes, which I shall try my best to convey to you. During sips of coffee, he examined the stub of his finger which Doc had carefully rebound for him.

"They were sittin' on me," he began, "giggling and eating their rice balls and I was scared to death that the two of 'em would catch on an' work me over with their machetes."

All of us knew what Clyde sometimes did to corpses, cutting off ears, hands, genitals and that sort of thing.

"I could see my M-16 lying on the ground beside us," he went on, "and I came close to grabbing for it when the two of them suddenly jumped up and stripped me. I had made up my mind that if they started mutilating me, I'd grab my rifle and light a fire to its muzzle and go out in style."

He told us that after they had taken his watch, they tried to remove his highschool classring off his finger, but he could tell by the feeling that his finger had swollen and that they'd have to cut it off.

"I knew the jig was up," he nodded, "when they couldn't twist it off. I figured to myself, 'uh oh, man, here comes a machete job on all my fingers at once.' I was convinced they'd just lay my hand up on the side of a tree and carelessly whack all the fingers off at once, just to get at my ring."

Doc observed that the pucker factor in the normal human being at such a moment would be enormous.

"Hell's fire," I said admiringly, "how did you keep from -just dying of fright, right there on the spot, Chief?"

"Funny," he smiled, "how I wasn't that scared. I think I had already accepted the fact that I'd be dead as soon as I grabbed my rifle and used up all my ammo anyhow, because there must have been a hundred enemy soldiers eating in that clearing.

"Dead men don't bleed," said Doc matter-of-factly, "you should have bled like a stuck hog when they chopped off that finger, Chief. How'd they miss that?"

Chief said that one of the NVA grabbed that ring finger and laid it up on the side of a tree and cleanly whacked it off with one stroke of his machete and had to run off a few feet and pick up the finger. He said that at about that instant, one of their leaders started shouting something and they all saddled up and immediately left the area. He said that his boots must have been too big for them to use, as they left them behind and he had chewed through the rawhide lace as an improvised tourniquet. He said that he had gotten out of the area as fast as he could, but once it had gotten dark, fearful of the enemy's whereabouts, he had crawled all night long toward the sound of our mortars, afraid to slap at any of a million insects which had bitten him.

"I had to laugh to myself as I crawled along last night," he admitted, "with the kind of luck I have always had, was I now crawling toward the sound of enemy mortars?"

The three of us discerned the sound of the incoming medevac ship and Doc and I shook hands in farewell with Chief.

"You know," he smiled, "they hung that nickname on me in my rifle platoon, and rightfully so—no complaints. But, if the Army lets me come back here from the hospital, I'm gonna insist that everyone calls me 'Chief Seven Fingers' he said merrily, waving his two thumbs in the air, "'cause these two don't count."

What a guy. That medevac crew must have thought we were nuts. Chief looked like he'd just escaped from a butcher shop and there Chief and I were, standing there laughing until the tears rolled down our cheeks and slapping one another on the back.

I boosted Chief aboard and he didn't look back or wave.

I never saw him again, but I'll bet Chief's doing o.k. now. He sure had more than his share of guts.

The Switch

It came as a shock to all of us when we read John D's obituary in the "Killed In Action/Died of Wounds" section of the *Army Times* when the mail clerk brought it to the fire support base for us to read. John D had been one of our bravest troopers and had been hospitalized in Walter Reed Army Hospital at

Washington, D.C., for about four months before we were surprised to find that he had finally succumbed to his wounds.

I asked Doc how a wounded soldier could hang on like that for so long and then die and he explained that sometimes someone with severe liver wounds like John D had suffered, could drag on and on and then suddenly—it's all over.

My mind flashed back to that fateful day, months before when our new Battalion Commander, Colonel Johnnie, had decided it was our turn to fly down to Bravo Company's jungle location and visit them. He had already visited the other three rifle companies, spending the night with them, discussing policies and getting acquainted in general. In my mind's eye, I recollected every facet of that visit and the events which followed, as I do even now. Pete, our expert Huey pilot had a very difficult landing to negotiate, but he had done it many times before and knew exactly what he was doing.

A few days before, the Aviation Company's First Sergeant had told me that Pete was one of the best pilots that he had ever known. He had been shot down twice before and had spent some time in the hospital on the second go-round. His crew trusted his steel nerve under fire. He was a superb Warrant officer, and person in general. As we landed, Colonel Johnnie told him to pick us up here early the following morning and after we jumped off, Pete took off. We were met by Chingo, the acting first sergeant and as he guided us to Bravo's CP area in the gloom of the jungle, I told the colonel that Bravo had lost its share of fine leaders before the colonel's arrival, during the Battle for Hill 830. He asked me for my opinion on how to boost Bravo's morale.

"Relieve their XO back in the rear, sir, and replace him with a seasoned lieutenant whose time is up in the jungle." He stared at me. "It'd be a smart trade, sir. He's new and needs some jungle experience and he is not looking out for the jungle troopers."

I told him to look at Bravo's troops. These poor guys had been wearing the same jungle fatigues now for over forty days, all still caked with the bright yellow clay from Hill 830, which had been gooey from the monsoons.

"The survivors are still wearing what they had on a couple of weeks before 830, sir, and they are cruddy and smell ripe—plus they are half ripped to pieces. As you know, the men wear no socks or underwear, but the jungle is rough on fatigues!"

"Smell me, colonel," laughed Chingo, "I'm one of those cats with the yellow fur." We had to laugh.

"He's tellin' it like it is, sir. And it's complicated by the fact that our brigade rear area in its entirety is currently in the process of moving about 300 miles up from Bien Hoa to An Khe."

Chingo told him that the supply sergeant had rotated to the states and the other supply sergeants were real scroungers, who had already gone to other outfits and gotten fresh fatigues for their troops. He told us that his best jungle fighter, John D, had just returned from the hospital and had been retained by the XO as acting supply sergeant, but he wasn't interested and was itching to get back into Chingo's platoon in the jungle. He said that Bravo's First Platoon Leader had been in the jungle the longest and should be traded for the XO.

The colonel told us that if Bravo's Captain concurred, that we'd have the old lieutenant on the C&C ship with us the following morning. We followed Chingo away from the clearing, down a dark path.

As we approached the CP, Chingo told us to skirt the scout dog as Devil tended to bite strangers! While the colonel talked to the captain, I told Chingo that Bravo's new First Sergeant would be coming in from An Khe in a couple of days and Chingo was happy with the prospect of returning to his platoon. He told me that he could hardly wait until John D returned also.

"Which one's John D, Chingo?" I puzzled.

"John D. The big black corporal who taught you all those tricks with the M-79 Grenade Launcher while we was in that crazy fire support base that got the shit mortared out of it back in June. Remember?"

"How could I forget that. I've carried one ever since, along with this rifle." I patted my velcroed M-79 vest and ran my fingers across its projectiles—three rows of three on each side for a total of eighteen of the death-dealing accurate missiles.

As Chingo and I inspected Bravo's perimeter, he told me that John D operated more like Clyde in the jungle than Clyde did. He and I went around the entire perimeter of Bravo, talking to the troopers as they dug in for the night. When we got back to the CP, the Colonel's RTO, Stan, already had our foxhole about a foot deep, so I told him to take a break while I dug and he snapped our two ponchos together and started to stretch them out as a watertight hootch for the colonel and him and I for the night. He already knew to make sure that the mosquito nets were low enough to keep those hordes out.

The mountain laterite was extremely hard. All of us had tough, calloused hands like leather from digging foxholes. I dug for a couple of hours with Stan spelling me and each of us taking his restful turn holding the sandbags open for the digger. Then we cut bamboo and roofed over our foxhole with sandbags to protect us from mortar or grenade fragments if we got hit.

After this, I went and got with the colonel and worried him until he agreed to break off chewing the fat with the captain and came and ate the "C" rations which Stan had warmed up for us all and then we hit the sack. The colonel had not gotten too much sleep lately and the welfare of our battalion depended upon his maintaining a clear head.

I was awakened just before first light by a stiff breeze stirring the tops of the 200 foot high ancient trees. Most combat troopers sleep like cats. You live longer that way. Some inner sense drives one wide awake at least once each hour. You get so that you can go right back to sleep in just a couple of seconds after ascertaining that all is well.

As any good company does in eminent danger, Bravo Company maintained one hundred percent alert during "standto" a half hour before daybreak and a half hour following it and after standto, Stan and I jointly tore down the hootch and emptied the foxhole's sandbags, refilling it with its own dirt. We replaced the empty sandbags on the outside of our rucksacks and opened some "C" rations to fix for breakfast.

Stan remarked on how lucky he and I were not to have spent the previous night out on ambush or perimeter watch. After humping an eighty-pound rucksack all day long, then digging in for the night, all my troopers had to spend 50 percent of the rest of the night taking their turn at one of the two above mentioned duties. It made for tired bodies and minds, month after month, but my guys did it one day at a time. Stan observed that the rest of the world rocks along, going their merry way, never knowing the rigors of combat, but that once a person had experienced it, he was proud to have been able to accomplish it. Made sense to me.

During the daylight, prior to Bravo's moving out, I went to the CP and spent twenty minutes with Chingo going over the promotion roster for the battalion, showing him where Bravo's troopers stood on it, recording new names for purple hearts into my book and so forth. I reached into my rucksack and pulled out five or six of the little hardbound notebooks and some ball point pens for him to distribute to his leaders.

Right about 0700 hours I heard the faint whopping of Pete's massive rotor as it approached our location and soon he was centered over the small hole in the sky surrounded by the 200 foot high trees, preparing to start his expert descent into our small clearing. You have to ride a chopper down through that hole to believe it. It's like settling down through a well, with the sides of the well being trees and the massive rotor seeming to miss their trunks just by inches. Many a chopper has ended up wrapping the blade around such trees and freefalling to the bottom of that well. Few survived such catastrophes.

When we boarded Pete's chopper, I noted with satisfaction that the First Rifle Platoon Leader was sitting right there beside me.

"Made the grade, huh, lieutenant?" I smiled innocently. He'd never know that I had been instrumental in his change of status.

"Yeah sergeant major—wonder of wonders. I sure hope all my troops have such good luck and survive this war."

He knew, as did I, that U. S. Army policy was that officers would spend only six months in such combat assignments, while enlisted personnel spent the entire year in the jungle. There were exceptions, if the officer volunteered to remain in a rifle platoon or company by extending his Vietnam tour six months at a time, but everything had to be approved through channels.

The theory here of course, was that shorter tours would result in the maximum number of officers receiving the combat training, but the flip side of that was that the rifle troops kept getting new, inexperienced officers and it was a natural inclination to distrust the new leader until he had proven himself under fire. This whole book could have been written about such situations. The majority of new officers realized that as the new kid on the block, one should rely on the advice and guidance of the senior NCO involved, and not come in like a bull in a china shop.

Once in a while we'd run into a meatball who hadn't gotten the word on how to operate and the rifle company's commander or first sergeant would straighten him out.

My mind was jarred back to reality as the draft from our huge rotor blasted debris consisting of woodchips from the troops' axes, all over the LZ, causing troopers to duck their sting as Pete poured the coal to the C&C ship with the powerful surge necessary to negotiate our completely vertical trip back up through that dark well of foliage and tree trunks until we once again emerged triumphantly into the bright sunlight above.

While watching that massive rotor seemingly just missing those treetrunks by inches, I marvelled at Pete's keen visual acumen and steady hand enabling such a difficult ascent under such dire circumstances. I knew Pete and both his great door gunners very well. All three extended their Vietnam tour after my time was up. It was with great sadness and dismay, a few weeks after my own return to the States, that I read where they were missing in action. It's a huge jungled area in wild parts of Vietnam and there are many circumstances caused by foe or accident which can cause a chopper to crash and be hidden completely in some inaccessible area. I never did find out the circumstances surrounding their crash. They were great, brave men.

Upon our emergence from that tiny hole in the trees, within a few seconds, Pete had us skipping merrily along, just a few feet from the top of the bright green, tangled canopy of trees beneath us. I smiled to myself at the joke which Colonel Johnnie had whipped on me only a day or so before when we were making a very early morning recon and Pete had to negotiate a long, thick fog bank on the way to our destination.

"You seem unconcerned and nonchalant, Sergeant Major Arthurs," he spoke over the intercom system which our flight helmets were plugged into, along with Pete and the rest of the crew. "Doesn't Pete scare the pants off you, roaring around here in the blind?"

"No, sir," I scoffed, "I made my peace with the man upstairs a while back on all this stuff. You can't keep sweatin' it out or you'd drive yourself crazy. If you are going to get killed, you are gonna go and if it's not your time to go, you get the brass ring instead of buyin' the farm, sir."

I know Pete was getting a kick out of all this because he laughed out loud when Colonel Johnnie whipped the punch-line on me!

"Yeah," agreed Johnnie, "but don't you go, too, if it's the pilot's turn?"

Darned if he didn't almost get me to worryin' again, but the man upstairs came through for me and I know I owe him forever.

Pete took us up a couple of hundred feet above the canopy and we could see why as we entered a slight bank of fog consisting of those curious vertical long columns of mist which, in the Central Highlands, portended thick fogbanks ahead. I found myself once again thinking of Johnnie's punchline. Visibility got dimmer and dimmer until we were rolling blindly along, seemingly immersed in the center of a feather pillow.

Just as suddenly, we emerged, flying once again through those vertical flecks bordering the other side.

"Top," Johnnie keyed his mike, "Pete'll let me off at the FSB, and then you guys go on into Dakto and trade lieutenants at Bravo and bring John D. back to where he belongs. While you are at it, drop by Headquarters Company and pick up that dud who got drunk the other night and fired off that flare into the ammo dump. Send him with John D. to Bravo. He goes right into a rifle squad when he gets there."

I rogered the transmission and told him that the lieutenant sitting beside me had already figured out who his new supply sergeant would be; a good trooper from his old platoon who was recently returned from the hospital and was in Bravo's rear area awaiting transportation back to the jungle. Johnnie grinned and gave a thumbs-up to Bravo's new XO who was already straightening out the company's biggest problem. Johnnie winked at me. He was giving me tacit credit for having suggested that switch in XOs.

As we landed to let Johnnie off at the FSB, we picked up two of our troopers whom Doc suspected of evincing symptoms of malaria. After the fifteen minute flight to Dakto, Pete sailed us over the large Montagnard village by the river at the west approach to the strip.

"That's the 'happy house'" Buck, the right door gunner pointed to a long hut on stilts, sitting at the village's edge closest to the river. Bravo's new XO had donned the colonel's flight helmet and listened with interest as Buck explained about 'Yards.

"See how the roof is much higher than all the other huts?" Buck continued. "The happy house is where all the bachelors reside. It's a big party every night in there. The little guys drink all this fermented hootch they make, but they never heard of a glass."

"How do they drink it?" queried the young lieutenant.

"Through a long, thin tube-like reed. Smells like formaldehide crossed with rotten eggs," he declared, "and if you get it past yer nose, it ain't half bad, and I mean, that stuff will knock you on yer ass." he smiled knowingly.

"Any hangover?" inquired the lieutenant.

"I don't remember, sir," replied the impish Buck. "Come to think of it, I don't remember nothin' so good the next day after a session with them bachelors in their doggone happy house."

Pete canted the ship toward the airstrip as though to make a run at landing, suddenly veering off course as Buck pointed below us where a huey was streaming madly by at full speed, multi-colored smoke grenades spuming their billowing streams of smoke into the ship's slipstream.

"Old custom among chopper pilots," Buck explained admiringly, "means it's his last flight in Vietnam. He's rotatin' back to the world."

Pete patiently stayed at a safe altitude as the celebrating pilot swiftly turned his ship, once again swooping the entire strip at low altitude until the grenades, one after the other, began exhausting themselves, dissipating one bright stream of smoke after another, the ship once again resuming normal flight, headed toward the parking pads. Somehow, the fireworks seemed fitting to such an occasion, befitting the return of a brave pilot to his loved ones. I thought it was great.

"He'll get his ass chewed for it," Pete intoned into the intercom, "once he lands, but it don't mean nothin' 'cause the next pilot to rotate will do the same damn thing—no matter what."

I wondered if the senior pilot who would be doing all that ass-chewing would spew his own smoke when the time came. I'd bet on it.

As we settled on our designated pad by the airstrip, Pete turned and looked questioningly at me. I drew my forefinger across my throat and he cut the engine. As the whirling rotor grew slower and slower, I told him that it might be a golden opportunity for him and his crew to enjoy some hot chow at our rear area's mess tent, where the lucky cooks and rear area personnel got two meals daily of fresh food while the boonie rats got one every fifth night.

Buck stood by with the tether to throw over the rotor as soon as it stopped spinning. It grew slower and slower, finally stopping with a wavering motion, then suddenly changing its mind, making a counter-rotation in the opposite direction for about a half a turn, then stopping for good. This was something new to the lieutenant as Buck expertly slung the tether over the rotor. I explained to him that in such a congested parking area, the wash from other landing ships could snatch the rotor upward and the last thing that anyone wanted was to fly around in a ship with a damaged rotor.

I told Pete that we were looking at about an hour and a half for departure time, and escorted the two malaria victims down the strip to the clinic and during this ten minute walk I gave them my standard lecture regarding malaria. I explained that one trooper from the First Bat had died of falciparum malaria scant days before and admonished them that if it turned out that they were lucky enough to have only contracted vivax malaria, that they could thank their lucky stars and to quit playing games regarding malaria prevention once they returned to the jungle. Smart guys who wanted to get out of the jungle, would "tongue" the pills administered by their platoon's medic, pretending to swallow them, in order to contract vivax and get a month's "rest" in the hospital.

"The game," I explained, "is Russian roulette in the Central Highlands. Unlike the rest of Vietnam, this place is crawling with Falciparum, which can kill you in a heartbeat, or, can burn up just enough of your brain to where for the rest of your life, you keep forgetting things—like whether or not a full house beats a flush. Don't listen to these jackasses who tell you to tongue your pill. They might have pulled it off down in the delta or over on the coastlands, but you are really askin' for it up here in the highlands."

They both looked sufficiently worried as I turned them over to the senior medic at the small clinic by the strip, and headed toward Headquarters Company's rear area. It turned out later that one had vivax and the other almost died of falciparum.

Our messtent was located in the Headquarters Company area, and when Lynn, the Mess Sergeant saw me coming, he told one of the cooks to fix me my favorite snack; a sandwich with a thick slice of bologna and a half-inch slice of onion, with a canteen cup filled with cold powdered milk.

"You've found a home in this Army, Wolf," reproved Lynn, "you are the sergeant major. You can have a steak sandwich, with iced tea. And look at your idea of a feast! I'll tell ya, I think you've been over here too long!"

I sent one of the guys for the first sergeant with the message for the meatball who had almost blown up the ammo dump to quickly pack his ruck sack and to put plenty of ammo in it, because he was going to need it in Bravo Company.

I was still enjoying my sandwich when Owen brought the miscreant to me.

"He's had his ruck packed since the night it happened, Wolf," said First Sergeant Owen Schroeder with a chuckle.

I looked at the sober and sorry former clerk and told him to go to Bravo's supply tent and to tell John D. to pack his rucksack, that I was on my way down there in about twenty minutes. Owen had fought in World War II, Korea and in the jungle. Next to him, I was the oldest man in the Fourth Bat. He had been hit by a ricochet a few weeks before on Hill 830 and that's how Chingo had come to be Bravo's acting first sergeant. The nearly spent bullet had hit Owen in the back, nestling between his ribs and skin and he had humped his eighty-pound rucksack for several days, wondering what the knot was until the medics cut it out.

I didn't have to fight him to pull him out of the jungle and put him in the rear area where he belonged. The law of averages were inexorably piling up on Owen. He was a helluva man.

We shot the breeze for a few minutes and I headed for Bravo to get John D.

Wait until you see the kind of jungle fighter that John D. was.

The Saga of John D.

John D. had his ruck packed and was waiting for me when I got to Bravo Company's rear area. He and I and the ammo dump meatball made our way to the chopper pad where we had about a ten minute wait for Pete and his crew to show up from eating chow. John D. told me that his favorite pastimes had always been hunting, fishing and basketball, in that order. Built like a tree, the huge black corporal had to be the tallest trooper in the 4th Bat.

Bravo's old XO was staying one more night in the rear, so that he could brief the lieutenant from the jungle. The rest of us were soon airborne, winging it back toward our jungle fire support base and as soon as Pete landed, I took John D. and the ammo dump guy up the slope to see Lieutenant Colonel Johnnie. He was sitting on some sandbags right outside his little tent, marking his map with a grease pencil and readily agreed to talk to the two men, one at a time. I told John D. to go and see Stan, the RTO and to tell him I was back while Colonel Johnnie gently read the riot act to the kid who had almost blown up our ammo dump. Johnnie seldom raised his voice. He didn't have to! First, he patiently explained to the ex-clerk that his folly within the ammo dump was an exercise in stupidity which could have caused a lot of friendly casualties and that he had wrestled with the idea of incarcerating him in the "LBJ"—the Long Binh Jail—but had decided to let him earn his way out of that jungle instead.

When it was John D's turn, Johnnie praised him for his fine combat record mentioning that he had recently approved a Bronze Star For Valor recommendation on John D's behalf, to higher HQ.

A couple of weeks went by, during which time Bravo's new first sergeant arrived and Chingo went happily back to his platoon with John D. and his other four dozen riflemen.

I already covered Chingo's exploits on Hill 823. This is an extension of that battle, in explanation of some of John D's amazing feats. If you remember, a superior force of NVA had us surrounded and were busily bellying up to us around our perimeter. It was late in the afternoon of 6 November, 1967 before we got the more seriously wounded troopers evacuated. We were still being sniped at frequently and we lost a fine soldier as he was carrying a wounded trooper to safety from just a few yards outside the perimeter. The wounded trooper was also killed at that time.

They were all over the place. Right before dusk, I accompanied a great sergeant, Larry K. Ohda and his squad in locating a fine lieutenant and seven of his men who were missing. As we suspected, they had been ambushed and those not killed outright had been wounded and overrun and dispatched with a close shot at the nape of the neck. Anyway, Larry O. and I figured we could carry all those guys back up to the perimeter in two trips and we hadn't gone thirty yards outside the perimeter when we heard the fuse pop nearby on an NVA grenade.

"Grenade!" Larry yelled, "Get down!"

Just as he did, several things happened simultaneously. I remember seeing the grenade floating lazily in slow motion toward us and just before it exploded, an enemy soldier jumped up and let us have the entire magazine of his AK-47. The slugs whopped harmlessly just over our heads as Larry killed the enemy.

Later, Larry commented that the dumb-assed enemy rifleman had done everything in reverse. Had he shot first, with all of us still standing, he would have gotten some of us for sure, instead of Larry getting him. Larry was one of the few of my sergeants who made it through O.K. after what happened to my battalion in the next seventeen days. What a fine NCO, but so were the rest of them.

Just at dusk, the NVA mortared our perimeter. This is a clever tactic designed to make your enemy keep his head down while you swiftly move groups of riflemen up close to the perimeter where they are immune to enemy mortars, artillery and gunships. You could actually hear their equipment jostling around as they quickly moved those last few yards toward us.

It was going to be a long, interesting night. The company commander passed the word to immediately cease all digging. Otherwise, on about the third "tunk" of a digging entrenching tool, that soldier would immediately receive a live grenade for his indiscretion. This will definitely get your attention.

I crawled quietly to the next position and noted with satisfaction that John D. was our neighbor on our left side. Chingo was at the CP coordinating with the company commander and Jeff, the dog handler and Vicki, his beautiful German Shepherd, were setting up on the position Chingo had chosen for the four of us. John D. had a half dozen grenades sitting on top of his rucksack, with his M-79 leaning against it, its muzzle ensconced in a sandbag.

"Got a flechet round down its tube, Wolf," he whispered. He was wearing a .45 pistol he had scrounged from a previous battle and cradled his M-16 rifle across one knee. He was an expert with every one of them.

"What do you think," I whispered, "of the price of rice in Hanoi, John?" He stifled a giggle.

"See that little gully comin' up through that bamboo out yonder?" he whispered. I squinted my eyes because by this time it was getting pretty dark and finally I saw what he meant.

"Yeah. It's not too far from ussens to them'uns considerin' that gully to be them'uns, John."

"Well, I got somethin' fer their asses. If I was ole Clyde, I'd damn sure try an' crawl up that gully. I got some empty ration cans with little stones in 'em tied up around twigs with string in that gully an' up above that, I've got me a Claymore Mine set up." He handed me the wire to feel, that ran from his rucksack to the mine.

"One tinkle from those cans," he giggled "an' I'll give 'em a few seconds an then the last sound ole Clyde hears is gonna be a loud one."

I shook his hand and turned to crawl off. He caught hold of my jacket and told me that all the troops were tickled to know that the sergeant major and battalion XO were both out in this hot spot with them and that it gave their morale a shot in the arm. I patted him on the shoulder and quietly crawled back to where Chingo now was, with Jeff and our hound.

At this point, any talking around our entire perimeter was done in guarded whispers. Chingo was back from the CP and Jeff was catching some Z's in anticipation of taking his turn on radio watch that night as Chingo's RTO had been one of the wounded evacuated earlier and the three of us would be taking turns all night long.

"Psst, Ted," he whispered, "Vicki's as nervous as a kid makin' his first night jump. Somethin' terrible's workin' up out front. Put yer paws on her once an' see for yourself."

It was true. She was a nervous wreck. She was sitting upright, taut as a bowstring and her eyes and ears must have been really straining in the dark, not to mention the messages which her cold, wet nose was sending to her brain. Chingo and I were probably lots better off not knowing what she knew, or we'd have had heart failure. I told Chingo that there were some Clydes who were certain to meet their maker tonight if they tried to sneak up that gully to John D.'s front.

"Yeah," he chuckled, "an' if their maker's the same one we got, we've got a good chance o' JOININ' em, buddy-row, the way Vik's actin' up. How many grenades ya got?"

We had sixteen between us, counting the ones I had taken from the first sergeant as he was being evacuated. He had told me to keep his rucksack as he didn't need it in the hospital and I had jumped off the C&C ship with just my rifle and M-79 and vest, but my own ruck was still back in the FSB. We knew that Jeff had at least eight, so Chingo decided to crawl over to John D.'s position and to give him four, because of the gully, in case the NVA poured out of it like a herd of turtles.

When he got back, I crawled the forty feet to our rear to the CP, which should always be further than that from the perimeter, out of grenade range, but this was a skinny perimeter, with the CP located in the bottom of one of the bomb craters.

I told Major Dick Scott, our fine 4th Bat XO and Captain Ron Leonard, Bravo's new commander, about some of the activity which Vicki was picking up on and they told me that Colonel Johnnie was going to try and lay a ring of steel around us that night with artillery and Spooky, the C-47 with its Gatlin Guns—which was music to my ears. We all knew, however, that the fat was in the fire with all those NVA bellied up to us. What it all translated to was that for our artillery or gunships to reach them, they had to reach us, TOO! That firepower would prevent enemy reinforcements, but like a head full of lice, the ones we already had were the ones we couldn't get rid of. We had wall-to-wall Clydes around us, each one with a pack full of grenades, it would seem in short order.

It was good and dark by the time I had crawled back to our little position on the perimeter, and as I started to impart my recently acquired knowledge to Chingo, we were interrupted as a close friendly artillery round from one of our batteries at our FSB made us duck as it sloshed in, splattering red hot shrapnel all through the bamboo around us. Some pieces were close enough to splash us with the warm water contained internally within live bamboo stalks. Soon thereafter, Spooky arrived on the scene and flew a constant circle overhead, lacing probable areas of enemy troop concentrations. Spooky sits up there at a couple of thousand feet, and when he starts to hosing down the area with those guns, it is something to see and to HEAR! First he drops a flare so that the gunners don't shoot up the friendly area. As he makes his approach nearest to you and belches his fire and brimstone, it sounds as though a gigantic foghorn has been turned on!

"HHOOOOOOOOOOORRRRRRUUUUMMMMM" thousands upon thousands of rounds of machine gun fire sprays into the suspected area. In the black of night, we could glimpse myriad red hot tracers melting together to form a solid cascade resembling molten lava. We could only see him when he crossed our cleared portion of the jungle. Spooky kicked out another flare, which brightly lit the entire area as we squinted into the eerie bamboo shadows around us, straining for a sight of the enemy we knew was there. "HHOOOOOOOOOOOR-RRRRUUUUMMMMM" more molten death poured into the hills surrounding us. This was very sound tactics, considering the fact that there were several regiments of enemy in the immediate vicinity and any one of a plethora of hiding places could be harboring a nearby enemy force which was gathering to overrun our small unit through sheer force of numbers and kill every one of us.

"HHODOOOOODOORRRRRUUUUUUUUUMMMM-MMM"—music to the ears of our poor combat soldiers lying there with fear in their hearts of being overrun. As the hours trickled slowly by, the chill of the night air was accentuated by the cold of the ground as the temperature dropped to that which was appropriate to the mountains of Dakto in November.

Poor Jeff, Vicki's handler, was sawing logs and I didn't have the heart to awaken him, so I stood his radio watch, too. All night long Clyde cracked fuses on Chicom grenades and heaved them at our troopers all around the perimeter. Every few minutes you could hear a fuse being activated—very similar to the sound of cracking a beercan's tab. This is guaranteed to raise your hackles.

We had a lot of activity in our vicinity, starting about midnight.

"CHHT" from somewhere near our left front, "clackity-clack" through the bamboo, one came "ALLAAM"—it busted right in front of John D.'s position. "CHHT-clakity-clack-clack-BA-LAMM" right to our right front. Then "CHHT-CHHT-CHHT-clackity-clack RAMM-RAA-RAMM"—three of them burst directly to our front, sending singing shards of death around us.

A Chicom—Chinese Communist—grenade in the pitch black of the jungle night lights up an area about the size of your bedroom to white hot intensity and a much larger area to a limited degree. If you turn your head sideways on the ground and watch it explode at night, it spews—in addition to the concussion—an awe-inspiring cascade of pinkish white fragments and burning material that somehow might remind you of a miniature cascade of molten steel you have seen being poured from a ladle in a steel mill.

Our captain immediately had his Weapons Platoon to crank in some 81mm mortar rounds and bring them in as close to us as he dared. Right in the middle of this barrage, John D. shot and killed two NVA riflemen with the same M-79 flechet round. They were both crawling at the time, very close to one another, and only two or three yards to his front. Since this vicious round contains a bunch of miniature steel darts, it is comparable to a very healthy shell being fired from a mammoth shotgun barrel. That same round undoubtedly wounded other enemy who were crawling along behind their buddies.

"Here they come!" John D. screamed, grabbing the activation device to his Claymore mine facing down the gully and squeezing it enough times to detonate the mine with an earth-shaking blast. The light from the mine disclosed four more enemy to our immediate right. Chingo and the now awakened Jeff and I all seemed to fire simultaneously on full automatic and got them all with our M-16s.

Some more came pouring out of John D's gully. They must have been too far behind the Claymore blast to be affected, but as they appeared, John D. fed them two more grenades and two flechet rounds, with immediate results. We heard more screams and an immediate scuttling around to our front resulting in us getting two more incoming grenades and some AK-47 fire. Chingo and I each tossed a grenade into that area, which quieted down.

The two men on the other side of John D.'s position had their hands full from the sound of it. The captain brought our mortars in a lot closer and he must have cut up a bunch of them out there judging from all the screaming.

There were still some a lot closer to us, as we could hear the moaning of the enemy wounded in the darkness nearby. About this time, the enemy probed the southwestern portion of our perimeter and they had fun and games over there for about a half hour or so. Our mortars got quite a few of the probing NVA, with only one of our own men being slightly wounded by the closely striking rounds.

During this same period, we had a couple of comedians somewhere out in front of us, one of whom spoke a little English. One was off to the left of John D and one was directly out to our front. They put on a show for about an hour for us all. The one directly to our front was either psycho, or high on dope—maybe both! He was a hair raiser.

"YIIIEEEE," he'd shriek, "Die, G.I., die. YAAAAAH-HHRRRR. Die, G.I., die! Heee heeeee!" He only knew two English words, but he was getting everyone's attention.

Jeff's theory was that both of the screamers were squad leaders, and that the screaming back and forth was their way of coordinating a forthcoming probe. The second guy, we nicknamed the English Professor. HE was a real nut.

"YEEEE," he'd holler, "YeeeEEEHHHEEEE!" You die, I die, we die. Chop-chop-machete-chop!" over and over again, and he was a real attention-getter.

It's a very scary situation to be surrounded by a large force of determined fanatics whose only goal was to overrun us and kill and chop up every last man.

When daylight came, it was easily determined that John D had certainly killed more than his share of the attacking force of NVA Infantrymen. This one man Army survived Hill 823, only to be shot through the liver on Hill 875 just about two weeks later.

John D. was a hero of the first degree, and it was a great honor to serve with him.

For John D. the battles for Dakto had finished. There were more to come.

Dedicated to the memory of
Corporal John Davis Willingham

Winchester's Round Trip

Winchester was almost human. Thinking back on it now, I am convinced of it. When I first met him, however, I could have sworn he was a pig. He certainly closely resembled most of the other semi-wild pigs which hung around the big Montagnard Village located about two miles from the Dakto Airstrip.

Our 4th Bat had recently participated in some fierce battles and needed 335 replacements, so our general moved us near the Dakto Airstrip. We had it made for about three days, sleeping on cots in twelve man tents, taking showers, eating fresh cooked food and my men even got to attend outdoor movies at night.

This would be one of two times during my year as sergeant major that my men were brought out of the jungle for a short rest. The second time was just for one overnight stay. My troops had just spent eight months of steadily humping the rucksack, eating "C" rations, with one meal of freshly cooked rations every fifth night being flown into them by "firefly" resupply choppers.

For this reason, Colonel Johnnie had been in the outfit for several weeks and never once seen his own battalion mess! On this particular day when I first met Winchester, the colonel had gone to the mess tent for a cup of coffee and had just returned.

"How long," he asked, "have you been in the Army, Sergeant Major Arthurs?"

"Right at twenty-two years, sir. How 'bout you?" I had him by five years.

"Have you," he laughed, "ever seen a pig in a messtent before?"

"Heck no. Wait a minute, sir. Two legged or four egged?" He laughed his head off at that one!

"Are you, or are you not," he probed, "believin' that we have a real live, cruddy stinkin' razorback hawg meanderin' around in our mess kitchen, like he owns the place?"

"Gee, sir," I was shocked by such a prospect, "could he have come from that Montagnard Village?"

"Exactly. Probably found his way over here, saw what a good deal that mess kitchen is, got hooked on the garbage and now you couldn't blast 'im out of there. How 'bout if you have some guys catch that hawg and have Stanley take him to the village in his jeep?" I nodded and hollered for Stanley.

"Come on, Stanley. Now we're nursemaidin' hawgs."

"Look, Top," Johnnie laughed, "you don't have to catch the pig. But you speak a little of the local lingo and that might help in taking the pig back."

"I don't mind, sir. I was just kidding. I have to buy one of those doggone Montagnard crossbows for my boy and some brass bracelets and stuff for my daughters anyhow. Those 'yards crack me up. I learn something new each time I get around them!" Colonel Johnnie asked me to buy a crossbow for his own son, also. Stanley was the colonel's RTO in the jungle and had never seen his jeep before and probably would never see it again, once we got the replacements and headed for the jungle. He drove up with the jeep and we drove to the mess area. In retrospect now, thinking about catching that pig, I remember my mother one time telling me about an old Welsh recipe for a rabbit dinner. It began, "First, catch the rabbit . . ."

Lynn, our mess sergeant, was gone for a few minutes and Stan and I saw the pig and set about planning our strategy. Don't ever try and catch a pig in a mess tent. This pig only looked to weigh about thirty-five or forty pounds, but he was all dynamite, believe me.

"Now," whispered Stan, "let ME have first go at ketchin' this here pig. Ya gotta sorta nonchalantly sidle up to' im like ya ain't really trying to ketch him or nothin' like-an'—gotcha!"

With one flying leap, Stan snatched that pig by one leg and it flew sideways with a horrific squeal, upsetting a three-legged Montagnard stool upon which the baker had just placed one of those huge rectangular Army issue pie pans. The trouble with that was that it contained piping hot pumpkin pie, fresh from the oven.

You ought to have heard the howling out of both Stan and the pig when that hot pumpkin hit them. Stan released the death grip he had on the pig, which went one way, bowling over the screened bread box and Stan yelled and jumped backwards, flipping the hot pumpkin off his hands and arms and in so doing, he backed into a huge serving receptacle full of freshly mashed potatoes, turning it upside down in the chow line.

Lynn, the mess sergeant, came running in along about then and couldn't believe his eyes! His kitchen was a complete shambles! Horrified, he stood there dumbly contemplating the magnitude of the damage while Stan and I ran outside, following the squealing pig, which looked to be exceeding the speed of sound—down through the 4.2 Mortar Platoon's area. I yelled at the mortarmen to join us and eventually we had twelve or fifteen of those paratroopers chasing that doggone pig around.

By the time they finally pinned him, it took three of them to hold him down because of the slippery pie filling he was still covered with. One guy brought up a puptent rope and we tied his legs and threw him into the jeep and moved out for the Yard village. We found out later that Lynn had taken a grease pencil to some cardboard and spelled out a huge sign for the chow line which read:

"Chow delayed two hours. Courtesy of the sergeant major and Stanley."

I could imagine that he and the cooks were cussing up a storm and I couldn't blame them. Stan and I took the pie covered pig to the village and someone got the chief. He in turn, sent for an interpreter who didn't do much good, but finally we got the message to him that he was getting his pig back and we wanted two crossbows and trinkets which we'd pay for. The chief acted real glad to get the pig and for the economy boosts.

By the time we got back to our area, the story had circled the entire globe about Stan and me and the pig wrecking the mess and it having taken half the battalion to catch one scrawny pig. Colonel Johnnie harassed me about it quite a bit and I gave him my firm stand concerning future pig escapades.

Chow was finally served—quite late—and it came as no big surprise to me when Lynn asked to speak to me when I had finished supper. He told me that we had just set the messhall back at least six months and I apologized, but told him that we had been under orders to capture that pig. He understood and said that wasn't the problem. There was plenty of pie and mashed potatoes.

I couldn't figure out what his beef was at that point. I had been his first sergeant for years in different airborne rifle companies and I could tell that he was dead serious. He was the best mess sergeant I had ever had and I wanted to make amends if I could.

"You know Slim, our first cook, don't you, Wolf?"

Everybody knew Slim. He had been in the 4th Bat longer than anyone else and after three wounds in a rifle squad, he had been moved to the rear and became a cook. He was absolutely the hardest working and the nicest cook that you ever saw. I nodded.

"Well," he continued, "he was goin' down tomorrow to sign an extension for another six months, but that was before you guys kidnapped Winchester an' now he's not—"

"Kidnapped whochester?"

"Winchester!" Lynn smiled that little smile of his, "Slim's pet pig, Winchester. I thought you knew all about him, Wolf. Honest." I shook my head dumbly.

"I know it sounds screwy, Wolf, keeping a pig around a mess is frowned upon but the doggone troops didn't mind an' they all liked Winchester. He can do some swell tricks and—"

"No, Lynn. Hell no. No pigs in the mess area. That colonel would have both our hides if you ever got written up for it and that's it. I'm sorry if Slim won't extend, but in his case, it's either him or us.

He turned on the soft soap. He said that all these years we'd been together, that the troops always trusted me to represent them in a fair manner. He suggested that we retrieve the pig and build it a sandbagged pen away from the mess. He looked at me entreatingly, his long, lanky frame accentuating his lean weather-beaten face as he appealed to me. I thought to myself about some of the great hunting trips he and I had taken around Fort Campbell, Kentucky. He had been born and raised in nearby Hopkinsville. He had never asked me for much before.

"Well, I don't know, Lynn," I offered.

He knew he had me at that point and pressed it. He asked me to please come back into the cooks' tent and talk to Slim, so I followed him. Some of the off duty cooks were playing poker back in the rear of the tent, but Slim was lying on his canvas cot, just staring up at the vast ceiling of the tent. He got up when I spoke to him and just stood there looking embarrassed. He bit his lower lip and looked at the deck of the tent. I noted with amazement that he had been crying and his eyes were all red.

Lynn told Slim to tell me the story about Winchester, from start to finish and that perhaps I could figure a way, for him to keep his pet. We all sat on cots across from one another and the tall black haired Slim folded his arms and looked very serious as he began.

"Well, sir, when I was in Bravo Company, we was cleanin' out some spider holes full of Clydes near this hamlet. I was in the forward element and we was feedin' hand grenades to the holes, ya know? All in all we was still under fire an' the situation was pretty furry. Ya know what I mean?"

We nodded. Slim continued his story. He said he heard and saw a quick rustle in the thick, high grass only about eight or ten yards to his front.

"Well, you bin through this sort of stuff before, Top. You know a smart rifleman can't take no chances with nothin' at a time like that or he kin dang sure become a dead rifleman an' real fast. Right?" We agreed. "So," he went on, "I cut down on that area immediately an' emptied my rifle on full automatic—I mean I dumped that entire magazine in a few seconds as I could've been dead in a instant if I hadn't done it." It sounded reasonable to me!

"How many of 'em did you get, Slim?" I asked.

"All of 'em. Kilt all 'cept three an' two of them was so badly wounded, I just hadda go on an' finish 'em off. Winchester was the only one of the litter who survived. He's a orphan now, just like me. So ya see, I made a orphan outta him an so now he's my responsibility."

"You mean," I laughed in surprise, "there was a passle of doggone pigs in there?"

"Yep," he said, "a mama pig musta bin nursin' her litter. Why, one round might'a got most o' those piggies as they was all lined up like that! Anyhow, I took Winnie an' put him in my ruck an' carried 'im off. Fed 'im "C" rations an' all."

"You," I shuddered in disbelief, "carried a pig on top of an eighty-pound rucksack?"

He shook his head matter-of-factly. "A orphan pig. 'Course he weren't near as heavy as he is now—probably went four or five pounds was all, I'd guess."

"What about all that squealin' and givin' away the column's location, Slim?"

"He never done it," declared Slim. "Winnie is a natural borned trooper. Plus he's a trained pig. They's a big difference in him an' regular pigs. He started out so young, he just naturally fell in step with the rest of us. He's smart as a whip an kin do tricks a-plenty an' he's as clean as most jungle troopers."

He told me that he took Winnie to the shower point with him and he scrubbed him at the same time as he scrubbed himself. Lynn nodded his head, his eyes mirroring the amusement he had felt when witnessing such a spectacle at the shower point!

"O.K." I looked from him to Lynn and back, "You've convinced me. Now, I'll have to convince the colonel to let you have your pig back—but—the deal is that the first time he wanders into that mess." I made a cutthroat sound and gesture. "Porkchops. Is it a deal?"

Slim looked horrified at the prospect of such cannibalism, but nodded that he concurred.

"Gee, thanks, sergeant major. Where's Winnie now?"

Lynn and I looked at one another. I suddenly visualized Winchester to be already butchered and resting on the Montagnard Chief's dinner table with an apple in his mouth!

I told Slim to get his steel pot and weapon and to run down the hill and have Stan to bring the jeep and as he was getting his gear, I told him the whereabouts of his pig and he almost tore the tent down getting out of there to go and get Stan.

I told Lynn that we might have to unload Slim's rifle if we got to the village and found that the pig had been eaten. Those Yards are pretty old-fashioned about pigs. Even orphan pigs. As soon as Stan arrived, we all boarded the jeep and headed for the village. On the way, Slim told us all that his ambition was to stay in Vietnam until he had saved a down payment on a small Kentucky farm.

"Then, too," he looked pensive, "Winnie's air fare to Kentucky is going to cost a lot."

Stan grinned from ear to ear at this prospect and almost ran off the road. Lynn and I looked at each other and struggled to keep a straight face at this idea of shipping Winchester by air from Vietnam to Kentucky.

"We've only got each other," he declared. "I can't put a price on his friendship an' that's all they is to it."

We arrived at the best place to park near the village, dismounted at the swiftly running stream and walked across the rickety wooden and bamboo bridge leading to the edge of the village. No one could find the interpreter. Someone got the chief and we started a powwow. He couldn't get much at all out of my Vietnamese. The Yards speak their own lingo and not much of it is Vietnamese.

The old chief and I were making some headway. With a little oinking here and there and a lot of sign language, he finally grinned and nodded his head up and down about a hundred times and motioned for us to follow him. That, in itself is enough to crack you up. When a Montagnard makes the 'follow me' motion, it is just exactly the opposite of the motion we make. Rather, it resembles the motion an American mother teaches a baby to make when waving 'bye byes.' That means, "come here" or "follow me."

We all laughed and followed the chief to the stream and instead of crossing the bridge to where our jeep sat, he turned left down a path through some thick bamboo which bordered the stream. We went a hundred or so yards and came out onto a small swampy area.

Finally we came to a big wallow which must have contained three dozen pigs of all sizes, shapes and assortments. They were all wallowing around in that filthy stinking mud, squealing and rolling and playing and having a good time in general. Most of them looked exactly like Winchester to my uninitiated eye.

"There's Winnie," pointed Slim joyously, "see him? With those four in that group over on the right."

"Here, Winnie, here, Winnie PHHHHHEEEEEET" he whistled, "come on, boy!"

Suddenly one of the pigs in the group he had indicated, straightened up, all covered in mud and slime, squealed and made a beeline for us. He was filthy and stinking from head to hoof and gamboling about Slim on his hind feet, looking for all the world like an excited Dachshund in a butcher shop.

The rest of us were trying to keep out of Winnie's way. Along about this time, the chief said something in broken Vietnamese.

"Toi muen piastre." He said it over and over again, grinning amiably, gesticulating all the while. At Lynn's urging, Slim had picked up his mucky orphan and dropped him into a pool in the stream, and was cleaning him off.

I was listening, carefully to the old Montagnard Chief, who was speaking a broken mixture of French, Vietnamese and what must have been his own tribe's dialect of Montagnard.

"What's the old feller sayin'?" asked Lynn.

"He's holdin' Winchester for ransom," I laughed, "in at least three different languages. Possession's nine points of the law, that sort of thing. He wants coins for Winchester!"

"How much does he want?" Lynn grinned at the prospect of us being held up by the simple old fellow.

"Eighteen hundred piastre," I replied, "about fifteen bucks." Lynn's grin faded.

"Tell him we'll give him three hundred, Wolf."

I did, and after much haggling, we settled upon four hundred "P." Stanley had the piastre and I gave him five dollars in script for it and paid the old man, whose ancient wrinkled face and eyes brightened as he gave us the nod that Slim could have his orphan back.

"I ain't believin' this shit, Wolf," laughed Stan, as he cranked the jeep. "That was about a quick four hundred 'P' for that old duffer! You give him the pig in the mornin' an' he holds us up an' sells it back to ya in the evenin'." I looked at the happy Slim and the happy Lynn and the super-ultra-happy Winchester.

"Storage, Stan, storage. Cheap at any price. Whizz by the shower point and drop Slim an' ole Winchester off, as it's their turn. Then take us home. They can walk across the strip."

I thought Colonel Johnnie was going to bust a gut when I told him the whole tale. He just roared.

"You gave that old Chief five bucks to ransom that cruddy ole stinkin' pig, Top?"

"Right, sir. A orphan pig—one which kin do swell tricks an'—"

"Yeah," he jeered, "like makin' good chow disappear an' gettin' me in hot water if the food inspector's report ever lands on our commanding general's desk. He wiped his eyes and laughed some more.

"Also, sir," I hastily added, "You mean that WE gave that dear old feller the five bucks. We didn't want to disrupt local relationships did we? We're supposed to be winnin' hearts and minds here, aren't we?"

He withdrew his wallet and good-naturedly gave me three dollars toward the ransom money and also paid me for his son's crossbow.

He said he'd be glad to get back into that nice, quiet jungle.

As I recall now, when I returned to the U.S. a few months later, Winchester looked a lot heftier than he had when we kidnapped him.

I lost track of Slim and Winchester and never did find out if they made it to their little farm in Kentucky.

Dedicated to the memory of S/Sgt Duard Lynn Adams

CHAPTER 11

Doc

Doc was the best surgeon there ever was. Although he was a captain, he had little patience with all that military courtesy stuff which entranced other officers.

He lived under a poncho with Stanley and me! At twenty eight, Stan was the same age as Doc, while I had them both by ten years.

Doc stayed in the Army after Vietnam, but Stan didn't. He was a great radio operator, though.

The three of us went anyplace the colonel did, except when one company was slated for an extra hazardous mission, at which time Doc and I would join it.

He saw more than his fair share of the horrors of war in his capacity as our battalion surgeon.

Normally, the colonel would be in our jungle fire support base, with easy access to our Tactical Operations Center which was a CONEX container, easily slung below a chopper for quick transport.

Doc was an easy-going giant, having played football in college and built about like a chimney. Stan and I used to harass Doc because we could do more pushups than he. I used to conduct calisthenics for the three of us each morning, and following one such session, we got on Doc's nerves with our friendly taunts.

"Let's hit the outside of that perimeter there," he challenged caustically, "and I'll take on both of you pushup champs in a little free for all wrestlin' match."

Stan, who was smaller than each of us merrily raised his eyebrows and grinned at the prospect of any two guys taking on Doc—let along two guys our size. But, what the heck! There's not much entertainment in the jungle unless you manufacture some for yourself.

We had cause to regret taking on Doc, because he tossed us around like ragdolls until he tripped over a vine and both of us gleefully pounced on him, rolling around.

Well, it was one of those with huge thorns like barbed wire growing out the sides of the vine and by the time the three of us finished thrashing around in the whole bunch of vines, we looked like we had received a direct hit with an 82mm mortar.

Things got worse as we walked back to the edge of the perimeter to re-enter it.

"Uh oh," said Doc, "Poison ivy, men." This was his nickname for our new major who stayed back in the rear all the time as it was his job to supervise the staff back there.

The major was kind of strict, or you might say straitlaced about regulations and we knew that he'd take a very dim view of a captain and sergeant major wrestling around on the ground with a buck sergeant like Stan.

There he stood, tapping his foot at the clearing's edge, eyeing the three of us disdainfully.

"Firin' squad's comin'" whispered Doc, which set Stan off to laughing uproariously, which didn't help our situation one whit.

"Crank up your radio," the major told Stan, "and report to the TOC, as they are having radio trouble." As Stan took off on the double for the poncho hootch which the three of us shared, the major eyed Doc and me disapprovingly.

"You two," he snorted, "come with me to see the colonel."

Our colonel's tent was about five times the size of your bathtub. Easily portable, we simply chopped bamboo for its poles wherever we went. He was sitting at his field desk, doing some writing as we approached its open flaps.

"Look a' them, sir," he pointed to our bloodied faces, hands and arms, "a captain and a sergeant major. Rolling around on the ground like—like privates—and with your radio operator, too, sir."

"Stanley?" says our surprised lieutenant colonel.

"Yes, sir," nodded the irate major. "I got suspicious when I saw the three of them walk outside the perimeter without their weapons or steel pots, sir. Look what one soldier with an AK-47 could have done to the battalion with one burst, sir."

The colonel looked at me with that look he gives when he is about to burst out in laughter, which wasn't often, given our tactical situation! Then, he turned the look on Doc!

"Sir," began Doc, "the Wolf, here, was just showin' Stanley and me some holds because he used to instruct hand-to-hand, and we—"

"That's B.S. sir, they were all three fighting. I saw it all as plain as day. Also, captain, this is our sergeant major, here—not the Wolf—even though he wears no stripes, lets even the privates call him Wolf and he—"

Colonel Johnnie held up his hand. He told the major that we were not on parade and that he was happy with the rapport which I enjoyed with the men. Then he dismissed me and Doc and kept the major there for a little chat.

Neither of them ever mentioned the incident to Doc or to me again, and eventually the major became a lot more down to earth in his dealings with the three of us. He turned out to be a very fine combat officer, but him being new to our ways, I guess I had destroyed some of his illusions about what a parade ground sergeant major should look and act like. The powers that be considered Vietnam to be a training ground for officers, I suppose.

For this reason, officers were rotated, after six months, from combat assignments, to be replaced by new ones—usually neophytes.

As a result, for example, I had three different lieutenants colonel as battalion commander of the 4th Bat during my year as its sergeant major.

Enlisted personnel spent the entire year in their combat position. Quite often, this resulted in a situation where a guy

like me—although vastly outranked—had a lot more knowledge and/or experience than the newly arrived officer who
was his boss.

This was the rule rather than the exception in ninety percent of the cases involving new lieutenants, most of whom had
never been in combat previously.

Well, it was finally Doc's turn to leave the jungle. During
our week's R&R together with our wives, this was Doc's favorite
subject as we drove around Hawaii and relaxed on its pristine
beaches.

Stanley was counting the days for Doc as the three of us lay
beneath that poncho hootch at night.

"Twenty-six more days and a wakeup, Doc."

"Shut up, Stanley. Don't remind me. That's like twenty six
years."

"Yeah," laughed Stan. "Wish it was me. Wolf and I both have
a hundred and sixty days to go in this jungle."

"A hundred and fifty nine and a wakeup, Stan," I interjected.

Inexorably, Doc's last day came. The colonel and Stan and
I walked him to the chopper pad to say goodbye. Doc was in a
great mood.

"You guys'll make it," he assured the three of us. "Just grind
'em out—one day at a time. I heard that the guy who is
replacin' me is a real brain. He knocked 'em dead in medical
school is what I heard from the C.O. of "B" Med, back there in
the rear, so you guys'll be much better off. You ain't losin'
much," he smiled merrily, "when you lose this dummy."

We said our goodbyes and waved as the chopper took him
away. We knew that he'd end up in an evac hospital over on the
coast somewhere, for the rest of his tour, and we'd never see
him again.

Doc's new replacement was due to arrive in our FSB early
the next morning. An hour or so after sunup, I was briefing the
colonel on the first sergeants' recommendations for who
should be promoted to staff sergeant when the chopper landed
at the pad down the slope from where we were.

We both stopped what we were doing.

"Want me to police up the new Doc and bring him up here to you, sir?" Yep.

I was putting on my steel helmet and just getting ready to grab my rifle, where it leaned against the sandbags surrounding his tent, when the look on his face caused me to pause and turn around.

It was Doc, already making his way up the slope. Our Doc. As he got closer, he looked like he had seen a ghost. He sure didn't look like the triumphant, euphoric Doc that we had bid farewell to the day before. He tossed his rucksack onto the ground disgustedly and threw his steel beside it, the helmet bumping and spinning.

"That dirty, rotten, little, skinny son of a bitch," he exploded, "weasiled his connivin' ass outta the jungle, sir!"

He turned his steel helmet upside down and sat in it as I did the same and the colonel sat down beside his field desk.

"Where I screwed up," Doc shook his head woefully, "was when I wore my rucksack into the "B" Med C.O.'s office when I met my replacement."

He told us that the commanding officer had told him to go ahead and remove the heavy ruck and sit down, which he did.

"How my replacement got through jump school," said Doc mournfully, "I'll never know. I mean, the guy wasn't fakin' it— his arms wasn't any bigger around than a mop handle—and he couldn't pick up my rucksack. Do you believe this shit? He couldn't lift my rucksack off the floor, let alone carry it in the jungle."

The shocked colonel and I looked at each other sadly.

"So, I'm back. I'm all yours. Oh, he called A.G. and that Adjutant General Major told me he'd send out a TELEX this very afternoon, to get me replaced as soon as possible. Both of you know how short the Army is of doctors right now, so I'll be old and gray before I ever get outta the 4th Bat—if it ain't feet first."

The colonel assured him that he'd cut him as much slack as possible and Doc sadly trudged back to our poncho shelter.

That night, he was in a little better mood when I told him about my experience during the Korean War, with a brand new battalion surgeon.

In those days, the government unceremoniously drafted doctors, who sometimes found themselves in combat units in Korea in the blink of an eye.

By the time Vietnam rolled around things were far more organized, with newly conscripted physicians attending a mandatory orientation course at Fort Sam Houston, Texas' Medical Center before sending them to Vietnam.

"It was on the tenth of May, 1953," I explained to him and Stanley, "and I was First Sergeant of my battalion's George Company.

I explained to them that medevac choppers in Korea were few and far between. We used litter jeeps and for mass casualties, we resorted to piling them into the company's deuce and a half or three quarter ton truck in order to get them back to the battalion aid station.

It was daybreak on the morning of the eleventh before we got the casualties to the battalion aid station and my men were bustling around, unloading our blanketed litters onto the frosty ground.

We found out later that the aid station was already filled with casualties from Fox Company and that our wonderful captain who was the outgoing battalion surgeon, was working like mad to save lives inside the large bunker.

Our medics were doing what they could for our guys, when out of the bunker comes what turned out later to be our brand new battalion surgeon, who immediately starts taking flash pictures of our critically wounded.

I tried as diplomatically as I was capable of, to explain to him that the custom of the Army dictated that no one ever take pictures of our own wounded or dead and he whipped it on me.

"A captain is higher than a master sergeant, right?" he says haughtily, taking another picture.

"Right, sir," I agreed, "but that doesn't mean that he's smarter—or more experienced, sir. You're taking your life in your hands if you don't snatch that film out of that camera right now, sir. Can't you see how all these riflemen, carrying their buddies, are looking at you, sir?"

I patiently explained to him that these buddies loved each other more than brothers ever could.

"They know by that caduceus on your collar, sir, that you are a doctor, and they think that you ought to be working on some of these seriously wounded instead of taking pictures, sir."

"O.K." With an angry sigh, he handed me the uncoiling film from his camera, and he strode over to a litter containing one of our best lieutenants who had burpgun slugs in both legs and one arm.

This lieutenant's really hurting.

"And, how are you, this fine morning?" the captain said in his finest bedside manner!

"I never had it so good, you stupid son of a bitch!" breathed the young lieutenant!

"What?" his jaw drooped. "Did you hear what this lieutenant said to me, sergeant?"

"Yes, sir," I admitted. "he said that some lieutenants are smarter'n some captains, too, sir."

He was probably the Army's original hippy or something. I guess he turned out all right once he got into the swing of things, because I never heard about anyone shooting him.

Doc got a big charge out of the story.

About six weeks later, we walked him down to the chopper pad again. He was replaced by another fine surgeon who did his best for the fine men of our Fourth Bat.

The last I heard of Doc, he was a lieutenant colonel in the Medical Corps. Doc was a fine surgeon, who saved a lot of lives.

Dedicated to
Capt. Ed Gallagher, M.D.

In Memory of Pete

The massive rotor on our Huey strained as Pete changed its pitch while we made our third run in order to attempt to land inside Charlie Company's small perimeter which lay a few miles out in the jungle from the Dakto Airstrip. Soon, it would be dark and we'd never get in.

Charlie's "laager" site was located in very thick timber. Two hundred foot tall heavy, thick-trunked trees lay about on the jungle floor, all helter-skelter where our Paratroopers had felled them with axes and chainsaws. From our altitude in the gathering dusk, the fallen trees looked for all the world like the results of a giant game of jackstraws. Around the small clearing, the dark, ominous jungle loomed below.

After superhuman efforts of the cutting crews, the landing zone was not quite large enough to permit an amateur Huey pilot to land. Our expert C&C ship's pilot, Pete, however, had been through this drill many times before and he knew to adroitly bring the ship up short at exactly the right spot, before we began our drop into the tiny dark clearing far below. The WHOP-WHOP-WHOP of the loudly protesting rotor attested to the strain being placed on it.

All of us trusted and admired Pete. I watched in awe as our rotor seemed to come within inches of the thick tree trunks surrounding our small shaft through them. A Huey weighs roughly twice as much as an automobile and when the rotor wraps itself around a treetrunk a hundred feet in the air, the result is usually a fiery crash. During the final few yards, I got the feeling that we were falling too fast but at the last second, Pete somehow trimmed the ship just right and we hovered a foot or two over the cluttered trunks below.

Colonel Johnnie knew that no more trees could be felled within the small clearing while our chopper remained, so he flipped the butterfly on the radio's console and told Warrant Officer Pete to disregard previous instructions, that we 3 passengers would stay the night and for Pete to return for us around 0800 hours the following morning. The tall, good-looking sandy-haired young warrant officer gave us a thumbs up while the colonel and Stan, his radio operator and I jumped to the sprawling logs below. We all watched fearfully as Pete completed the more dangerous trip back upward through the small hole in the treacherous jungle while we made our way to the edge of Charlie Company's clearing, jumping like lumberjacks from one fallen tree to another.

While Colonel Johnnie and Stan remained with Charlie's fine Captain, the First Sergeant guided me to that portion of the perimeter where Platoon Sergeant Janos Schalavin's platoon was. "Jan" had been a Hungarian freedom fighter against the occupying Russians, hated Communists with a passion and was one of our very best leaders. This well decorated NCO had insisted upon returning to Charlie Company even after having received over five hundred stitches in the aftermath of being on the receiving end of one of Clyde's super-sized command-detonated Claymore mines! What a guy! Before the night was over, he would demonstrate the instincts which made him be a superb jungle fighter.

Just before dusk, Colonel Johnnie and Stan joined Jan and me where we had already set up a poncho hootch for the three of us to try and spend a dry night beneath. Janos had already heated each of us a "C" rations dinner, which we were gratefully sitting on the ground savoring, when Jan suddenly raised a warning finger to his mouth, as the three of us stopped chewing.

"Ssshhh," he cautioned, "I smell Charlie! Smell that garlic?"

Colonel Johnnie gave Jan an amused look and continued eating! He didn't smell any garlic, and neither did I, but Stan did. Jan rummaged in his ruck and came up with three high explosive hand grenades, handing one to Stan and one to me. Once again indicating quiet, he stood and quietly made his way the ten yards to the perimeter's edge while Stan and I followed stealthily, each of us clutching our HE missile. At his insistence, we each pulled our pins and at his count of three, heaved them as far as we could out amongst the trees. The only time the colonel quit eating was when the three simultaneous horrendous explosions rocked the jungle.

He hit the deck along with the three of us, however, when all of a sudden, all hell broke loose and from outside the perimeter, several incoming grenades came into our perimeter down to the left of us and the same thing happened further up the perimeter to our right.

Of course, Charlie Company's troopers at that portion of the perimeter opened up with everything they had, to include more grenades of their own! The enemy probe ended up being broken up before it started and several blood trails were found during daylight the following day. Fortunately, the incoming grenades had inflicted only minor shrapnel injuries on several of our riflemen. Jan had made his point, though! Some of the guys could smell Charlie. At this writing, Jan is a famous retired command sergeant major. He was one Helluva soldier, let me tell you.

The following morning, right before Charlie Company started their hump out of the perimeter, the faithful Pete arrived to pick us up.

"Keep that sniffer of yours going," the colonel smiled to Jan as we left his area to walk to the LZ. He was really impressed with Janos.

Pete took us on our perilous journey back upward through the giant trees and deposited us at our FSB a few miles away.

One day not long afterward, Bobbie and Buck, Pete's two doorgunners, taped a red smoke grenade to one skid and a green one to the other, with strings attached, and as Pete circled our FSB, they pulled the strings and you should have seen those colorful streams of smoke.

"What tha hell—" started Colonel Johnnie.

"It's an old custom of Vietnam chopper pilots, sir," I explained to him and the gawking, astounded Stan and Doc, our surgeon. "It's Pete's last flight. His time is up. He's rotatin' to the U.S."

And it was.

Two years later, I opened the *Army Times* to the casualty section and saw to my dismay that Pete and Bobbie and Buck were all three carried in the MIA portion. They had returned to

Vietnam and gotten together in the same outfit again. What brave men.

It might be years before some little Montagnard kids or some hunter find what's left of their chopper in that thick jungle. For Pete and Bobbie and Buck, the battles had ended.

There were more to come.

Paratroopers Go Down Swinging

During my year as sergeant major of our wonderful battalion of outstanding paratroopers in Vietnam, we typically fielded between 650 and 750 riflemen on any given day.

During their year of fighting in the terrible, dark, triple-canopied jungles of the Central Highlands, this valiant battalion lost 125 fine, brave troopers and over five hundred wounded.

This sort of action makes you kind of crazy. The troops straggle around with the thousand yard stare. It's as though someone has stunned you with a blow to the head to have combat fatigue following a fierce battle.

A fellow certainly feels fortunate to have survived, but has mixed feelings of guilt and anguish that some of his buddies did not.

Each man, partly guided by instinct, still does his job, but he is certainly not thinking as clearly as he was before becoming exposed to the psychological punishment which he has just endured.

Late in each afternoon, every company stopped their search and destroy operation and dug in for the night. This protected perimeter was known as a "laager" site—its origin coming from the tactics of the Afrikaan Boers who traditionally dug their wagons into a huge circle each evening, as a defensive perimeter.

This was very difficult due to the hard "laterite" soil of the mountains. Two men would dig a foxhole, by one filling a sandbag as his buddy dug into the hard ground—then they'd exchange places. This three hour process would culminate by cutting bamboo to form overhead cover with the sandbags as a roof for the foxhole.

This roof was vital to protect from mortar shrapnel from tree bursts.

We wore no socks or underwear and the men stayed wet for a month or two at a time during the Monsoons, and the foxholes filled up with water, too.

At least a squad-sized ambush patrol was sent out at dusk to cover the avenue of most likely approach by the enemy.

As soon as the foxhole was completed, the men would eat some "C" rations and then spell each other for two hour periods while one slept and the other kept watch.

These guys, who have just been through terrible, life-threatening experiences, have seen their buddies' maimed or lifeless bodies being evacuated by helicopter, and these things are molding their thinking and their very being—for the rest of their young lives—which might be very short, if they could foretell the future.

An unknown—but very astute—Civil War combat vet said it all when he wrote:

"I asked for all things, that I might enjoy life, and was granted life, that I might enjoy all things!"

That kind of tells it like it really is, doesn't it?

It was time for our great lieutenant colonel to depart from the battalion. Commanders stayed only six months, the theory being that you could give twice as many commanders some combat experience through this policy.

The bad side was that it took a while until the new C.O. became completely effective, as there were too many variables in jungle warfare. My inexperienced new colonel had just arrived.

He asked me if our battalion had an official motto!

He thought that I had a defeatist attitude when I told him!

"It's 'go down swinging,' sir."

Our 4th Battalion of the 503rd Infantry—the outfit which jumped in and captured Corregidor in World War II—didn't need a motto.

We needed replacements.

And we needed rest.

We got the replacements.

The 173rd Airborne Brigade not only spent more time fighting in Vietnam than any other Army unit, it stayed in the field longer.

Troops like that don't need a motto.

They need rest.

"Tien Bing" is the 173rd Airborne Brigade's motto. It translates to "Sky Soldiers" in Chinese.

Killer's Epitaph

Jim was a quiet, efficient rifleman when he had joined Dog Company as a replacement in 1966. His squad members soon learned that they could always depend upon this tall, slim private when the going got rough. He was a nice-looking teen-aged kid who kept his brown hair in a neat crewcut, whose reassuring smile seemed to bolster the morale of his pals when they were tired and disgusted with life in the jungle.

Early on, his squad leader nicknamed him "Killer" for his eagerness to volunteer for the point at every opportunity. He became such a fine pointman that the C.O. and first sergeant of Dog had decided to form him and one other expert into a full-time team to alternate on point. Everyone knew that when one of these two guys were on point, they were all in good hands.

Killer had left Vietnam once, feet-first, before I ever met him, as I had joined the battalion in May of 1967 shortly after the 173rd had arrived in the Central Highlands. The first time, he had been awarded a well-earned Silver Star, and the second time, we had nominated him for the Medal of Honor for what he had done on Cemetery Hill.

Like the rest of the world, though, nothing's fair in love and war and this nomination had been downgraded to a final award of his second Silver Star. Such things never ceased to amaze me.

Killer didn't care, though. He was in it for the adventure, rather than for any personal aggrandizement. He had lost his right thumb and been shot through the lung on Cemetery Hill during the infamous 1968 Tet Offensive.

With such serious wounds, he spent a long time in Walter Reed Army Hospital in Washington, D.C.

A couple of years after Cemetery Hill, he called me and I invited him and a friend to come and visit us at West Point, where I was command sergeant major of a regiment of fine cadets. It was an Easter long weekend amid a period of brisk snow and they really enjoyed themselves. There are few places more beautiful than West Point during and after a good snow.

We were pleasantly surprised to learn that Killer had been working undercover for the FBI. Agents had gone to the Pentagon and made a computer scan in order to find a brave young man with an outstanding combat record, who knew his way around a motorcycle and they had taken one look at his record and found him to fit the bill.

The two agents swore him to secrecy and asked him how he'd like to join a motorcycle gang which was not only highly suspected of peddling hard drugs up and down the entire east coast, but some of its members were thought to have murdered a State Department official.

They could already prove that one of the dead official's relatives was thick as thieves with some of the gang's members and they believed that this person had enveigled the deceased into the basement of his own home, where members of the gang had lain in wait and then murdered him.

It was suspected that somehow the official had gotten wind of the dope distribution activities and had been on the verge of notifying the appropriate authorities when he was done away with in order to prevent this.

Well, Killer was used to playing for keeps with the VC and NVA and he had definitely been leading a different kind of life in that hospital, than his life in the jungle, so he was ready and willing to take on such an exciting project with those crooks! Killer already had a nice motorcycle and with the FBI paying his salary and all expenses, he had little trouble in joining the gang.

We were all sitting in the spacious living room of our quarters in West Point, sipping refreshments while Killer told us this entire intriguing tale. He told us that the gang consisted of over sixty members, many of whom lived in a big three story brownstone house which was headquarters for the gang. Only about half of them lived in the house at any given time while the others acted as dope couriers up and down the coast.

Well, Jim was a nice-looking young bachelor and it didn't take long before one or two unattached female members of the gang were shooting to partner up with him. He played one off against the other and worked his way into each one's confidence. Each of these gals knew where all the bodies were buried and whose closet contained which particular skeleton! Accordingly, over a few weeks' period, he was able to pass onto the agents enough information for them to sack up the murder case as tight as a drum. He said that by the time the FBI got through using informants who had turned state's evidence in order to save their own skins, the murderers were all facing imprisonment for life in Maryland.

Not only that, but the same process had put several dozen dope couriers behind bars.

"It's hard for a guy to keep his thumb into the informant business," joked Killer, waving the nub of his missing digit for emphasis, "when the word gets around and all the crooks are lookin' for a one-thumbed motorcyclist, so I'm retiring from huntin' crooks and Charlie here, and I are thinkin' of headin' for New Orleans to see about a job on an oil rig."

I had previously told our son, Patrick, about Killer's exploits on Cemetery Hill, and the wide-eyed ten year old, was quite interested when Killer explained why he hadn't stayed in the Army.

Killer explained to Pat that some archaic army regulation stipulated that if a right-handed soldier lost his right thumb, he could not stay in the Infantry because he couldn't cock a .45 caliber pistol. Accordingly, Killer had chosen to be discharged rather than to have to serve in a branch other than his beloved Infantry.

He asked Patrick to go and fetch the small bag which he was travelling with and after Pat brought it to him, Killer unzipped it and strapped on a brand new Python .357 Magnum which he had extracted from the bag's depths. With a confident smile, Killer struck a Hollywood gunfighter's stance and with lightning speed, he drew the weapon, cocking its hammer with the nub of his missing right thumb.

"I rest my case, Pat," he enthused, confidently using the nub to lower the hammer into its safety position! "So much for all those darn know-it-all bureaucrats," he crowed triumphantly.

"Is that thing loaded?" gasped his friend, John.

"'Course it's loaded," Killer demonstrated this fact by ejecting the six large "hollow point" cartridges out onto Marlene's living room rug.

"You mean -" the astonished John went on, "I've been driving all over the State of New York—where they'll jail you in a minute under their "Sullivan Act" for having a concealed weapon—with a loaded one in a bag on the back seat of my car and—"

"'Course ya have," laughed Killer, "you don't think I'm dumb enough to run around all over New York City with all those crooks an' not be prepared, do ya?"

He had a good point.

In memory of Sgt. James Eli Mahon

Jungle Cowboys

When Westy was a two star, he commanded the 101st Airborne Division at Fort Campbell, Kentucky. I had fixed up my company dayroom and messhall to look like "The Old Army" of the 1880's and Westy loved it. Periodically he would bring dignitaries to my company for lunch, which was quite an honor.

He was frequently called to my telephone by his headquarters, and noticed that I had a chain running from a pipe to my desk, said chain securing my stapler and hole puncher.

"Top," he once said, "if I ever see that this entire barracks has been levelled, I'll know that some SOB stole your stapler."

When I got to Vietnam, I was told that each sergeant major lived in his battalion rear area, in a tent, where he could greet and brief all new replacements. These most senior NCOs actually wore starched fatigues and spit-shined boots. I cut off my stripes and patches, turned in my fancy tent and hit the jungle with my troopers. The colonel told me that the battalion had a high incidence of malaria.

We were humping eighty-pound rucksacks, and he carried his own as we joined our Bravo Company for the day's operation. That night, I accompanied a squad on an all night's ambush patrol.

To help prevent malaria, jungle troops must roll down their sleeves and button their collar starting at six o'clock each evening because mosquitoes are night biters. Also, each man was supposed to carry a plastic bottle of mosquito ointment beneath his elastic camouflage band around his steel helmet. In the evening, he must apply this ointment to his hands, face and neck.

Every man in Vietnam was required to take a large red pill each Monday, to prevent vivax malaria. This was the mildest form of malaria, comparable to a bad case of the flu—and recurrent up to fifteen or so years.

The troops knew this, and many of them caught malaria on purpose, so they could spend thirty to forty-five days in the nice, safe hospital, while their more gungho buddies were getting killed and wounded.

On this all night ambush patrol, I noticed that sometimes ten or twenty mosquitoes at a time would land on your face and hands if you had no ointment—and these troops were completely out of ointment! I passed my bottle around.

Then they told me that there was only one or two rifle cleaning rods in each squad. At that time, the M-16 was bad about jamming an expended cartridge in its chamber, and the panacea was to run the rifle rod down the bore, and knock it out, but meanwhile, the enemy was shooting at you.

The next day I flew back to our battalion rear and gave the battalion supply sergeant twenty dollars. I told him to go back to the rear warehouse areas, convert the money to whisky as trading material, and to find some thirsty supply people and get us 8,000 bottles of mosquito ointment and also 4,000 M-16 cleaning rods.

I told him to immediately send 2,000 bottles to our troops in the jungle, plus 700 cleaning rods. I told him to keep thirteen hundred rods, and then for him to personally deliver the remaining rods and bottles to the full colonel who was in charge of the brigade's staff, as the second ranking officer in the outfit.

The colonel didn't like it that I had single-handedly supplied four battalions of riflemen with the life-saving equipment! He flew into our fire support base and threatened to court martial me.

He stated that my circumvention of the supply system was a serious violation.

I told him he should court martial his supply officer and the entire crew. I was in very hot water with the general, but I didn't care, because I knew I was right.

I had also had my supply guy to scrounge up a thousand big olive drab handkerchiefs for my men to wear around their necks like cowboys. At night, they would pull it up over their face like a bandit, protecting most of the neck and face from those swarms of mosquitoes. Worked like a charm.

But I was still in very hot water with our general and the staff colonel. That is, I was until General Westmoreland's visit.

One day we were informed that he and some of his staff would visit us the following afternoon. Accordingly, the colonel who was teed off at me, had lined up every lieutenant colonel and sergeant major on the edge of the airstrip which supplied the Special Forces Camp at Daksut, about an hour before Westy's arrival.

Each of these important people were decked out in starched jungle fatigues and spit-shined boots, and the colonel nodded happily as he inspected each one, until he came to me. He voiced his displeasure and I told him that I had been on an ambush patrol all night.

I still had blood on my fatigues from carrying some poor guy a week before. He didn't like that and I told him that his staff was supplying my men in the field with fresh fatigues an average of every forty days, and I didn't think that any of us were any better than they were. He shook his head sadly, because Westy's aircraft was landing, and saved me further trouble.

I mentioned that everyone in Vietnam had to take the big red pill each Monday, but the smaller amount of soldiers in the Central Highlands had to take an additional daily pill to prevent the horrible falciparum malaria, which burned up the brain and killed a lot of soldiers.

All the evacuation hospitals were used to administering the red pill weekly, but they didn't all give the daily one because they weren't used to patients from the Central Highlands.

As a result, some of my men were contracting falciparum malaria while in the hospital, because of neglect on the part of the medical chain of command.

So, I had written Westy a letter from the jungle, explaining the problem.

Our general met Westy at the aircraft, and our colonel came back from the plane with a brigadier general who was Westy's new chief of staff. Turned out that he was brand new in country and didn't know beans. He inspected us, starting with the 1st Battalion's commander and sergeant major. My colonel and I were last, as we had the 4th Battalion.

We could hear him asking everyone questions, and it turned out that he was kind of a sarcastic fellow. When it came my turn, he wrinkled up his nose at my sour bloody smell, and his eyes darted all over my filthy, blank jungle fatigues.

"And who," he crinkled his nose in disdain, "might you be?"

"Sir, I am the 4th Rifle Battalion's sergeant major, sir."

Some of those in the rank tittered when he asked his next question in a very scornful tone.

"How," he demanded, "can you tell?" No chevrons.

"Well, sir," I replied brightly, "on paydays, the battalion clerk brings us our pink pay slips to the jungle, and it says right on mine 'Sergeant Major Ted G. Arthurs'!"

"Fall out to the rear," he said darkly, which I did. He joined me and proceeded to give me hell for wearing the plastic "bug juice" on my helmet.

"This is not a cowboy outfit, sergeant major," he admonished. "Remove that ridiculous bandanna—right now."

At that moment, Westy arrived, with our general, who was eyeing me and that brigadier general apprehensively, like "What now?"

My general's apprehensive look turned to one of great astonishment when Westy grabbed me.

"Ted Arthurs," he said, hugging my shoulder, "I got your letter, and I mean, I rattled some cages. You've saved hundreds of lives from being ruined, and I am sending a letter commending you for this."

Then, he greeted the entire formation and praised everyone for our recent actions.

At the conclusion of this, there were refreshments by the airstrip. Westy told his one star Chief Of Staff that they would be on the ground for three hours, and while he went with our general and the staff colonel, he wanted me to brief the chief on my "Combat Tips" poop sheet that I was writing up.

"I loved your 'olive drab bandanna' suggestion, Ted," he said, "and I see you've got one on. How does it work?"

"It's great, sir. The troops love it."

After Westy departed the area, my general and his staff colonel converged on me and my battalion commander.

"Do you have a copy of that letter which you wrote to General Westmoreland?" asked the general apprehensively.

"No, sir. I wrote it by hand and put it on the mail chopper."

"I see, uh—um—you didn't mention to him our shortages of rifle cleaning rods and mosquito ointment, did you?"

No, sir, I solved that problem, sir."

"Yes, and quite well, I should say," he ventured in a complimentary manner.

"Would you do me a favor, sergeant major?"

"Of course, sir."

"For future reference, would you run any of your ideas by my colonel, here, who can brief me on them, and then we can send them onto General Westmoreland, if you like?"

Would I?

I had to laugh to myself when I thought of those three hours I spent briefing Westy's Chief of Staff, who was taking notes a mile a minute.

The fortunes of war.

Going from rags to riches.

Sometimes the bear eats you, and sometimes you eat the bear.

It's usually the bear who does the eating, though.

That colonel wasn't through with me yet.

Snoozin' Riflemen

You could put an American G.I. in a closet full of NVA riflemen, all meanern' a snake and tell him that if he went to sleep first, he'd die. A lot of 'em would go ahead and die and say "to hell with it."

They only walked daily for eight hours up in those mountains of Vietnam because the next three or four hours had to be devoted to digging a foxhole in that awful laterite ground.

Webster's definition does not do it justice.

"A red residual soil in humid tropical regions, used as ore of iron, aluminum, manganese or nickel."

Thunk! A mighty stroke with your entrenching tool produces a chunk about the size of a postage stamp or a bottle cap.

How many such licks with that shovel do you think two guys have to make before they produce their foxhole for the night! Then they fill their sandbags which they've been carrying on top of that rucksack all day, with the removed laterite and fix up overhead cover by placing the bags on bamboo laid across the top, or else die sooner or later from a tree burst from a mortar some night.

Now, it's your turn to sleep, only I forgot to tell you that your foxhole's got a foot of water in it, and rising fast, so you crawl beneath the poncho hootch that you and your buddy have stretched and you lie on his poncho which is the floor of the hootch supporting you on two inches of mud beneath.

The ketch to that situation is that you are one poncho short to protect your pal who now has the two hour watch in the driving rain of the monsoon, while you "sleep" if that's what you want to call it.

So, somehow he tries to remain halfway beneath the top poncho and keep from drowning in the rain while he "watches."

"Listens" is the word. You aren't watching anything in the black hole of triple canopied jungle. It's about as unspeakably black as being in a coal mine at midnight. That is no exaggeration.

If you move through that black of night, you must keep hold of the man to your front. Try that sliding downhill some time.

In an area completely saturated with NVA like Dakto sometimes was, it's a terrifying experience to get tapped for ambush patrol! You leave the safety of your company's perimeter, where at least you have three other platoons to rely on and you rob the rest of your platoon in order to produce a full squad of twelve un-wounded men to go out on ambush.

Just prior to dusk, off you go. Where? The C.O. has looked on the map and he's hoping he knows where you are. He says to himself, "If I were Clyde—I'd sneak in on us from here."

That's where you go—hoping against hope that Clyde is not already there.

Your leader sets up the ambush the way he wants it and you are now back to just you and your buddy and the dark. You each decide who gets to sleep first and of course, neither one of you has a watch. Watches are issued to leaders, not to us riflemen. That lovely, expensive luminous-dialed watch which does everything it's supposed to do in combat, except to resist the acid-like action which G.I. mosquito repellent has if it's accidentally spilt on the watch's face! Mosquito ointment.

It'll kill anything. You don't want to get it into your eyes, so they go for your eyelids. And if you don't have the ointment on, you can scrape twenty of them at a time off your face and the backs of your hands!

It used to bolster heck out of those kids' morale when I joined them for the night's ambush patrol. It must be going to be safe tonight. The sergeant major's out here with us.

Once in a while I got the feeling that most of those guys were snoozing away, to include the ones who should have been awake. But that's what that rucksack'll do for you, day after day, week after week.

One morning the first sergeant of the company that I was humping with told me that they were going to have to call in a medevac to evacuate one of their best riflemen, because he was coming apart at the seams. He had been out there almost eleven months.

"Maybe I can send him back to the rear and they could make a clerk out of him or something," I suggested.

"He's too far gone for that, Ted," he declared. "We had to rope him to a log last night and gag him. Damned shame."

I could see two figures making their way up to the edge of the small clearing where we stood. The weight of the big guy they were carrying, strained their handholds on the poncho.

"The senior medic has looked at him, Wolf," he reiterated, "and he says he has to go."

I had seen bad combat fatigue cases before, but this kid was not a complete basket case.

"He turns on and off," said Top.

The kid sobbed and cried and he told me how ashamed he was to have to go out like this. He knew exactly where he was and who I was.

"The rucksack got me, sergeant major," he cried, "and it's going to kill everyone. Do you think that these guys can hump it month after month and still pull fifty percent alert every night? Can't you see that Clyde's going to come through that perimeter one of these nights and kill everyone in their sleep? And, it's not the guys' fault, sergeant major."

I told him that a hero need not be ashamed, that hardly anyone in the whole outfit had humped a ruck as long as he had and that I wanted him to get a nice long rest in the hospital and not pay any mind to all of this stuff anymore.

He grasped my sleeve as I squatted beside him.

"I care about my buddies," he sobbed. "Our perimeter watch is being conducted by the mosquito hawks and the crickets, sir," he told me.

When the dustoff ship finally arrived, one of the men grabbed the back of his poncho and I grabbed the front. We put him on feet first and he grabbed my wrist in a grip of iron, his tearful eyes burning into mine. He wanted to say something, so I put my ear against his mouth to combat the pandemonium of the ship's rotor.

"I'm sorry," he cried. "I'm sorry, sergeant major. I'm not yellow."

"Of course not, son," I told him, "and no one thinks you are. You are a proud trooper, who gave his all, and don't you ever forget it."

He squeezed my wrist in thanks.

"But," he breathed loudly into my ear, "our perimeter watch is being done by the hawks and crickets, sir."

I broke loose from his grasp, and patted his shoulder as I gave thumbs up to the pilot with my other hand.

"There goes a good kid," said the first sergeant as we watched the ship hit the top of the two hundred foot hole in the jungle's thick ceiling.

"But," he added, "you know and I know that they ain't all asleep, Wolf. They've still got something for Clyde's ass if he ever tries to breach our perimeter."

That kid knew something that Top and I didn't and it had driven him batty worrying about it.

It took me years to figure it out that he had been humping that ruck all day long and staying awake all night, every night, and that's why he had to be taken out in a poncho.

"Don't ever make fun of the one man who's afraid," goes an old infantry adage. "HE might be the only one who completely understands the situation."

Julian and the Bamboo Viper

Julian was a fine NCO, but he was scared to death of snakes, which I found out the hard way early one morning.

He and I had been foxhole buddies and during the cold, dark night, a Bamboo Viper had crawled into the hole with us—probably attracted by the warmth of our bodies—and was coiled up between us.

At first light, when I climbed out and stretched, I had glanced back into the hole and seen him.

"Julian," I hissed loudly, "Julian, don't move a muscle, pal. A bamboo viper is coiled up behind you, ready to strike."

He took a deep breath, like he was going to scream.

Hopefully he looked at me from beneath his steel helmet, his eyes searching mine for the hint of a practical joke.

"Don't move," I whispered, never taking my eyes off the snake as I furtively fished behind me on the ground for my entrenching shovel. Clutching its handle, I struck at the snake, grimly realizing that if I missed his head, Julian would have to immediately be medevaced to the nearest hospital.

Whop!

"Bingo!" I shouted as I severed its head.

The writhing snake didn't make three turns before Julian had erupted out of that foxhole like Vesuvius in 79 A.D.

Staring in disbelief as I held up the headless serpent, he backed away in shock, thinking what had almost been.

"Sergeant major," he said firmly, his face as white as snow, "I'm not afraid of Charlie, out here in this jungle, but that thing—well, you'll never see me in another foxhole in this country, I'm here to tell you."

And come to think of it, I never did.

My battalion got into some bad-news places during the terrible Dakto Campaign of 1967, so every chance I got, I would accompany the troops.

The poor squad of a dozen men who had to go out into that dark jungle at night, knowing that we were surrounded, and set up an ambush, would find me tagging along with them for the night.

"Hey," one might say, "couldn't be as bad as all that—here's the sergeant major with us."

We had one black guy who was one helluva pointman. He knew his stuff, and everyone trusted his judgment because he had survived a lot.

We were humping eighty pound rucksacks containing maybe seven or eight hundred rounds of M-16 ammo—plenty of grenades—and plenty of "C" rations, etc, and it's a cumbersome load.

I was backing this guy on point one day, as he carefully made his way through the jungle, when I heard him give a cross between a huge gasp and a stifled yelp.

I thought he had stepped into one of those huge beartraps which the Montagnards set out for big game and I hurried up to his side. He was scared out of his mind. This didn't help me.

He pointed to his left, and I could see vegetation moving.

"A f-f-f-freight train," he stammered, "as big as a snake just crawled by here."

We went to the right.

One of our greatest pointmen was a fine kid from Louisiana named Ross. He had a barrel full of guts. I have a picture of him and me and two other guys carrying a huge rock python that he shot one day. We were carrying it on our shoulders, and he was dragging the ground in two places, he was so long.

Well, my guys just had to slice him up to see what that one huge lump in him was, and out tumbled the remains of a half-grown pig.

Sadly, Ross was killed a few weeks later during some fierce action, but that's another story. Every time I see a snake on TV or while I'm hunting or fishing, I think of Ross. He was the finest.

In memory of PFC Gene Autry Ross

CHAPTER 12

Another Huge Snake

As I fixed us some "C" ration coffee, I told the still-shaken Julian about our big snake in Jump School, almost eighteen years before.

I had only been out of the USMC a very few weeks when I maxed Fort Benning's PT (physical training) test in Jump School, and was retained to run the quitters barracks at Fort Benning, Georgia.

My fighting weight was right at two hundred, and it was a good thing it was, because all those quitters were washouts from jump school, had a very sour attitude toward the world in general, and at me in particular because I was required, as one of my duties, to force them to "G.I." the barracks every evening after chow.

The whole place had to be scrubbed clean enough to eat off, to include washing the windows. I probably averaged at least three fistfights a week in the pursuit of these duties!

I was a private, so many of them outranked me. The only thing I had going for me was the fact that I was a member of the jump instruction staff, and could put anyone on report to the battalion commander for disciplinary action.

I never did this—I just duked it out with any real trouble-makers, and our commander was happy with the results. My best pals were Louie, the first cook, and Cholly, the mail clerk. Louie had just been released from a German POW camp, five years before, and he was still kind of nervous.

Cholly was a quiet guy from Boston, but he had one helluva sense of humor, and was always dreaming up ways for the three of us to play tricks on the rest of the jump instructors.

Probably two times each week, the three of us went catfishing at night in the nearby Chatahootchee River. We'd filet the cats, and Louie would open the messhall and fry them up for us, which we would enjoy along with a cool beer.

The old wooden barracks were firetraps and would burn to the ground in a very few minutes, so it was very important that the company's charge of quarters should make periodic fire-checks of the barracks.

When a big, burly corporal broke his leg on his first jump, the first sergeant gave him the permanent duty as C.Q. each night until the medics cut his cast off. As he had to stay awake all night, he got to sleep during the daytime. Louie told Cholly and me that he had caught the guy sleeping on two separate occasions, when he should have been acting as C.Q. and fire-watch.

We fished by the light of carbide lamps, and one night Louie and Cholly yelped, and dropped their fishing rods and jumped back from the river. I ran over there and they excitedly told me that a huge snake had come out of the river between them! I grabbed a carbide lamp and went behind them, in the direction that the snake had gone, and found him all coiled up among the roots of a tree which had been downed by swirling high water, some time in the past.

"I'll hold the light," I suggested, "and you guys pin his neck with a stick and we'll capture 'im."

"You get the stick," said the jittery Louis, "we each have a light. You capture him." We followed the plan.

It was the biggest snake I had ever seen up until some pythons in Vietnam, seventeen years later.

When I scrambled from beneath that fallen tree, I had a good grip on its neck, and it immediately wrapped itself around my arm from wrist to shoulder, and still dangled at least two feet toward the ground.

Cholly was really an innovative thinker.

"You know our sleepy fire watch? Well, we've got somethin' for his sleepin' ass, here."

On our way back to the company, he planned the caper. We would look through the side window and if he was sleeping, Louie would sneak the enclosed porch's screendoor open, while Cholly and I tiptoed across the porch. Then, Cholly would sneak the screendoor into the orderly room open, giving me and the snake access.

Worked like a charm! As I passed through the second door and approached his sleeping form, he was snoring away, with his head on the desk.

"Snake!" I shouted, and thrust it across the desk as he awoke with a start.

The best laid plans of mice and men and Cholly went astray with a bang as the terrified fellow knocked over the first sergeant's file cabinet, and with a horrifying yelp, went through the closest screendoor, scattering Louie and Cholly like chaff.

The catch was that the outside screendoor, leading from the porch to the outside steps, opened in. The big guy went right through it, tearing it from its hinges and taking the steps three at a time, charged bellowing into the darkness.

We got into trouble in spades on that deal, because the next day, the doctor called our battalion executive officer and told them that the guy had run the cast off his leg!

The first sergeant thought it was funny as Hell, because he put the guy back on permanent C.Q. and fire watch.

"And snake watch," said the C.Q., who promised not to sleep!

A Million Dollar Leg

My battalion was operating a "search and destroy" mission against the enemy in the jungle near a place named Dakto.

It was mid-November '67 and I was out with our Dog Company for a few days. Dog was our smallest company, and performed recon missions when called for.

None of us knew that within two months, nineteen of Dog's 83 men would be killed on Cemetery Hill, and all the rest would be wounded, during the infamous Tet Offensive.

It was to be my lot to accompany Dog in that assault. I would imagine that the other survivors thank the Lord daily, as I do.

It was the end of the rainy season, and the muddy ground witnessed to the ferocity of the previous two months' assault by the Monsoons.

Some of my men had never been dry during that eighty some days period. We lost a lot of men during the Dakto campaign.

Several fallen trees lay like jackstraws across this one clearing and many men were lying on the trees, trying for a few minutes rest without becoming completely immersed in the mud.

The sniper's bullet hit with a thunk, knocking the rifleman lying nearest me off into the mud. A second later we heard the rifle's report, across the river to our right. So much for the mud. I crawled to the young fellow, screaming my lungs out for our medic.

He had been shot in the right thigh, with the bullet penetrating his pants pocket. The medic and I stared in amazement at his wound. The high-powered rifle bullet, instead of breaking his bones, had penetrated the leg muscle only about a quarter of an inch. A packet of Polaroid film had absorbed the shock of that slug, permitting only part of the bullet to penetrate his leg.

It was the damnest thing I ever saw. Each of the films had concentric circles etched into it by the shock of the round hitting. I have one of them which I saved as a souvenir.

"Those dirty, atrocity-committin' sons of bitches," cursed the kid. "Look what Clyde did to five bucks' worth of brandnew Polaroid film!"

As the laughing medic bound up his leg, the kid wanted to know what we found to be so funny!

"Tell him, Doc," I said.

"Listen, pal, you're new in Vietnam. You have got to thank God that you've still got that million-dollar leg."

Wives and Wallets

As mentioned, my battalion suffered terrible casualties during the Dakto Campaign in the mountains of Vietnam's Central Highlands.

We would average a little over one hundred and fifty men in each rifle company during that time.

In one four day period, we received 335 replacements, which should give you an idea of our losses.

During my year, we received three Green Beret NCOs as replacements. These men were not washouts by any means. Each was outstanding, but each one had run afoul of some policy or some officer's idiosyncrasy, and took the best way out by asking for a transfer to a conventional Airborne infantry outfit.

We were lucky we got them. One became an outstanding, brave first sergeant. One was killed in action. The third was Marty.

Marty was a staff sergeant. He liked being a staff sergeant because this meant that he would be held responsible for only twelve men, to include himself. To Marty, this was child's play, because he was quite a soldier, who really knew his trade, and I admired him quite a bit.

I laugh to myself every time I think about the day he arrived in my 4th Rifle Battalion of the 173rd Airborne Brigade. I was interviewing him.

"Are you married, Sergeant Marty?" I asked.

I thought he was going to show me pictures when he reached for his wallet.

"My wallet," he said matter-of-factly, "is my wife. You might say that I keep my wife in my wallet."

'Nuff said.

"Anything you want to discuss, Sergeant Marty?"

He told me that the airborne community is very small when compared to the rest of the Regular Army. For that reason, he pointed out that I might hear the rumor that he was a dud, and had been given the bounce from the Green Berets.

He went on to say that nothing was further from the truth, that he had done a good job, and had turned down promotion after promotion. He admitted that he kind of shunned higher ranking individuals, and would rather stay with the Montagnards, whose culture he respected.

He explained to me that there are perhaps three dozen main tribes, whose main mark of distinction is that they have never been captured and governed by any conqueror. The main reason is that their dialects are in such disparity of one another.

To illustrate his point, he emphasized that if you have three tribes in a row, that the middle one can barely communicate with the tribe on either side.

Chinese conquerors couldn't put a dent in the tribes and just ignored them and governed the Vietnam lowlands, for example.

I already knew, from listening to them at night, that the tribes communicated amongst themselves by thrumming and drumming on hollowed logs—their beautiful music lulling one to sleep.

They were tough little allies, in more ways than one. I will never forget the one whose wounded foot could not be sewn shut by our medic because the sole was as tough as the horn of a cow.

I didn't press this wiry little guy for details, but he told me the whole story.

They had gotten a new lieutenant colonel from the states, on his first tour of Vietnam, who had been determined to make a name for himself.

"He was still peeing stateside water," explained Marty, "when he choppered into my little camp and started trying to push me and my 'yards around—who just ignored him!"

"But, YOU," I laughed, "couldn't do that, right, Sergeant Marty?" "Right! This guy whipped the maddest scheme on me that you ever heard of."

"Try me."

"He had this fancy .22 pistol," he went on, "with a huge chrome silencer on it! I had to put G.I. tape on it before I could take it into the bush. First of all, I had to take quite a bit of target practice with it, because you are not gonna believe what he told me to do with it."

The colonel had written up an operation where Marty would take four of his 'yards on a chopper ride and be inserted into some wild territory, thickly populated with NVA soldiers.

After making four or five false insertions, to confuse the enemy, they would be inserted at their correct location, just at dusk. Early the next morning they were to set up an ambush on a thickly travelled trail, with two men on one side and three on the other.

"This operation had all kinds of holes in it," declared Marty. "First of all, the place was crawling with NVA, who are gonna romp over the rise like locusts at the first shot."

Their orders were that Marty could incapacitate a single NVA soldier, by lightly wounding him with the pistol. Then they were to quickly truss him up, and beat feet cross country to the extraction point, having radioed for the chopper, in their spare time!

"From first light on, hundreds of NVA went up and down that trail—and the least number we ever saw at once was three of 'em. Of course, we are so well camouflaged beside that trail that this one Clyde stopped and peed right on one of my best 'Yards—and I thought he was gonna let him have it right then and there—and that would've been the end of us."

He said that they were getting discouraged, all cramped up—couldn't move a muscle for long periods of time, when it must have been time to cook the noon rice, because traffic came to a screeching halt.

After about fifteen minutes, they heard it. One Clyde was whistling a catchy tune as he strolled down that trail like he was in his own hometown, with his AK-47 slung over his shoulder.

"This guy only looked like he was ate up with the dumbass," winked Marty, "because when I aimed for his knee, I just missed and got him in the fat part of the thigh, between his knee and his hip. Of course, with no noise, he thought he'd been hit by a bamboo viper or something, because he gasped and halted and started batting at his leg like he was trying to kill whatever was hurting him."

Marty explained that with the guy dancing around, he missed his other knee on the second shot, and got him in the thigh again.

"Well! This guy ain't no dummy. He whips that AK-47 off his shoulder and blindly sprays the whole area, wounding one of my 'yards, and bustin' his arm—he like to bled to death as we tried to bandage him up on the run, after my other three 'Yards sent Clyde to his maker."

"We were scared to death that the whole NVA Army would ketch up with us—but they never did—and when we heard the most welcome sound in the world—that Huey's beatin' rotor—we were on that chopper like a shot, I can tell you."

His wounded guy made it O.K., which was the main worry.

"We're toolin' along up there over that wild jungle, Top, and I got to thinkin' to myself—'that madman is just gonna send someone back OUT there again with this pistol'—or even worse, he's gonna send us."

He nodded his head as he recalled the event.

"I fed it to the jungle below," he said.

Alan B.

I met some fine captains in Korea and Vietnam, but, Alan B. was tops. His men knew it, and I knew it, and our old colonel knew it, who was departing at the conclusion of his tour.

Alan B. looked after his troops first, and worried about his military career second. It sure didn't hurt him, because he is a retired colonel now, with an outstanding reputation with his combat troops.

On the last operation before our colonel left, he and I and our artillery captain were sitting in my colonel's command and control chopper at perhaps a thousand feet, observing the massive artillery and air "prep" of an objective which Alan B's men were about to assault by helicopter.

Open areas suitable for choppers to land on in the Central Highlands were few and far between, and as a result, were quite often manned by large enemy forces, who knew that sooner or later, American Infantrymen would land on them.

For this reason, minutes prior to landing your assault force, you pounded the landing zone with everything you had. It was good insurance.

As soon as Alan B. had most of his troops on the ground, his unit began receiving heavy fire. Two or three hundred feet above our C&C ship, was the general's C&C ship. He and his staff colonel were closely monitoring what my colonel did, and what Allan B did on the ground.

Now, the catch to all this is that only the man on the ground can actually appreciate the exact situation. That jungle is so thick, with triple-canopied cover, that the commander on the ground must pop smoke grenades periodically, so that the smoke may filter up through those thick treetops, and give the commander in the air an idea of the ground troops' position so that he could call in air strikes and/or artillery and gunships to support them.

On this particular day, the general started interfering with Alan B's decisions and his conversations by radio with my colonel.

Alan B. had enough of that in short order. Although he knew that the general could easily relieve him and ruin his military career, he put it all on the line.

"Respectfully request that you don't interfere," he told the general. "This area down here might look like a golf course to you at fifteen-hundred feet, but only I can see the terrain. Over."

Well, generals and colonels don't like to have everyone on the net hear some young captain tell them how the cow ate the cabbage.

It all came to a head a few days later when Alan B's company was performing perimeter security for our artillery fire support base, and he and I were meeting our brand new colonel for the very first time, when he arrived with the general and his staff colonel by chopper.

As we were introduced, the staff colonel pulled his rank on Alan B.

"I want to talk to you," he said abruptly, "about golf courses, young captain."

"Know what you mean, sir," Alan B. adroitly turned the tables on the colonel, "look at these letters which your adjutant general sent for me to sign. They are letters of condolence to the families of my men who were killed in action and some are illiterate, and two of them are addressed to the wrong parents, sir, and I'd like to suggest to you, sir, that you talk to your A.G. Major—"

"You," snarled the colonel, while the general and our new lieutenant colonel looked on with interest, "sound like the sergeant major here, who thinks I should court-martial my whole staff."

"Sir," I chimed in, "the captain is right. Your A.G. owes us orders on over 200 Purple Hearts and Combat Infantryman's Badges and—"

"He's solved that problem, damnit," he said acidly, "when a man's tour is up in the jungle, my A.G. is giving him a records check and those orders are cut right on the spot and inserted into his records."

"But, sir," I protested, "we have had hundreds of wounded evacuated, and they don't get a records check. They are not here for your A.G. to give them a records check. One of my wounded sergeants just wrote me from his new unit in Germany, and they let him wear his Silver Star, because they have its General Order in his file—but they will not let him wear his C.I.B. or his two Purple Hearts—this records check crap is for the birds, sir. Now, we're trying to point out—"

"You are trying to tell me my business," he sputtered, and Alan B. had laid his helmet on the ground to show the colonel the letters.

Alan B. kicked his helmet down the slope and threw the letters on the ground.

"Come on, sergeant major," he said, "No one wants to hear about our problems with wounded and dead riflemen as long as all those rear echelon sons of bitches have an eight to five job back there in the rear with the ice cold beer."

He and I trudged down the slope to where he could retrieve his helmet.

An hour or so later, the new colonel talked to us both.

"Both the general and the colonel told me, sergeant major, that you have a big mouth, and a heart of gold for your troops—and the colonel told me about the golfcourse transmission," he eyed Alan B.

What could we say?

"I observed that scene up the slope," he said sadly, "and I'm telling you both now, that I get paid to do all your fighting for you with that colonel and that general. I guarantee you that I will do everything in my power to influence them to straighten out such problems. O.K.?"

Sure, it was O.K. and he was a great commander, and as good as his word.

I think of Alan B often—drop-kicking that doggone helmet down that slope. A fine, dependable captain, with balls like the proverbial burglar.

Dedicated to Col. Alan Burgess Phillips (Retired)

Boneyard Luck

Stan Jones and his lovely wife, Cathy, owned and operated "Stan's Boneyard" in Phoenix until his recent tragic death. They had 300 ancient Pontiacs.

Stan learned about life in the jungle. The radio operator that Stan replaced, was killed at Dakto. He became my colonel's radio operator.

Stan and I and "Doc", our battalion surgeon, slept beneath the same poncho hootch for weeks on end. Doc played football while in college—and you can imagine the horrors he experienced during the terrible Dakto Campaign. He never pulled his captain's rank on me or Stan—he'd get you in a wrestlin' match in a minute—so he was a helluva guy.

Well, if you can survive for a month in the jungle—it's a good month. I had a bad week one time, though, and Doc and Stan were eyebrow deep in the three things which happened to me.

The first thing wasn't hard to fix. I reached down in the dark to pick up my helmet and evidently one of those big red mountain scorpions nailed me right between the knuckles of two fingers of my hand. Kinda painful.

Doc shot novacaine into my knuckles and my hand swelled up like a board for a day or two.

The second thing was tougher. He and I and Stan had gotten hold of some "C" rations cheese and crackers and made a meal of them beneath the dark ponchos.

Well, at about zero dark-thirty, a big ole jungle rat bit into my "good" hand. I involuntarily clamped my hand shut on his head and shoulders in my sleep, and choked him to death.

"Rabies," announced Doc, as Stan held his zippo for us to look at the rat, "one hundred percent fatal," said Doc matter-of-factly, "if we don't get you evacuated for fourteen days' treatment with 'duck embryo' vaccine!" "Evacuated?" I couldn't believe it.

"Yep," said Doc, "they told us at Fort Sam that all these monkeys and rats have got it, and not to take any chances. We'll have to get you out in the morning."

Well, he was finally able to get a small icechest sent out, with the required two weeks' supply of vaccine. Every few days, a chopper would bring us a few pounds of ice.

You get the shots, one a day—right in the belly. Sounds horrible, but it's not that bad. The medics go by the "clock" system, with your bellybutton being the center of the clock.

The first day, you get one at twelve o'clock, and the next day at six—and so forth. They must hit a nerve once in a while, because you can go two or three days in a row with the painful shot not being too bad and then the next one is like a teacup of molten lead being slowly poured over your entire stomach!

Vastly preferable to the undertaker, though. The rifle troops got a big kick out of watching Doc shoot me every morning, but they didn't have much entertainment in the jungle, so I didn't mind.

Well, the third thing which happened to me that week, happened to Stan and Doc, too.

It just so happened that we had operated in this same area a couple of weeks before, and killed some enemy soldiers. During the Monsoons, things grow fast—plus that heavy rain plays hell with the ground—so, how did we know that we had set our hootch up, in the waning light, right on top of some of those shallow graves.

In the middle of the night, either Stan or Doc awakened the other two. I was the last one to awaken, and they were comparing notes.

"Do you feel it, Doc?" asked Stan.

"Damn right I do. Do you feel it, Wolf?" Doc used my nickname.

"Feel what? Are you guys nuts? I—hey—yeah. You mean that electrical tingling? Yeah!"

Stan lit his lighter beneath the poncho, and with a yelp, went right through the roof, extinguishing the lighter and causing Doc and me to scramble out from under that poncho like it was filled with snakes.

There aren't many things which will make a combat-hardened paratrooper like Stan, to act like that, and it will get your attention right now.

Stan was beating at his jungle fatigues and tearing them off like they were on fire.

"Maggots," he loudly whispered, because we were in a bad place to be talking loudly, "Thousands of 'em," he hissed, as Doc and I swiftly joined him in the divesting of our jackets and trousers. We wore no socks or underwear in the jungle, so we were soon down to our boots, which were also teeming with the maggots.

We started shaking our fatigues as hard as we could, and I would imagine that after fifteen or twenty minutes, we had gotten rid of most of them, although we still had them in our hair and armpits.

"They can't eat you," lectured Doc, "unless your flesh is putrid, you know, decaying, then they can get their little mouths into you. That electrical tingling was thousands and thousands of those little mouths trying to eat us."

"Thanks, Doc," whispered Stan. "We needed that, Doc. I probably will never get another night's sleep in this God-forsaken home of ours."

"Let's move this poncho," I suggested, "and see."

Within fifteen minutes, Stan was snoring like a sawmill.

Clyde's Big Feet

It might have been a month after the incident with the maggots or it might have been a week. After all these years, I couldn't tell you, but every other facet of this incident is etched in my mind—much clearer than a bell.

The book says that under ideal circumstances, when a unit settles in for the night, it should not only select the best ground for defending itself, but must take into consideration a lot of other things, like placing the CP in a concealed spot that cannot be reached by enemy hand grenades from outside the perimeter.

That's all well and good if the terrain is cooperating with the basic tenets of the book.

Our Alpha Company had suffered its share of casualties recently, so I thought it wouldn't hurt to tag along with its smallest platoon. We were still about as high in the mountains as you can get in the Central Highlands. I'd say that they averaged a tad more than two thousand, four hundred feet in elevation.

The monsoon was still raging, which exacerbated a situation which is very bad even under normal conditions. The men hadn't been dry for weeks and the chill of the night air had started to descend upon us as I accompanied the first sergeant and we checked each position around the perimeter's edge, making sure that each trooper knew the latest scoop, to include the password.

The perimeter ran around the edge of the top of a razor-back ridge. One of the reasons the captain had selected this position was that it could be more easily defended with a smaller number of men.

Top didn't mind the men's questions about their status for R&R, which was a very big thing to a bunch of troopers whose one pleasure in their current existence was to know that they had seen daylight enter the dark confines of the jungle that very morning. Now, if I could only do that 364 more times.

Most of their other questions involved the status of close buddies who had been wounded in action recently. Any word on how he's going to end up? Blind on that side of his head? Lame? Even paralyzed in some cases.

Or did he get the brass ring and win a stateside trip, but would suffer none of the above? Lucky dog! God bless the others who weren't so lucky, Top. In a rucksack outfit, the medic humps a rectangular piece of canvas which becomes a litter once a bamboo pole is inserted through a channel along each side.

After a guy is evacuated, the poles are tossed and the litter canvas becomes once again part of the pack. That works great for one or two casualties, but for mass casualties, the troops used man's best friend—their poncho.

I was bushed from the day's hump, so I just lay on one half of my poncho, rested my rifle across my chest and covered up with the second half, the rain drumming on my poncho having the same affect as it does in lulling a person to sleep who is fortunate enough to be lying beneath a tin roof.

I'd guess it was nine or ten o'clock at night, in thickly falling rain, when some clumsy clutz clomped right smack in the middle of my stomach, knocking his rifle from sling arms as he fell, its muzzle hitting me right smack in the neck.

He was frantically groping backwards for the rifle, was the way we figured it out the next day. I thought he was one of our riflemen who had gotten lost somehow in our perimeter and was trying to find his own foxhole when I admonished him verbally. I became completely awake in one second, however, when he began excitedly whining fearfully in that high-pitched piercing Vietnamese voice.

We didn't have a Kit Carson Scout with us at that time, so it had to be an enemy soldier.

I sounded off at the top of my voice to alert the perimeter, but he was gone. He had beat feet with those clumsy back paws of his.

I didn't have very many friends in the outfit the next day because, of course, the captain placed the perimeter on one hundred percent alert! Wouldn't you?

In broad daylight, Top and I tracked the guy's footprints in the mud. He had come strolling into our perimeter, walking between two foxholes in the dark, not having any idea in the world that he was anywhere near a perimeter filled with G.I.s armed to the teeth.

When he fell backwards on top of me and I had sounded off in English, the poor guy had put two and two together and come up with the idea of getting the hell out of there.

He had to be a loner. Either a trail watcher who had gotten himself lost and disoriented, or some NVA private who had gotten separated from his unit and was trying to find them.

It's not hard to get lost in that jungle in the daytime, but at night, it's unspeakably dark.

Top had a chat with the four guys occupying the vicinity of those two foxholes and they all swore they were as wide awake as night watchmen when it was their turn to be so the night before. Could be.

CHAPTER 13

Hill 875

Like a string of unlucky, ill-fated pearls, Special Forces camps of the U. S. Army's green berets were located at strategic points along the Republic of Vietnam's northwestern border with the countries of Cambodia and Laos. In general, manned by a small contingent of Americans, who supervised a force of Montagnard "Civilian Irregular Defense Group" sometimes directed by a cadre of Vietnamese Special Forces personnel who came under our green berets, they were fine, willing soldiers.

Many brave soldiers in all three categories lost their lives when these camps were overrun by numerically superior NVA Army troops during the camps' inception.

All of our friendly forces were fighting with one hand tied behind their back due to the restrictions placed upon them by the politicians who were catering to world opinion, instead of letting our forces pursue the enemy across those borders.

Instead, the NVA would cross into these safe sanctuaries where they were safe from our air and ground forces while they trained new replacements and received new supplies and ammunition. As soon as all the cards were stacked in their favor, back across the border they would come, threatening our Special Forces camps and the area in general.

On two separate occasions during the summer and fall of 1967, the 173rd Airborne Brigade was moved into this threatened area in order to thwart the enemy's plans. During both of these periods, the 1st, 2nd and 4th battalions found themselves to be fighting numerically superior NVA forces. The outfit's Third Rifle Battalion was late arriving in country and the powers that be decreed that it receive its baptism under fire in Phu

Yen Province in Tuy Hoa's coastal area. Their action was not as fierce as that being met by their sister battalions in Dakto, but any man killed in action in the Third Bat was just as dead, so it was all very serious business indeed!

The 4th Bat locked horns with the NVA in its first full-blown battle during the July 10, 1967, battle for Hill 830 at Dakto, as covered in another story.

On its second trip to Dakto in November, the battalion's first fierce battle took place with Dog and Alpha Companies in the vicinity of the Ngok Kom Leat ridgeline while Bravo was in fierce contact on Hill 823, several thousand meters away. The battalion commander ordered Company "C" to enter the fray with Alpha and Dog, but after a ninety minute fight with an NVA blocking force, Charlie had to set up a night position well short of their objective.

In the middle of the battle, Bravo's Captain and First Sergeant became casualties and when Colonel Johnnie landed his command and control Huey on Hill 823's LZ to evacuate them, our XO, Major Scott took over as Bravo's C.O. and I took over as its First Sergeant.

Colonel Johnnie med-evaced a whole chopper load into Ben Het FSB and returned a few minutes later with our S-2 Officer, Captain Leonard, to take over command from major Scott, who remained to coordinate firepower. That night, all four of our companies were probed time and again by the NVA who had bellied up to each perimeter in order to escape our arty and air. During one such probe, one of Bravo's fine platoon sergeants was killed a few yards from my own perimeter position.

After a very eventful night, the newly-appointed acting first sergeant, "Chingo," suggested that at first light, it would be a good idea for me and him and Jeff, our dog handler, to follow Viki, the great German Shepherd scout dog, down the furriest slope of Hill 823 and make a recon.

I was vastly against this scheme from the start, and it was with great reservations that I advised Captain Leonard of this plan and asked him to pass the word around the perimeter for the troops to not shoot anything furry or bald-headed. During the first fifty meters, it was still pretty dark as we crawled and tripped over enemy bodies and weapons. Perhaps a hundred yards out, we ran into what had to be the NVA aid station, a ten yard square area containing fourteen bodies and four critically wounded soldiers. The whole area was littered with empty glass vials printed in French.

Maybe thirty yards beyond this area, we shot a tree sniper and killed two NVA stay-behinds with grenades, at which point, Captain Leonard radioed that he was sending a rifle platoon down there and for us to stand fast, which met with my swift approval!

This platoon killed one officer and two more NVA, and policed up 56 AK-47s and a bunch of other weapons while I talked myself into going back up into the perimeter.

The afternoon before, I had taken two riflemen and we had made four trips down this exact same slope, retrieving seven of Bravo's seriously wounded troopers who were in danger of being headshot, as had been the fate a few minutes before of one lieutenant and six of his men as they lay strewn wounded nearby, as the area had been just crawling with NVA.

That evening at dusk, I had led Sergeant Ohda and a recovery detail to retrieve those bodies when, a few meters outside the perimeter, an enemy soldier sprang up and threw a grenade. At Ohda's warning shout, we all hit the deck just as this NVA loosed a lethal spray from his AK-47 at the location where we had been standing! The quick-thinking Ohda tossed two grenades in rapid response, killing the enemy soldier and we continued our detail, taking two such trips to complete.

So, as I ambled back up to the CP, I was thinking to myself that I had made seven hazardous trips down that slope in a very few hours and a Vegas bookie would probably start laying odds on the NVA. So, with a clear conscience, I once again resumed my duties as the 4th Bat's sergeant major.

Within another half day, Colonel Johnnie had arranged for the survivors of all four companies to be choppered back into Ben Het fire support base to re-group and hopefully gain replacements.

I finally got to go on leave.

Well, suffice it to say that I was very excited at the prospect of being with Marlene for a week, and when it finally came about, it was great. We were permitted to stay at Fort Derussey's U.S. Army R&R Center right on the beach, which was a great discount from what a fancy civilian hotel would have charged us. We had been married for about eighteen years then, and our three kids were staying with friends in California during Marlene's visit.

She and I were enjoying a wonderful Thanksgiving dinner at one of the fort's great restaurants, when the TV flashed that following a very serious battle at Dakto, the 173rd's Fourth Battalion had taken Hill 875 after having relieved the Second Bat, which had been accidentally bombed by friendly forces. The Fourth Bat had gone ahead with the assault, emerging victorious after having themselves suffered severe casualties during a four day siege of the extremely well-fortified hill.

I had missed the battle of all battles, which with my luck, could have saved my life, depending upon the whims of fate. I had also lost many good friends, some of whom I had known for years, as the airborne infantry is a very small community within a big Army.

As our R&R ended, we sadly bid one another farewell and I headed back to Dakto to my beloved battalion, which our general had moved, along with the others, to the Dakto Airstrip awaiting replacements. The full realization of our losses started to hit me when I heard of the things which had happened during my absence. First of all, on Saturday, November 18, 1967, a one-in-a-million error by Dog Company's artillery forward observer lieutenant had caused a direct hit by one of Bravo Battery's 105mm artillery rounds, with the round landing directly on Dog's CP group, instantly killing the lieutenant, as well as Dog's great captain and its fantastic, seasoned first sergeant, in addition to some other fine troopers, including Mac, who had been the colonel's radio operator and my poncho mate for many weeks.

This ill sign proved to be a portender of more bad luck to come not only for the 4th Bat's troopers, but for the 2nd as well, because the very next day, they made their first unsuccessful attack upon Hill 875, whose fortifications must have been dug and improved for months, and ran much deeper into the bowels of the huge hill, providing a safe sanctuary for its defenders while the air force's fast movers pounded it and our artillery did its best to "prep" the hill's military crest and probable areas of its strongest fortifications.

The 2nd Bat was finding out the hard way, what the 4th would soon discover, that this was no ordinary hill with conventional trenches and foxholes as its only assets.

For these reasons, the 2nd Bat's initial assault was a fiasco with quite a few friendly WIA and KIA. These casualties were moved into a protective perimeter in preparation for evacuation as soon as possible. It was not to be. During this undertaking, the battalion of fine troopers ran up against exceedingly bad luck in the form of a miscommunication between a ground observer and the pilot of one of our friendly fast movers.

The tragic result was that the pilot dropped two 500-pound bombs on the hard-luck battalion, already beleaguered by many casualties. One of the bombs actually landed just outside the perimeter, killing a group of NVA which was preparing to assault the perimeter. Sadly, the second bomb landed right in the perimeter. It wasn't hard to figure out what time this happened, because at precisely two minutes until seven in the evening, those monitoring the Second Bat's radio traffic heard a tremendous blast, followed by complete silence as the perimeter's unfortunate occupants were either killed, wounded or suffered severe shock from the horrible explosion.

In effect, for a while, the 2nd Bat had been rendered to be completely helpless. Had the NVA mounted an attack during this initial period of dazed confusion, the result would undoubtedly have been horrendous.

Within the hour, our fine general had given Colonel Johnnie the order to immediately move to the assistance of the poor

2nd Bat. He landed his chopper onto FSB 12's LZ, where Alpha Company of our battalion was already being readied by the colonel. As Bravo Company was located at FSB 16, already the closest to Hill 875, the colonel informed Captain Leonard that he would be the first to move to the beleaguered 2nd Bat's aid, that he should brief his leaders accordingly and be prepared to move out at first light.

He had his staff to immediately coordinate for Chinooks to move Alpha Company from FSB 12 to 16 at first light, so that they could follow Bravo and that Charlie would come next. Because of the proximity of the troops, Colonel Johnnie was able to personally brief Alpha's Captain Muldoon and Charlie's Connolly in order to give them the benefit of every facet of what he knew. He told them that they would have a wall of artillery fire moving along with them on their approach march to the hill. These basic facts had already been imparted to Leonard, who knew that both battalions were depending upon his success in the initial phases of the 4th Bat's move to help the 2nd.

I am convinced that the 4th Bat was very fortunate to have had Colonel Johnson as their CO. I knew from my many conversations with him that he was not only an experienced, savvy commander, whom I explicitly trusted to look after our troops' welfare, but who had also striven, throughout his military career, to stay in command of troops, consistently deferring staff assignments in order to extend the command periods beyond the normal parameters. I knew that he completely disdained the "ticket punching" syndrome where some very fiercely ambitious officers used every wile at their disposal in order to arrange "career benefitting" assignments. In my time as first sergeant and sergeant major, I had come to regard commanders such as he, with the most "troop" experience, to be head and shoulders above the rest.

Well, the fat was in the fire and some very excited 4th Bat troopers embraced the first light of the forthcoming dawn of Monday, November 20, with mixed feelings. I am sure that some of them were telling themselves that this was their lucky day and to not sweat the small stuff, while a much smaller percentage of the more experienced gungho Paratroopers might greet the rising sun with the misgivings that this could be their last dawn.

As Ron Leonard led his troopers on essentially the same route of march on which the 2nd Bat had recently approached 875, he silently thanked Colonel Johnnie as the forepromised wall of artillery arrived on schedule. So far, so good, he thought.

His column had not set out from FSB 16 until sometime after 0900 because of the time it took for clearing patrols to return from their recon and the fact that Colonel Johnnie had choppered into the base in the interim in order to give Leonard an extensive briefing. He explained the order of march of the other companies and encouraged the captain that he would soon have plenty of support in case Bravo was ambushed en route.

At this time, Colonel Johnnie approved for Bravo to eventually swing wide and to approach Hill 875 more from the northwest, in order to catch the enemy forces unaware who might be expecting the column to take a direct route from FSB 16. Whatever he was cracked up to be, our enemy was certainly no fool. Most of those NVA commanders had experienced many such battles and sometimes their bag of tricks seemed boundless.

By now, on Hill 875, several wounded lieutenants, the ranking survivors, were taking action to get the wounded moved downhill to a better area for med-evac, but it was still too dangerous to bring in dustoffs due to severe enemy fire. When they got the word of the 4th Bat's pending arrival, the morale of all the troops shot skyward.

Within about three and a half hours, Leonard had led Bravo to about 1700 yards of 875. On the way they had seen plenty of NVA sign in the form of dead soldiers, bloody bandages and discarded supplies.

Meanwhile, it had taken the Chinooks a couple of hours to ferry Captain Muldoon's Alpha Company to the point of departure, where they immediately hit the trail, soon to be followed by Captain Connolly and Charlie.

A while later, Captain Leonard made contact with Lieutenant O'Leary, giving him their azimuth of approach so that they would not be fired upon by the wary Second Bat survivors.

About four in the afternoon, Sergeant Leo Hill, Leonard's pointman, discovered the base of 875. Hill, from Cleveland, Ohio, was one of the more experienced pointmen and he soon came upon quite a few bodies, both American and NVA. The ragged bamboo and shattered tree trunks bespoke the ferocity of the bullets expended during some very fierce firefights.

Colonel Johnson, knowing that choppers could not land on 875, had wisely ordered that every trooper double up with food, water and as much ammo as possible, in order to re-supply the grateful 2nd Bat guys, which worked out like a charm, believe me.

Captain Leonard made his way to the front of the column, where he was immediately briefed by Lieutenant O'Leary, word of which was radioed to Colonel Johnnie a bit past five in the evening. Leonard placed Lieutenant Lindseth's platoon in the center of the line facing uphill into the enemy positions, with Moore's on the right and Proffitt's on the left.

It wasn't hard to find a fallen tree as many had been knocked down by the original prep of air and arty and some of the smaller ones had fallen victim to enemy RPG and mortar fire. Clumps of ragged bamboo were sprinkled everywhere, its jagged slivers as sharp as any razor.

Lieutenant Remington was another of the ranking survivors, whose many wounds and bloody clothing made him look to be more dead than alive. At this writing, he is a prominent judge in Fort Walton Beach, Florida. I wonder how many slick operators come before him figuring to whip a combat story on him that he hasn't heard before.

Four hours after Bravo's arrival, Alpha entered the perimeter, followed in about an hour and a half by Bill Connolly's Charlie Company, taking their places to the left and right of Bravo.

Most intelligence estimates place several NVA regiments to be in the Dakto vicinity during the period in question. While the 173rd was so engaged, elements of the 4th Infantry Division and several ARVN battalions were also vigorously engaged with the enemy. It seemed as though you could put troops in just about anywhere and they would soon be engaged with some large force.

Hill 875 itself was less than four miles from the Cambodian border. By this time, the CG had placed Colonel Johnnie in charge of both battalions, and from his position in his C&C ship overhead, it became apparent to him that the current LZ was a death trap for dustoffs, so he ordered Leonard, the ranking captain on the hill, to cut a new LZ in a more concealed spot down the hill. Meanwhile, incoming mortar barrages were causing many more casualties.

Leonard decided to move most of the 2nd Bat's able-bodied troopers downhill to cut the new LZ while the others moved the wounded to that general proximity for immediate evac as soon as choppers could be safely brought in for them. Even though enemy small arms fire could not reach the casualties on the new LZ, mortars still could. The fly in the ointment was that the dustoffs themselves were extremely vulnerable to small arms fire as they arrived or departed. Leonard and Johnnie got their heads together and coordinated arty and air against the enemy's locations while a chopper sortie was in progress and once the LZ was finished, this system worked quite well.

Meanwhile, Colonel Johnnie had radioed Leonard to prepare to attack the enemy at 1100 hours, which had to be ultimately postponed until the LZ was finished and the evacuation in progress. He knew there would be further casualties among the 4th Bat once the attack progressed, so it was the correct sequence of events to follow to get the 2nd Bat's guys out first.

At a little after two in the afternoon, the first dustoff took out a load of the more seriously wounded, followed by more ships to make hay while the sun shone.

A new time was set by Johnnie to attack at 1500 hours, and at a few minutes past three, Leonard gave the order to his three companies on the ground to start the assault.

Even though a dozen fast-movers had dropped tons of ordnance and napalm on the enemy during the interim while the LZ was being fashioned, the assaulting Paratroopers were unpleasantly surprised to find that the enemy was obviously alive and well, having escaped deep into the bowels of the hill, only to emerge safe and sound to combat the assaulting force. The advantage was all theirs as they could place fire upon anything which moved up the hill toward where they were dug in.

The attacking Paratroopers found themselves to become the recipient of some very accurate automatic weapons fire, augmented by mortars and RPGs. An occasional B-40 rocket would swoosh downhill from enemy bunkers, leaving death and destruction in the wake of most of them! As groups of troopers in the assault element, found the fire to be too severe, they tried to find cover behind downed trees and logs. Many of the men who were more lightly wounded patched each other up in the absence of the medics, working on the more seriously wounded. As a general rule, the lightly wounded would move the serious ones downhill for evacuation and then make their way back up to their former positions and either make another trip with badly wounded buddies, or resume the fight.

Sometimes a lull in the severe incoming fire would permit elements of the various companies to advance a few yards, only to become once again bogged down by casualties.

In the long run, Alpha Company made it closer to the top, advancing up the steepest portion where the enemy had least expected their presence, but when they were found out, they were met with the same severe fire being placed upon Bravo and Charlie who were almost completely bogged down by this time, causing Colonel Johnnie to cancel the assault at that point.

In retrospect, some of Alpha's leaders thought that they might have made it to the top, but the volume of live grenades being rolled down the hill into their ranks tells the story that there were still many live NVA between Muldoon's company and the military crest of the hill. They would probably have paid dearly, had they continued the attack at that point.

"The fortunes of war," is an oft-quoted adage, but after two wars in the Infantry, I think that it is an ill-quoted adage. An experienced combat man might say "The ill-fortunes of war," or indeed, "The misfortunes of war," would have to be a much more accurate description of the outcome of war.

Today, I sat down and tallied the casualties from my thirty-eight-year-old rucksack green book, which reflects that during the two hour period of Tuesday, the 21st's assault, culminating around 1700 hours, HQ Company lost 3 medics KIA, Alpha lost 4 KIA and 58 WIA, Bravo lost 11 KIA and 35 WIA and Charlie lost 1 KIA and 12 WIA.

There were no "fortunes of war" on Hill 875 on Tuesday, and the fortunate part of Wednesday was that the scheduled attack was called off. The LZ was still clogged with wounded being dusted off from the previous day's battle when Colonel Johnnie landed on the hill and consulted with his three brave rifle company commanders. He told them that our CG had left it up to them if they felt that they could successfully take the hill and if so, that the Fourth Infantry Division would provide two rifle companies to attack up from the North slope of the hill.

Those three warriors looked at one another and they looked at their fine lieutenant colonel and they all came to the same conclusion; that the assets they most prized in this world had been already invested to the hilt in Hill 875. They wanted revenge for the lives and limbs of the men, already expended against a cruel enemy who had never given any quarter, but had consistently murdered our wounded and then ravaged the bodies of the dead! It would have been a stain upon the honor of our dead and wounded, not to defeat this enemy, was the consensus of the opinion of the three valiant captains!

The proud lieutenant colonel shook hands with his three brave captains and took off. The three of them returned to their units, confident that Colonel Johnnie would ensure that they got all the support they needed for the following day's final assault upon that terrible, foreboding bastion above.

They briefed their leaders, who set about the myriad tasks confronting them at this fearful time. Each one knew that their fine troopers would follow them up that hill without question, each one hoping to at least make it through the operation alive, already figuring the high odds of being wounded by lead or steel.

As the ranking officer present, Captain Leonard wouldn't ask anyone else to further tempt the odds, so he personally moved to the most exposed and dangerous position on the perimeter's edge and coordinated the artillery and air strikes in preparation for the following day's assault. He did the same thing again the next day, ensuring the accuracy of the bombs, other ordnance and artillery just prior to the assault.

These unselfish acts of bravery on his part, coupled with other feats eventually earned Captain Ron Leonard the nation's second highest award for valor; the Distinguished Service Cross!

As the gungho Paratroopers prepared themselves for the forthcoming assault, Father Roy Peters set up his altar, distributing the sacrament to all comers, regardless of denomination. His presence encouraged these hardened combat veterans, who knew the odds they would soon face. Father Peters was still emotionally jarred by the very recent loss of his friend, Father Charles Watters, killed by the bomb on this very hill, not too many hours before! No one could have known it at the time, but for his own valiant exploits prior to the bomb, Father Watters would posthumously be awarded the Medal of Honor, along with PFC Carlos J. Losada, a fine 2nd Bat light machine gunner.

At about 1100 hours on Thanksgiving Day, Thursday, the 23rd of November, 1967, Captain Leonard gave the signal for a pre-determined 81mm mortar barrage by all three companies, to be placed just forward of the assault element of his Bravo Company on the left and Connolly's Charlie on the right. They would be followed by Muldoon's Alpha Company, by now the smallest in strength, and about 24 members of Alpha of the Second Bat, led by their Lieutenant Harrison! Following them all were the remaining able-bodied members of the Second Bat, acting as litter bearers. The Second Bat was well-represented in looking for their own revenge against the formidable NVA, with their own axe to grind.

The entire assault was over in less than half an hour. The intense fire from every type of NVA Infantry weapon previously experienced, was not there. It was no cakewalk by any means, as the enemy mortars and automatic weapons fire had killed one and wounded nine in Alpha, killed five and wounded twenty-four in Bravo, and also killed three and wounded thirty-five in Charlie Company, but the troopers killed all the enemy in evidence and when everyone understood that the hill was ours, a victory cry went up from the cheering troopers.

The three suspicious captains, naturally expecting a possible counterattack, emplaced their troopers accordingly, but it never came. Colonel Johnnie landed his C&C ship among his victorious troopers, walking around shaking hands with them and congratulating them on their success. Captain Leonard had been shot through the fleshy part of one leg, missing the bone and Captain Connolly had been wounded in several places by mortar shrapnel.

It was over! Most of the mortar fire had come from surrounding hills still occupied by NVA. Intel from the bodies of NVA on 875 indicated that we had been fighting elements of the 2nd Bat of the NVA's 174th Infantry Regiment. As it turned out, the two lucky companies from the 4th Infantry Division's 1st Bat of the 12th Infantry had encountered absolutely no NVA whatsoever in their move up the north side of 875.

It sure didn't take much C-4 for the Engineers to blast an LZ along the balding top of 875 and after they did, casualties were dusted off right from the top of the hill.

Brigadier General Leo "Hank" Schweiter, our fine CG, landed his C&C ship on the LZ to congratulate his troopers. He was accompanied by his sergeant major, Vincent Roegiers. Known by the nickname of "The Pope" for his strong religious beliefs, Vince was a fine soldier and like his general, had a fine reputation among Airborne troops.

Right on top of their visit, a Huey "firefly" supply ship arrived with a very welcome Thanksgiving dinner. The delicious contents of those hot marmite cans further enhanced the morale of a bunch of troopers who knew that they had hit the jackpot of all Thanksgiving miracles; they were alive to enjoy the dinner.

The next day, dozens of NVA bodies were buried in a mass grave. To give you an idea of how confusing the task is to tally mass casualties—especially for the wounded, the final official word was that the 2nd Bat had lost 87 KIA, 130 WIA and 3 missing, while the 4th Bat had suffered 28 KIA, 123 WIA, and 4 missing.

The troops knew that none were missing, because those four had been involved in a massive explosion, but the 173rd's Adjutant General had insisted they be carried as unaccounted for, despite my violent arguments to the contrary, as I had bitter experiences as first sergeant during the Korean War with that same situation, where the bereaved next of kin needlessly and hopelessly awaited the return of loved ones when their own comrades knew that it was futile. A whole book could be written about situations like that, but no one listens to the rifle troopers—until it's too late.

My green book proves that the Fourth Bat actually had over 180 wounded on 875. Exactly 184 Purple Hearts were issued to live troopers, and of course, 28 more to the next of kin of our dead heroes.

Two days after the Thanksgiving victory, the physical ordeal of Hill 875 was over and the Fourth Bat was choppered off the hill and moved to the Dakto airstrip in order to receive replacements, of whom we received 335.

I say that the "physical ordeal" was over, but as is the case with all other battles, the participants will never forget Hill 875 and what they and their comrades did there.

Dedicated to the valiant captains and men of
Company "A" James Muldoon
Company "B" Ronald R. Leonard
Company "C" William J. Connolly

And to the memory of:
Sgt. Thomas Curtis Mays
Sgt. Arthur Turner, Jr.
Sp4 Roy Ronald Lee
PFC Jesse E. Smith
Sp4 Louis George Arnold
Staff Sgt. Roland Will Manuel
Sp4 Michael Jay Gladden
Sp4 David Richard Reynolds
Sp4 Leonard J. Richards
PFC Thomas Joe Wade
Sp4 Robert W. Lindgren
PFC Roger Dale Mabe
PFC Kenneth Grant Owens
PFC James Worrell
PFC Angel R. Flores-Jimenez
Sgt. Thomas Louis Corbett
PFC Raymond W. Michalopoulas
Sp4 Earl Kennon Webb
Sgt. Merrel P. Whittington
PFC Gerald Klossek
Platoon Sgt. John Lewis Ponting
First Lt. Tracy Henry Murrey
Platoon Sgt. William Lloyd Cates
PFC Robert Edward Paciorek
PFC Richard Floyd Mason
PFC John William Smith
Sgt. Leroy Edward Fladry
PFC Billy Ray Cubit

and to
Sp4 Richard Dale McGhee
Capt. Michael A. Crabtree
First Sgt. William A. Collins
First Lt. Douglas G. Magruder
Sp4 Harry Conrad Wilson II
PFC Charles H. Robinson
Sp4 John D. Willingham (died of wounds in Walter Reed)

Father Charlie

"Ever seen a sandbag filled with hand grenades, Top?" asked "The Moose," who was our senior chaplain at the time, charged with the responsibility, among other things—of physically shaping up any new non-jumping—non-Airborne qualified—chaplains as they arrived in the outfit, getting them ready for jump school in June 1965. The Moose was Maj. Conrad N. Walker, who had been a renowned boxer and quarterback.

"Lots of 'em, sir," I replied to the jolly Lutheran captain as he introduced our latest candidate for the rigorous jump school training.

"This," he playfully poked the older chaplain, who was also a captain, in his ample stomach, "is Father Charlie Watters. He's been livin' the good life up there in New England, and those aren't grenades bulgin' here an' there, that's Charlie in there."

The priest broke out into good-natured laughter and stuck out his hand for me to shake.

"I cannot tell a lie, first sergeant," he allowed jovially, "it is definitely me, but I haven't always been chubby, it's just a reflection of the company I've been keepin' and judging from you two, I'm in for it."

I looked at the tall candidate chaplain, who as it turned out, was about my own age, and I knew from the look in his eye, that he had considered Moose's "sandbag" comment to be the challenge that it was meant to be. Big Moose had thrown down the gauntlet and Big Charlie had accepted it immediately.

Moose and I have had many a discussion since then, that the Lord was the only one who could have known at that time, that within thirty months, Father Charles V. Watters would have become one of the more famous posthumous recipients of our nation's Medal of Honor.

I had three other close friends who were MH recipients, and I was proud to know them all.

Moose and Father Charlie and I all ended up in the famous 173rd Airborne Brigade, although Moose went over before we did. Moose ended up being awarded the Silver Star for keeping some wounded troopers from being overrun and headshot by our benevolent enemy. During WWII, there was a song about a famous chaplain who did essentially the same thing: "Praise the Lord and pass the ammunition." The Moose was that kind of guy, too.

I ran into Father Watters at Dakto in the 173rd. I was in the 4th Bat, and he was in the 2nd, and we met on the airstrip.

"Still runnin' the meatballs, Top?" he punched me affectionately in the stomach. "See ya still haven't gone to pot from old age."

"Not yet, Father," I laughed, "and don't forget, you and I are about the same age, so you'd better be keeping up that 'six miler'!"

It was the last time I ever saw him, but somehow I knew in my heart, that if push ever came to shove and it was his life or yours, that Father Charlie would lay his down for you and never give it a second thought!

In Ed Murphy's book, *Dak To,* he mentions some of the brave exploits accomplished by Maj. (CHC) Charles V. Watters which were epitomized also in his posthumous Medal of Honor citation: "To those who saw him that day Father Watters was an inspiring example of coolness under fire. Totally oblivious to the hail of enemy fire, he moved across the battlefield, tending the torn and mangled bodies, giving last rites to the dying. Time after time he advanced to the firing line, pulling the wounded to safety, carrying them to the aid station and recovering the dead. At the aid station, Specialist 4th Class Steer watched the chaplain work his way through the rows of wounded. The priest had words of comfort for each man. He held the hands of some as they cried from the pain. Others he embraced as they died, unwilling to let them depart this world alone."

Well, I could have told the guys in the 2nd Bat, what kind of chaplain they were getting when they got Father Watters. He was one of a kind.

The brave priest died with his wounded a few hours later, when they were accidentally bombed on Hill 875 at a couple of minutes before six on the evening of Sunday, November 19, 1967.

Knowing Father Watters, he probably would have wanted it that way.

In memory of Maj. (CHC) Charles V. Watters, M. H.

Red

Red was one of my best riflemen in the jungles of Vietnam. He was so dependable that they kept trying to make a leader out of him, but he turned those promotions down. He didn't want the responsibility for possibly causing injury or death to his comrades. He willingly went on ambush patrols and other missions, but he didn't want to lead them.

I asked Red on time if he had ever heard of Roger Young, but he hadn't. Can't fault him there, because Roger Young got his medal about twenty-three years before Red got his.

If you've ever heard the song about Roger Young, you might remember the story. A young fellow of modest means from a small Ohio town, he eventually found himself in the infantry, fighting in the New Hebrides Islands of the South Pacific. Like Red, he was a very dependable soldier, but unlike Red, he let them promote him to squad leader and then to platoon sergeant in charge of four dozen men.

After their latest fight, he turned in his stripes, telling the captain and the first sergeant that he'd rather be just a plain rifleman. Well, they weren't having any of that, because he was such a good platoon sergeant and they need him. So they argued against it. Young convinced them to take his stripes because he was losing his hearing, and he was fearful that in some future encounter with the enemy, he could be responsible for some good men dying. Reluctantly, the captain agreed to let him become just a rifleman, so he was right back where he had started. He was an unselfish hero and proved it when his platoon was pinned down and taking serious casualties from a Japanese machine gun. Charging the emplacement, he neutralized it, saving many of his buddies' lives but losing his own in the process.

On July 10, 1967, it was Red's turn to become a hero to his buddies on Hill 830 in the dark, dank jungles of Dakto in the Central Highlands. Many men died that day or were wounded like Red. During a lengthy hospitalization, he survived to receive a well-earned Silver Star medal, the nation's third highest decoration for valor and gallantry in action.

Years later, it became evident that Red was inadvertently administered tained blood during one of the transfusions. While many others had dodged the draft, went to Canada, or performed other subterfuge in order to avoid combat, Red volunteered for the airborne infantry. At the apex of his life, Red found that he had to battle liver cancer, caused by hepatitis C induced by those tainted transfusions.

The average citizen can become a life-saving hero, too, through participation in the organ donation program. Such a timely transplant would undoubtedly have saved Red's life, but sadly, after a valiant struggle, he lost his most serious battle.

In respectful memory of Dennis Richard "Red" Cooney,
January 16, 1944–April 4, 2002

Epilogue

My editor, Chris Evans, who has expertly and patiently guided this neophyte writer, has asked that I write a summation of this book's contents as viewed from the standpoint of its brave combat participants nearly forty years afterward. From both a psychological and physical standpoint, these fine warriors were well prepared to fight the more experienced enemy in Vietnam. Each had received an excellent, well-rounded basic training; was issued the finest equipment known to modern warfare; and was in turn led by outstanding, well-motivated leaders within the airborne infantry, which was composed of volunteers—the "cream of the crop."

On the debit side of the ledger, exactly like what was happening within every conventional U.S. battalion in Vietnam, all those newly arrived leaders had yet to learn the myriad specific little tricks of the trade which the VC and NVA had in store for them, not the least important of which was to fully understand that their enemy intended to murder every last one of our wounded and then, in many instances, mutilate their corpses with machetes. Once a unit suffers such an ordeal, the attitude of every survivor is that it's now payback time and each man is the paymaster.

We fought the war with one hand tied behind our back, guided by strict observation of the Geneva Convention's rules regarding war crimes, while our enemy was motivated by his own leadership to commit them. While we could certainly kill the enemy, murder and mayhem were strictly forbidden.

The second drawback was that during the 1967-68 period, the army had yet to discern that the wrong gunpowder was being used in the manufacture of our M-16 ammo and that this was the main culprit causing jamming of the weapon. Our riflemen tried to combat that deadly problem by taping their extended cleaning rod to the rifle, so that it could be immediately rammed down the bore to unclog a ruptured cartridge during a firefight, as well as by taking extreme measures to keep the weapon clean.

The third defect within our system was that the powers that be decided that if an officer spent only six months in a leadership position in Vietnam, then everybody would get a crack at combat experience, "spreading the wealth" more equitably throughout the officer corps. On paper, it appeared to be a sound procedure, but on the ground it wasn't for several important reasons.

To fully understand what was going on, one had to be aware that the enemy officers were in that jungle until the last dog was hung or he was carried out feet-first. Some of those senior commanders had fought the French as young officers, and by the time we were facing them, they had years of experience under their belt, particularly in jungle fighting, which was the name of the game. Until our officer got his feet on the ground and learned the ropes, our GIs were bound to have more casualties; this applied to the platoon, company, battalion, and brigade. Then, as soon as our officer gained enough know-how to pick up on most of the local tricks, he was off to some staff job, and there was a new kid on the block to replace him.

It's next to impossible to know the whereabouts of almost 800 men. We see one another at some of the reunions, but it is word of mouth concerning others. I'll name off a few that stick in my mind. Lt. Col. James H. "Johnnie" Johnson retired as a two-star, and he and his wife, June, reside in South Carolina. We stay in touch regularly. His great RTO, Stan Jones, tragically succumbed to cancer two years ago. Maj. Walter "Doug" Williams' lovely widow, Juliana, never remarried; she raised their then-newborn daughter, Margaret, who now works for the government. Col. Lawrence W. Jackley and his wife, Jo, live near The Wall and recently took me and Marlene and Carl "Doc" Noyes" there to honor Doug and all our other fallen heroes.

Chingo, with a string of Silver Stars, Bronze Stars, and Purple Hearts from three wars, retired from the army and settled in California. Neal Hagenow lost his right arm at Dakto. This indomitable trooper became a successful accountant, and he and his wife, Kathi, raised a fine family in Indiana, where he pursues his hobby as an accomplished woodworker.

Captains Bill Connolly, Johnnie Gilbert, Ron Leonard, Alan Phillips, and James Muldoon all retired as colonels, while George Baldridge was medically retired and died in Idaho of multiple sclerosis. Jimmy Jackson did not stay in the army but returned to St. Louis to pursue a career in law enforcement. Tom Baird, badly wounded during the November 6 battle, spent a long time in Walter Reed, eventually retiring from the army in New Jersey. He and his wife, Judy, recently visited us in Florida.

Our magnificent first sergeants didn't fare as well in the long run, starting, of course, with Bill Collins, who, along with Tom Baird's replacement, Captain Crabtree, was killed on November 18 at Dakto. Jerry Babb, Artis Knight, Eddie Crook, and Billy Duncan each retired as command sergeants major, as well as Irwin "Ray" Fraser in Colorado and Pappy Schroeder near Fort Campbell, Kentucky. Babb, Crook, and Fraser passed away in the last several years.

Medically retired and wheelchair-bound since Cemetery Hill, Lt. Larry Hawkins and his beautiful wife still remain active, politically and otherwise, in Florida.

John Ponting's lovely widow, Thelma, is a nurse in Florida.

I mentioned Earl Soucie and Wayne Hughes in the dedication. After having been terribly wounded by a land mine in Vietnam in another airborne unit, Earl retired with his wife, Dot, to Bangor, Maine. Sadly, this fine soldier succumbed to Lou Gehrig's disease several years ago.

Wayne Hughes was one of the toughest, yet sweetest guys I have ever known. Despite his terrible wounds from Dakto, he and his wife, Teresa, raised a big family in Indiana.

I'm proud of the men of the 4th Battalion. Now just think of all the other fine battalions in Vietnam and the experiences that their men had in fighting the enemy. They are all great units.

Our men came back, overcame every obstacle—and there were many—becoming members of every vocation, and they realized that above all, they were lucky to make it home. Like me, I am sure many credit the benevolence of the Lord, coupled with a bit of the luck of the draw, for having been granted life's spark a bit longer. Granted that one important advantage, they took it from there and did everything themselves.

I'm equally certain that each and every one personally thanks his lucky stars while silently paying tribute to our fallen comrades, who, in many instances, guaranteed our lives by forfeiting their own. I know that each of us keeps a secret place in his heart where he frequently visits our departed comrades and that the memories of who they were and what they did will never die.

So I salute you, Vietnam vet, and I say to you, hold your head up high and with pride. You have earned the recognition that you richly deserve. God bless you and yours.

Ted G. Arthurs
Their Sergeant Major

About the Author

Ted G. Arthurs was born in the small town of Uhrichsville, Ohio, on October 5, 1929—the same month as the occurrence of the "Great Crash" of the stock market, which heralded the world's terrible depression of the thirties.

After a poverty-stricken childhood, still poor but proud, he joined the U.S. Marine Corps on his seventeenth birthday. Following this three year hitch, he joined the U.S. Army's Paratroops, spending the better part of the next twenty-seven years in the Airborne Infantry.

He fought in Korea and Vietnam, during which time he was awarded two Silver Stars, two Purple Hearts, and more than two dozen other decorations and awards.

He served as first sergeant of rifle companies for well over thirteen years and as command sergeant major for eleven years, including four years in the U.S. Corps of Cadets at West Point.

An ardent family man, he saw to it that his wife, Marlene and three children accompanied him to all peacetime assignments.

Land with No Sun is the story of the brave paratroopers of the 4th Battalion, 503rd Airborne Infantry, of the famous 173rd Airborne Brigade. During his tour with them as their sergeant major from May 1967 through May 1968, 125 of his 750 brave riflemen were killed in action, and more than 500 were wounded. Most of these true incidents took place in the Dakto area of Vietnam's dark, triple-canopied jungles in the mountainous Central Highlands and some in Tuy Hoa's coastal area.

The purpose of his story is to assist the public in understanding how it really was.

Index

Page numbers in italics indicate illustrations

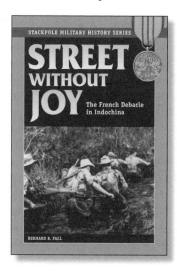

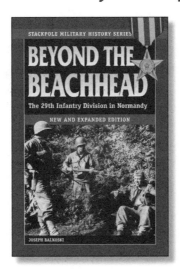

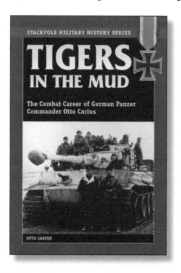

Stackpole Military History Series

ARMOR BATTLES
OF THE WAFFEN-SS
1943–45

Will Fey, translated by Henri Henschler

The Waffen-SS were considered the elite of the
German armed forces in the Second World War and
were involved in almost continuous combat. From
the sweeping tank battle of Kursk on the Russian
front to the bitter fighting among the hedgerows
of Normandy and the offensive in the Ardennes,
these men and their tanks made history.

$19.95 • Paperback • 6 x 9 • 384 pages
32 photos • 15 drawings • 4 maps

WWW.STACKPOLEBOOKS.COM
1-800-732-3669

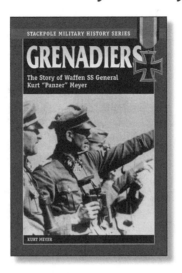

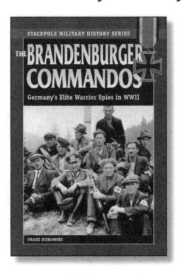

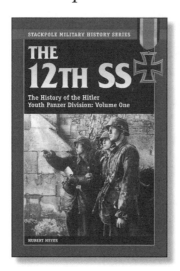 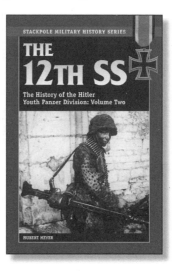